NAHUAT MYTH AND SOCIAL STRUCTURE

THE TEXAS PAN AMERICAN SERIES

Nahuat Myth and Social Structure

BY JAMES M. TAGGART

 UNIVERSITY OF TEXAS PRESS, AUSTIN

Requests for permission to reproduce material from this
work should be sent to Permissions, University of Texas Press,
Box 7819, Austin, Texas 78713-7819.

⊚ The paper used in this publication meets the minimum
requirements of American National Standard for Information
Sciences—Permanence of Paper for Printed Library Materials,
ANSI Z39.48-1984.

LIBRARY OF CONGRESS CATALOGING IN PUBLICATION DATA

Taggart, James M., 1941–
    Nahuat myth and social structure.

    (The Texas Pan American series)
    Bibliography: p.
    Includes index.
    1. Nahuas—Religion and mythology. 2. Nahuas—Legends.
3. Nahuas—Social conditions. 4. Indians of Mexico—
Religion and mythology. 5. Indians of Mexico—Legends.
6. Indians of Mexico—Social conditions. I. Title.
II. Series.
F1221.N3T34   1983   306'.08997   82-16033
ISBN 0-292-78152-0 (pbk.: alk. paper)

Contents

Tables

Acknowledgments

This study grew during a number of years of fieldwork among the Sierra Nahuat, an Aztec-speaking group in Mexico. In 1968, I began work in Huitzilan de Serdán, a community which lies deep in the most beautiful and isolated part of the northern Sierra de Puebla. That trip started a long and warm association with the Nahuat and their Hispanic neighbors in a number of communities during which I revised my views of their culture many times.

I shall never forget the storytellers, who generously gave me their time, who told me their stories, and who opened up their hearts and their homes to a curious outsider. Ignacio Angel introduced me to Nahuat oral tradition during the last months of initial fieldwork in Huitzilan. Appendix 2 presents short biographies of all Nahuat storytellers whose narratives appear in this book to illustrate how they fit into their communities. Through warm friendships with a number of Nahuat, many of whom did not tell stories, I came to understand how Nahuat oral tradition fits into a cultural and social context. They include Victoria Bonilla, Juan Gravioto, María Antonia Santiago, Aurelio Aco, Clemencia Cortéz, and Florentino Perez of Huitzilan, and Francisco Aparicio, Luciano Vega, Mariano Isidro, Francisca Vazquez, and Sofia Rodriguez of Yaonáhuac.

A number of foundations generously provided the funds for fieldwork in the northern Sierra. The Wenner-Gren and Mellon foundations supported the first two and a half years of fieldwork in Huitzilan. The American Philosophical Society Penrose Fund aided the research carried out during the summer of 1974. Franklin and Marshall College contributed to fieldwork during the summers of 1972, 1973, 1975, and 1976. The National Science Foundation, grant BNS 77-06660, funded the last period of fieldwork from 1977 to 1978, and provided salaries for assistants from Franklin and Marshall College, who helped code and analyze the data during the spring and summer of 1979. I am also very grateful to the Instituto Nacional de Antropología e Historia for permission to carry out all stages of the field research from 1968 to 1979.

Many colleagues provided wise guidance and support during fieldwork and aided in the preparation of this and other manuscripts for publication. L. Keith Brown, Pedro Carrasco, J. L. Fischer, G. P. Murdock, and Hugo G. Nutini made many thoughtful suggestions that helped focus the research over the years. Alfonso Villa Rojas and Nancie Gonzalez provided strong encouragement for carrying out this study. Carole Counihan, Linda Klug, Nancy McDowell, Mary Moscony, and Norman B. Schwartz read earlier drafts of this manuscript and made valuable suggestions that were incorporated into the revisions. Conversations with several colleagues, some of whom have read other manuscripts based on the Nahuat research, contributed to this book. They are Louise Burkhart, Leslie Dorit, Joel Eigen, John Holly, Charles Holzinger, Margaret Jackson, Murdo McLeod, Sally Falk Moore, Adebisi Otudeko, Maurice Richter, Thomas Schorr, and Edward Wilson. To be sure, all those who generously gave their advice contributed to the strengths of this work, but I accept all responsibility for errors in interpretation and fact.

I thank the Compañía Hulera Euzkadi, S.A., for their gracious permission to derive map 1 from their publication *Caminos de México*. I also express my gratitude to the School of American Research and the University of Utah for permission to paraphrase Arthur J. O. Anderson and Charles E. Dibble's translation of the Aztec myth of the Fifth Sun contained in Sahagún's *Florentine Codex*. Finally, I am grateful to the American Anthropological Association for permission to reproduce portions of my article which was published in the *American Ethnologist*.

Enough cannot be said to thank my wife, Sharon, who aided me on every field project since 1966. Our daughter, Marisela Cristina, did much to help us establish rapport in Yaonáhuac, and she brought joy to our lives. It is to Sharon and Marisela that I dedicate this book.

J. M. T.

A Note on Nahuat Orthography

The storytellers who told me the myths that appear in this book speak the Zacapoaxtla dialect of General Aztec or Sierra Nahuat. When I recorded and transcribed their stories, I could choose from a number of ways of writing their language. Harold Key and Mary Ritchie de Key had prepared their *Vocabulario de la Sierra de Zacapoaxtla* (Summer Institute of Linguistics, 1953) with an orthography designed to help Nahuat literate in Spanish record and read their own language. Dow F. Robinson, who wrote a very useful word structure, preferred writing Nahuat with a method adapted from H. A. Gleason's phonology. Both sources used orthographies different from those of the well-known dictionaries and grammars of Classical Nahuatl. While I found the dictionary prepared by Harold Key and Mary Ritchie de Key very useful, the words it contained did not correspond precisely to what I heard in Huitzilan and Yaonáhuac, the villages where I did my fieldwork and which are located near Zacapoaxtla. Moreover, their dictionary has some errors: principally missing or misplaced glottal stops. I decided to record the speech of the Nahuat storytellers with Gleason's phonology.

A number of developments in Nahuat orthography have taken place since I transcribed narratives in the Sierra Norte de Puebla. Principal among them was the appearance of Frances Karttunen's *An Analytical Dictionary of Nahuatl* (University of Texas, 1983) which would have made my task easier. Karttunen combined, systematized, and corrected information contained in several dictionaries including the one by Harold Key and Mary Ritchie de Key. I prefer Karttunen's orthography because it has the linguistic corrections and uses a minimum of diacritical markers. Those who wish to find in Karttunen's dictionary the Nahuat words appearing in my book will need to know how her words are spelled differently from mine. Readers can usually locate my Nahuat words in her dictionary by changing my k to her c or qu, č to ch, s to c or z, š to x, and w to hu or u. For example, change okičpil (boy) to oquichpil, siwapil (girl) to cihuāpil, masewal (speaker of Nahuat) to mācēhual, neiškwitil (lesson) to neīxcuītil, and kisayampa (it comes out of) to quīzayānpa. Readers will also be able to locate more easily the stems and compounds of Nahuat words by adding missing or misplaced glottal stops. The following glossary will be useful. The first column refers to Nahuat words as they appear in *Nahuat Myth and*

Social Structure, the second shows the same words written according to Karttunen's orthography, and the third gives the Nahuat defi-
nitions I obtained from my storytellers. Readers can find other
meanings by consulting Karttunen's dictionary.

kitahsota	= quitazohta	= he/she loves him/her
koyome	= coyōmeh	= Spanish-speakers
kwowta	= cuauhtah	= wilderness
kwošašaca	= cuauhxaxaca	= horned owl
kwoyo	= cuauhyoh	= mountain/forest
masewalme	= mācēhualmeh	= speakers of Nahuat
nagualme	= nāhualmeh	= witches
nepanta	= nepantah	= noon
owikan	= ohuihcān	= dangerous place
tahtakoke	= tahtacohqueh	= they sinned
takwa	= tacuā	= he/she eats something
tiačkauw	= tiāchcāuh	= elder brother
tikowame	= tīcōāmeh	= lightning-bolt
tonalme	= tōnalmeh	= days/animal companions

I am in the process of redoing my transcriptions of Nahuat
narratives with Karttunen's orthography and prefer to wait until
completing the changes before sending readers the promised
original-language versions of the myths appearing in this volume.
Correcting thousands of pages of transcription is a very time-
consuming job, but I have made some progress. Readers wishing
to see in Nahuat some of the narratives that I collected and transcribed in Huitzilan de Serdán can find them in the appendix to
*The Bear and His Sons: Masculinity in Spanish and Mexican Folk-
tales* (University of Texas, 1997) and also by contacting me for
information on the unpublished companion volume *Original
Language Texts for the Bear and His Sons.*

James M. Taggart
Lancaster, Pennsylvania, 1997

1. Introduction

Two storytellers

This book describes how two groups of Sierra Nahuat in Mexico tell the same stories differently according to their social structure. It illustrates how the position of Indians in Mexican society and the position of men and women can influence the way narrators develop the characters and the plots of their stories. It compares parallel stories, many of which derive from a common historical source, to control for the random factors in story collection that can lead to spurious conclusions about differences between bodies of narrative tradition.

The comparison of parallel stories for two populations can reveal subtle but important differences in collective beliefs. To be sure, storytellers distort and exaggerate events to hold the interest of their audience, and they consequently depict an abstracted view of their culture. Moreover, storytellers are sometimes deviant individuals who do not represent their communities. Among the Sierra Nahuat most storytellers are men, who express a masculine view of experience. But stories can reveal much about a people's view for several reasons. Stories contain collective images that accord with those expressed by the Nahuat in ordinary discourse and in ritual. The reason why stories contain widely held images when narrators are deviant and deliberately distort reality lies in the storytelling process. Narrators tell their tales in front of an audience which exerts a powerful effect on the storyteller's performance. The Nahuat tell stories when drinking in bars; they tell tales at all-night vigils; those who travel to the hot country in migratory work groups tell stories when resting in the evening camp; and workers in sugarcane processing groups tell stories to make the time go faster. On repeated public occasions a complex social and psychological process gradually shapes the story to reflect the personalities of the listeners as well as the storyteller himself. Storytellers of renown have the ability skillfully to connect their stories to the shared beliefs, concerns, and experiences of those in their audience. Those who impose their private views in their tales will not become renowned storytellers if those views differ markedly from those of their listeners. There is no formal selection of storytellers, but an audience can encourage some more than others by expressing approval or disapproval of their art. After numerous performances a story becomes much more than the reflection of one individual's personality.

Stories and collective beliefs in the two Nahuat groups have diverged as each group responded to different exogenous changes in social structure. Stories evolve with social structural changes because storytelling and narratives are inextricably linked to prevailing patterns of social behavior. First, the characters in stories stand for categories of persons in real life. The Nahuat identify with characters in stories and regard narratives as accounts of true events. They stress how the moral messages of tales are social lessons that apply to people living today, just as they did at the time the action of the story is said to have taken place.

Second, stories play a role in social interaction. Nahuat stories support the moral order, define social situations, and explain social dilemmas. They affect as well as respond to the prevailing patterns of social behavior. To take just one example, when Nahuat men describe women in stories as morally weak, sexually voracious, and inclined toward deviance, they justify patrilineal inheritance limiting women's access to strategic resources. But the stories men tell about women also change in response to shifts in women's access to land brought about from outside the society.

BACKGROUND

Competition between Indians and non-Indians for land and the creation of an ethnically stratified society have taken place throughout much of Mexico and Guatemala (Wolf 1959; Colby and van den Berghe 1969; Aguirre Beltrán 1973; Helms 1975). These processes left a deep impression on the oral tradition of the Nahuat just as they have for many other Indian groups in Mesoamerica. They began in the Nahuat area in the seventeenth century when the non-Indian population first moved into the northern Sierra de Puebla. I shall use the term *Hispanic* to refer to the non-Indians, recognizing that it is difficult to settle on the best term to apply to this group.[1]

The Nahuat who stood in the Hispanics' way lost their land and experienced intense pressure threatening their survival. Many could not support themselves at home and migrated elsewhere to ture. In some parts of the northern Sierra, the family changed due to the shift from patrilineal to bilateral land inheritance. This shift provided women with access to more strategic resources and gave them a stronger basis for initiative in family decision making.

Comparison of Nahuat communities can test hypotheses accounting for the relationship between peasant social structure and men's images of women. Nahuat men and women occupy different structural positions in various communities, and men express contrasting views of women in parallel stories. Hypotheses accounting for male-dominant sexual ideologies among peasants do not always make clear the type of ideology they purport to explain, but keeping this in mind, they appear to fall into three major categories.

The first hypothesis asserts that an ideology of male dominance develops among men in compensation for their actually weak position in the socioeconomic class structure (Michaelson and Goldschmidt 1971: 247; Rogers 1975; Gissi Bustos 1976; Brandes 1980). According to this notion, men, who lack control over important strategic resources and who occupy the lower strata of society, develop a view of women as morally weaker than men to compensate for men's actual powerlessness. Even though peasant men may monopolize local political office, they must carry out orders given them by superiors in district and federal capitals. They have comparatively little discretion to make decisions at the community level, they are held accountable for failing to carry out orders coming from above, and they are blamed by members of their communities for carrying out unpopular governmental policies. Men thus need a compensatory ideology of male dominance to help restore their self-esteem. It is possible to test this hypothesis with the Nahuat data because communities in the northern Sierra occupy different structural positions in the ethnic hierarchy, and the Nahuat express their powerlessness and their sexual ideologies in parallel stories. Chapter 8 compares stories from two Nahuat communities with different degrees of economic and political autonomy relative to the dominant ethnic group, and it supports this hypothesis. A comparison of parallel stories from the two groups reveals that those Nahuat who perceive themselves as the more powerless relative to Hispanics also have the stronger male-dominant sexual ideology.

The second hypothesis asserts that an ideology of male dominance is actually a myth that develops, sometimes with the tacit consent of women, to compensate men for their comparatively weak position in the family as well as the community and state political structure (Lewis 1949; Rogers 1975). According to this hypothesis, peasant men generally depend on women, who contribute substantially to the family income, who sometimes own land because inheritance is bilateral, who manage the family purse, and who have a closer relationship with children. To compensate for men's comparatively weak and marginal position in the household, they depict women as the morally weaker sex. A comparison of parallel stores in part III of this book does not support this hypothesis for the Nahuat. Men express the strongest ideology of male dominance when women actually have a weaker position in the social structure. The Nahuat data lend support to Michaelson and Goldschmidt's (1971: 345) argument that men develop the male virility complex when women acquire more land through inheritance (see chapter 10). But on balance, the Nahuat with bilateral inheritance express a more symmetrical view of the sexes.

The third hypothesis asserts that a male-dominant ideology develops as a functional part of a male-dominant family structure (Taggart 1977; Dwyer 1978a, 1978b). According to this notion, an ideology of male dominance develops to justify and maintain men's actual position of dominance in the family, and men use it to control women, who covertly undermine male authority. The comparative data from the two Nahuat communities support this hypothesis. To be sure, a number of factors go into defining the position of men and women in Nahuat society, but on balance men who express the most male-dominant sexual ideology also have the strongest position in the family. One can still argue that the androcentric family comes about primarily because of a compensatory ideology of male dominance that develops in response to Nahuat men's weak position relative to Hispanics (see hypothesis 1). It is true that those Nahuat who have the weakest position in the plural society also have the strongest androcentric ideology and family structure. These men probably apply this sexual ideology to justify patrilineal land inheritance, weakening the position of women by restricting their access to an important strategic resource. But the chapters in part I identify other exogenous factors that promote patrilineal land inheritance in some cases, and bilateral inheritance in others. These factors affect the pattern of interaction between husbands and wives and alter men's images of women expressed in stories.

Nahuat images of the sexes do not exist in isolation but form part of an ideational system expressed in myth. A change in any one part of this system can alter the configuration of ideas in the system taken as a whole. The comparison of parallel stories offers an opportunity to examine how different prevailing images of men and women derived from different degrees of sexual hierarchy in social structure co-vary with other details of Nahuat cosmology.

METHOD

I gathered the stories that appear in this book from fifteen men whom the Nahuat considered renowned storytellers. Their tales belong to the genre labeled with the Spanish terms *cuento* (story) and *cuentillo* (diminutive for story), or the Nahuat terms *neiškwitil* or *neiškwiltil* (lesson or example). Paradoxically the Spanish terms are in more common use despite the fact that storytellers tell their tales in Nahuat. The Summer Institute of Linguistics uses the Nahuat term *neiškwitil* to refer to the biblical stories they translate into Nahuat and distribute throughout the area, and some Nahuat apply this term to the narratives in their oral tradition.

I hoped to find a separate oral tradition for Nahuat women wherein they would express a view of the sexes complementary to the view expressed by men. Women in male-dominant societies in other parts of the world are excellent storytellers (see Sapir 1977b; Dwyer 1978b), and they present different images of the sexes than those presented by men. Nahuat women told some anecdotal tales and a few myths, but I found few women who told many narratives cognate with those told by men. The small sample of stories collected from women did not permit a comparison of oral tradition by the sex of the storyteller.

Many of the master storytellers from both communities have worked on plantations in the lowlands, and very possibly they learned some of the tales in their repertoires from storytellers of other communities. But most migrated long ago, and their stories have had time to adapt to local conditions. Moreover, these storytellers generally migrated to the lowlands with other Nahuat either from their own communities or from surrounding communities that do not differ much in terms of the variables of this study (see appendix 2, Profiles of Nahuat Storytellers).

All tales were gathered in Nahuat and according to the same procedure in Huitzilan and Yaonáhuac. I learned who the storytellers of renown were and visited their homes to ask them to tell their tales into a small hand-held tape recorder. I visted the Huitzilan narrators intermittently over a ten-year period, during which I lived in the community for a total of three years. I collected 105 narratives from ten storytellers whose tales appear in this book. They represent those stories narrators considered themselves competent to tell in public and do not necessarily represent all the stories they heard and only fragments of which they remember. I visited the Yaonáhuac narrators regularly over a nine-month period during 1977 and 1978, when I resided in that community primarily to collect stories. I obtained 175 narratives from the five story-tellers whose tales appear in this book and, again, they represent most of the stories they considered themselves able to tell in public and do not necessarily represent their entire repertoires. Story-tellers became very good friends and offered their views of what their stories meant to them. Stories were transcribed in Nahuat with the help of native speakers, who corrected my transcriptions and clarified the denotative and figurative meanings of words.

It was necessary to obtain stories through formal interviews to collect a sufficiently large sample of narratives. I found natural storytelling situations too infrequent for collecting the number of stories needed for this study. One can never rule out the possibility that the formal interviews might have shaped the way the stories were told (see Georges 1969), but the tales I heard in natural settings did not differ much from those told in more formal settings, in terms of the variables discussed here. Nahuat narrators tell tales with remarkable consistency, even when storytelling events are separated by considerable time. Moreover, the elicitation of tales took place under nearly identical conditions in both communities, and thus this method probably affects the results in parallel ways for both Nahuat groups.

To measure differences in social images which might be concordant to social structure, I compared similar—particularly cognate—stories from the two communities. Fischer (1956, 1958) applied this method to detect how folktales vary with the position of men and women in the social structure of societies in Oceania. This is the first study I know of to apply this method to historically related societies in Hispanic America.[3] Similar stories were compared to control for differences in story content attributable to the historical antecedents of oral tradition, and the random factors in folktale collection. I attempted to gather all stories known by all master storytellers in the two communities, but one can never be sure of complete coverage. If one compares nonparallel stories to identify differences in narrative thought, the results can be spurious if coverage is not complete.[4]

Comparing similar stories from two related communities shaped by different historical processes is one way to study ideational change. It is not without flaws, but it has advantages over other methods that elicit beliefs through discourse and dialogue. To be sure, Nahuat tales are told by men and do not necessarily contain views held by women. Both sexes express in dialogue private views of the men and women in their experience that sometimes diverge from the stereotyped images of the sexes that men depict in narratives. But trying to understand the Nahuat by listening to their stories can reveal things which other methods might overlook. Folktales contain surprises that might remain concealed with participant observation and in ordinary conversation. Narratives are highly compact, rich, and eloquent statements of ideas that contribute to understanding other kinds of behavior. The Nahuat themselves say they care about stories because they provide important perspectives on their experience.

Eliciting Nahuat ideas by listening to stories contaminates the results less than collecting ideology through discourse and dialogue. The gradual social and psychological process that shapes a story into a public product results in finely honed narratives. Nahuat storytellers are reluctant to tamper with their stories, which they assert ought to be told according to the way they heard them. They and their audience are quick to criticize those whose stories deviate from their expectations. Of course, no storyteller recounts a narrative exactly the same way twice, stories change over time, and some stories have entered Nahuat oral tradition later than others and have undergone less honing through the storytelling process. But the belief that stories should be repeated as one heard them and the use of mnemonic devices to remember stories make it less likely that storytellers, in any single storytelling event, will shape their narratives in radical ways to please an outside observer the way informants sometimes shape their responses to please their interrogators.

Many stories compared in this book probably derive from Aztec and Spanish prototypes.[5] Works of the Spanish chroniclers, particularly the *Florentine Codex* (Sahagún 1953) and the anonymous manuscript of 1558 known as the *Leyenda de los Soles* (Paso y Troncoso 1903; Lehmann 1906; Feliciano Velázquez 1975), contain texts of Aztec narratives parallel to the modern Nahuat ones. Indices of Spanish folktales told in Spain (Boggs 1930) and Mexico (Robe 1973) facilitate the identification of Spanish themes in Nahuat stories. Chapter 7 compares ancient Aztec and parallel modern Nahuat texts to gauge the degree of retention of Aztec ideas in the contemporary oral tradition, according to the degree of Hispanic domination.

But Nahuat narratives frequently contain mixed Aztec and Spanish elements, making the precise identification of their historical origins difficult. There are no historical sources for tracing the flow of narratives from pre-Hispanic times to the present in the Sierra Nahuat area. Stories appearing to have cognate episodes are not always parallel in every respect, but I considered nonparallel segments of cognate episodes important because they indicate how the Nahuat from different areas re-work the same core idea to fit the changes that have taken place in their communities.

One can argue that perhaps the Nahuat of the two communities compared in this study have similar narratives not because they acquired them from a common source, but because of their parallel experiences. While that can cause one to consider narratives as cognate, when in fact they have no common historical source, it does not present major problems for this study. The comparison of what are considered cognate narratives aims to discover how the Nahuat have re-worked parallel ideas whose source is of little consequence.

I matched similar stories from the two communities for comparison on the basis of their characterization, their plots, and their poetic style. One must tailor the comparative method to fit any particular situation, but general theoretical works and particular studies contain many useful hints on how to go about this task. I found that the motifs in Thompson's (1955–58) index do not incorporate enough Aztec ideas to organize many of the Nahuat stories according to their parallel themes. However, Propp (1979) makes several suggestions for dealing with similarities and differences in plots and characterization that one can apply to sets of parallel or cognate Nahuat narratives. Fischer (1956, 1958) has many ideas for how narrators portray male and female characters in similar stories according to their position in society. The structuralism of Lévi-Strauss (1963, 1967, 1969) is very useful for identifying analogies based on juxtaposed or polarized concepts which seem so prevalent in Nahuat myths. While Lévi-Strauss is primarily concerned with the logical transformations in poetic style, a number who draw from his approach make many useful points on how social experience can contribute to the formation of metaphors in expressive culture (see Fernandez 1974; Sapir 1977*a*).

Each story is a piece in a large mosaic of ideas, and to understand the design of this mosaic, one must fit stories together and observe the configuration. Cognate and parallel stories from the two communities were compared element by element to discern the pattern of similarities and differences concordant with social structure and other variables. Different methods were used to compare elements, episodes, and entire stories. Where comparisons did not require specific knowledge of Nahuat beliefs and values, I used colleagues as judges to ensure impartiality. This method is particularly useful for comparing many versions of the same story, especially when it contains numerous events and episodes. In cases where judges rated tales, tables containing all parallel episodes compared appear in the text so the reader can make independent ratings (see chapter 8).

All stories appearing in the body and appendix of this book are English translations of the Nahuat originals. Inclusion of the Nahuat texts alongside the English translations would be ideal, but it would add considerably to the length and the cost of the book. Readers interested in the Nahuat originals may write me for copies.

Part I. The People

Man planting corn

Woman placing maize in
the cooking pot

2. The Nahuat

The elder brother drinks before the younger

The northern Sierra de Puebla is a large and heterogeneous region suited for controlled comparisons to test relationships among numerous variables. This chapter places Huitzilan de Serdán and Santiago Yaonáhuac, the communities compared in this study, in the Nahuat area, and it describes the variables held constant. These background variables, which are similar for both, help account for the parallel ways narrators from each tell their stories. The map shows the location of these communities relative to all major geographical features mentioned in the text.

The Nahuat are scattered in nineteen *municipios* (townships) in the northern Sierra with a total population of 219,120 (México 1973).[1] Approximately 40 percent speak Nahuat in the home, but this figure varies considerably among *municipios* and among settlements within *municipios*. Strung out along the edge of the Central Mexican Highlands, the nineteen *municipios* lie in different climatic and agricultural zones. They are sandwiched in between the Nahuatl Indians and the Hispanics of the cool, dry high plateau and the Mayan-speaking Totonacs of the hot, humid coastal lowlands. The warm air laden with moisture rises up from the lowlands and meets the cooler air from the highlands, producing low clouds and drizzle through much of the winter following the summer rainy season. The continuous rainfall through most of the year, except for a brief dry season from mid-March to the end of May, produces lush vegetation and makes farm land very fertile.

The communities at higher elevations have different growing seasons and yield different crops than the communities at lower elevations. The Nahuat living above 1,200 meters reap a single corn harvest each year because occasional frosts prevent a winter growing season. Their cash crops are avocados, potatoes, apples, peaches, and pears sold in the domestic Mexican market. The lowland Nahuat produce two, sometimes three crops of corn, and they cultivate coffee sold to the international market. Aside from agricultural diversity, Nahuat communities specialize in a variety of cottage industries: some make pottery, others weave, some embroider shawls, a few produce reed baskets and make wooden spoons. The diversity of agricultural products and crafts and the rich farmland promote active local periodic markets and bustling commercial centers. Mining and a large smelting plant make Teziutlán one of the major economic centers in the state of Puebla.

Hispanics congregate in the commercial towns—Teziutlán, Tlatlauqui, Zacapoaxtla, Cuetzalan, Tetela de Ocampo, and Chignahuapan—but they have also settled in the rural farming communities, where they live with the Nahuat. Hispanics in these biethnic *municipios* are the dominant ethnic group because they own most of the land, run the major businesses, and control politics. Most Nahuat live in biethnic communities, a few live in monoethnic ones, but no Nahuat can entirely escape the larger hierarchical plural society because they all have economic and political ties with Hispanics in the commercial towns.[2]

SHARED ANTECEDENTS

Despite this variability, Huitzilan and Yaonáhuac share linguistic and historical antecedents, and they possess similar but not identical social structures. A comparison of communities that share linguistic and historical antecedents increases the likelihood they will share a number of cognate narratives with a similar poetic style. Narratives probably flow more easily among people who speak the same language and maintain social or political contact. The poetic style of stories is likely to be similar if those who tell them share historical antecedents because the possibilities for constructing metaphors are nearly unlimited. A metaphor consists of a tenor (the topic of discourse) and a vehicle. Storytellers can draw from a myriad of possible vehicles to explain, add insight to, and elucidate the same tenor. Some (Edmonson 1971: 50) argue that two groups will use identical metaphors only if they are in contact, although one must acknowledge the possibility of parallel invention.

Contact has taken place among nearly all communities in Mesoamerica since Classic or even Formative times, spreading similar mythical characters all over the region (see Hunt 1977). But narratives of the same linguistic region of Mesoamerica are likely to exhibit more parallels than those from different language groups. The Sierra Nahuat language varies from community to community, with the greatest variation occurring between groups at the extreme ends of the northern Sierra. Huitzilan and Yaonáhuac are noncontiguous *municipios* lying about 40 kilometers apart and separated by two ridges of mountains. But they are situated close

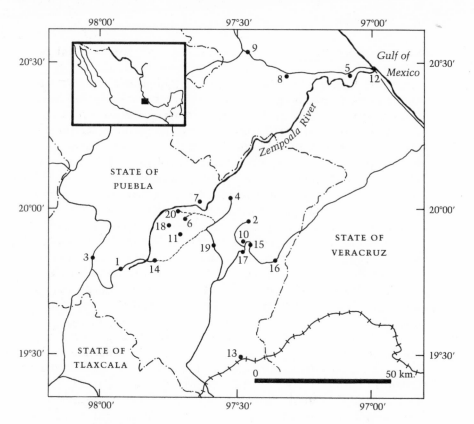

The northern Sierra de Puebla

1. Aquixtla
2. Atotocoyan
3. Chignahuapan
4. Cuetzalan del Progreso
5. Gutiérrez Zamora
6. Huitzilan de Serdán
7. Ištepek
8. Papantla
9. Poza Rica
10. Santiago Yaonáhuac
11. Tachco
12. Tecolutla
13. Tepeyahualco
14. Tetela de Ocampo
15. Teteles de Ávila Castillo
16. Teziutlán
17. Tlatlauqui(tepec)
18. Totutla
19. Zacapoaxtla
20. Zapotitlán de Méndez

enough so that the Indians of each speak very mutually intelligible dialects.

Huitzilan and Yaonáhuac share Aztec linguistic and historical antecedents. Common narratives flowed between the Sierra Nahuat in the northern Sierra de Puebla and the Aztecs of the Valley of Mexico by virtue of linguistic similarities and political connections between the two groups. Sierra Nahuat spoken in Huitzilan and Yaonáhuac today and Classical Nahuatl spoken by the Aztecs in the Valley of Mexico are closely related members of the Aztecoidan subfamily of languages (Robinson 1966; Longacre 1967). Mocte-zuma I (1440–1468) promoted the flow of common narratives by establishing political connections between the Aztec capital of Tenochtitlán and the Sierra Nahuat region. Determined to isolate and eventually conquer the Tlaxcalan Indians to the southwest of the northern Sierra, he brought the Nahuat communities of Tetela de Ocampo and Tlatlauquitepec under his domination. Huitzilan near Tetela and Yaonáhuac, some ten kilometers from Tlatlau-quitepec, probably paid tribute to Moctezuma and possibly contrib-uted troops for his battles against the Tlaxcalans (Davies 1968:27, 80). For these reasons, contemporary Sierra Nahuat narratives share many motifs with those reported for the ancient Aztecs by Sahagún (1953) and other sixteenth-century chroniclers who collected mythic tradition and beliefs in the Valley of Mexico (see chapter 7).

Spaniards began to settle in the Sierra Nahuat area in the late seventeenth century and brought peninsular Spanish tales from southern and central Spain.[3] The first Spaniards sought the mineral deposits and settled in Tetela de Ocampo (south of Huitzilan), Tlatlauquitepec (west of Yaonáhuac), and Teziutlán (east of Yaoná-huac). After exhausting the veins of gold, silver, and copper, they continued to settle the area to work the rich farm and pasture land.

SOCIAL STRUCTURE

It is necessary to control for social structure to reduce the number of social factors that can influence the way storytellers shape social images and social metaphors. Stories often contain multivocal symbols which have a variety of possible social referents in every-day life and can mean very different things. If many elements of social structure vary between the two communities, it will in-crease the difficulty of connecting differences in cognate stories to specific aspects of social life.

Nahuat stories from Huitzilan and Yaonáhuac have developed in conjunction with similar patterns of social relations. The Nahuat of both communities are the subordinate members of a plural society, and the men who tell stories about women are members of male-dominant families. These basic facts of Nahuat experience contribute to common images of the Nahuat as a class juxtaposed against Hispanics, and they affect men's images of women.

The Nahuat throughout the northern Sierra de Puebla are constantly reminded that Hispanics control the bulk of the strategic resources, monopolize trade, control the highest political offices in the region, make and administer the law, and are in control of the major instruments of ideational change—the church and the school. Of course Indians in biethnic communities feel the weight of Hispanic domination more than Indians in monoethnic ones, but no Nahuat can escape dealing with Hispanics in the major commercial and administrative centers. The Nahuat in both communities must obtain cash incomes by selling crops (coffee, avocados, plums, pears, apples, and peaches) to pay taxes on land or pay landlords for rented land, to buy medicine, clothes, tools, and construction materials. They must market their crops through a chain of intermediaries, the most important of whom are Hispanics. Many Nahuat of both communities must periodically migrate to work on Hispanic plantations in the lowlands to obtain additional income. While some Nahuat run their local community political affairs, all Nahuat participate in a political system whose laws and administration at the state level are in the hands of Hispanics. The Nahuat must contend with tax collectors who represent Hispanics in control of the state government. Indians must obey compulsory education laws by sending their children to schools where they learn values, knowledge, and new patterns of behavior from Hispanic teachers. While school attendance varies tremendously between communities in the northern Sierra de Puebla, no Nahuat can avoid sending children to school without risking fines or even imprisonment. Hispanics primarily control the church hierarchy by their support of the archdiocese if not the actual parish church. Hispanic priests and laypeople, with the help of bilingual Nahuat, assume the responsibility of religious indoctrination by giving classes in catechism, translating sermons into Nahuat, and conducting ritual dramas to teach Catholic doctrine.

Indians' feelings of powerlessness are partially mitigated by participation in the civil-religious hierarchy. In the northern Sierra the hierarchy consists partly of secular offices in the town council and committees organized among those who received land during the Agrarian Reform of the 1930s and 1940s. It also consists of religious officials, who include members of a variety of church committees, assistants to the priest, and sponsors of saints honored with elaborate rituals on days usually specified by the Catholic calendar. In Huitzilan as well as Yaonáhuac secular and religious offices have different rank and confer varying amounts of prestige on office holders. The degree of Nahuat powerlessness varies depending on Indians' access to the important local secular offices, particularly that of *municipio* president. Indians who control the town council have greater ability to determine how Hispanic law will apply at the *municipio* level, adjudicate disputes, influence the operation of public schools, can initiate public works, and can deal more effectively with Hispanic representatives of the state government because Indians are legal representatives of their communities. Chapters 3 and 4 describe how lack of access to secular office contributes to Nahuat powerlessness in Huitzilan and how fuller participation in the town council gives the Nahuat of Yaonáhuac more control over the above-mentioned matters.

Hispanic domination of Indians has affected Nahuat stories by imposing European-Catholic beliefs and Christian personalities into pre-Hispanic narratives. Hispanics introduced a large number of peninsular Spanish stories and motifs with no parallels in the Aztec oral tradition. Thus Nahuat narratives are a synthesis of two traditions tailored to fit the Indians' structural position in an ethnically stratified society. This synthetic oral tradition clearly expresses the powerlessness of the Nahuat relative to Hispanics, but the degree of Nahuat powerlessness varies according to the degree of Nahuat dependence or autonomy with respect to the dominant ethnic group.

NAHUAT FAMILY STRUCTURE

Androcentrism (male dominance) is a second theme running through Nahuat society and narrative tradition. Men generally have a stronger position in the social structure, and they depict women in stories as the morally weaker sex who should submit to control by men. It was mentioned that the Nahuat are a special case of a widespread pattern of androcentrism in peasant and tribal societies in many parts of the world. But Nahuat communities do not exhibit the same degree of androcentrism in myth or social structure. The comparison of parallel stories from different communities affords an opportunity to test hypotheses about the relationship between sexual ideology in narratives and men's and women's position in society. Before considering the variations, let us first turn to the common aspects of Nahuat family structure.

The Nahuat of both communities form households—the principal corporate kin groups—which function as units of food production and consumption. The members of a household work a
common corn and bean plot (*milpa*), they store their harvest in a
common granary, and the head of the household manages a single
purse filled by the sale of jointly owned cash crops (coffee, plums,
avocados, and pears) and domestic animals (chickens, turkeys, and
pigs), and supplemented by some of the wages of the household
members. Generally the household has residential unity, but the
component families frequently occupy separate dwellings on a
house plot and the women work in separate kitchens.

The household normally passes through an extended phase
when married sons and, more rarely, married daughters bring their
spouses into the group. But few couples remain in extended families for more than three or four years. The dependent couples often
establish their independence through a series of phases beginning
with the separation of kitchens for the mother-in-law and daughter-
in-law and ending when the couple plants a separate *milpa* (see
Taggart 1972).

Nahuat men and women have an interdependent relationship.
Men primarily perform *milpa* agriculture: they carry out most
stages of field preparation, planting, cultivation, and weeding,
although women help harvest crops in both communities, and
Huitzilan women and children cut coffee alongside men both on
their own plots and on the estates of Hispanics. Women primarily
carry out the arduous task of processing food, spin, weave, mend,
and embroider cloth, wash clothes, feed the domestic animals, and
care for children when their husbands are away in the field. Table 1
describes in more detail the sexual division of labor in Huitzilan,
which closely parallels that of Yaonáhuac.

Nahuat men and women express great pride in their work, and
they repeatedly assert that they cannot get along without each
other. Men and women give their interdependence as a major reason for marriage and re-marriage. When widows and widowers express grief over the loss of a spouse, they frequently remark on
their former dependence on each other and anguish over how they
will cope in the future. Nahuat men and women do not consider
the work of one sex more important than the work of the other.
Men do express a preference for male children but only because
they rely on their sons to help them work their *milpas* in their old
age.

Lewis (1949) argues that some Mexican Indian women have a
closer relationship with children than men because they are the

Table 1. Sexual Division of Labor in Huitzilan

Men	Men and Women	Women
Farming tasks by sex		
Prepare *milpas* for planting by clearing and burning debris. Plant, weed, cultivate, and fertilize plots.		
	Harvest *milpa* crops of corn, beans, squash, and chiles. Transport crops from plot to house.	
Plant and fertilize sugarcane fields.		
Harvest sugarcane and process stalks to make brown sugar (a single operation).		Cook for sugarcane harvesting groups.
	Transport brown sugar from press to house.	
Plant and fertilize coffee trees.		
		Women and children harvest most of the coffee crop.
Other nondomicile-based tasks by sex		
Collect and cut firewood in the forest.		
Hunt.	Gather crayfish.	
Migrate temporarily to lowland plantations to work in fields. Cut trees and work as stonemasons.		Cook for migrant labor groups.
	Market produce in local and neighboring markets.	
Lead prayers.	Perform sorcery and cure disease.	Assist women in childbirth.
Work as muleteers.		
Domicile-based tasks by sex		
Split firewood for kitchen.	Husk corn. Sell merchandise in local stores.	Grind tortilla dough and process other food, transport water, care for domestic animals, wash clothes, spin, weave, mend clothing, and embroider. Work in the homes of Hispanics as servants.

primary socializing agents and can exert considerable influence over family affairs through their children. The father has a more marginal position because he spends long hours away from the family, often drinks heavily, and remains more aloof from his children to be consistent with his role as disciplinarian and family head. But instead of supporting his position of authority, his marginality and aloofness actually reduce the amount of influence he has over family affairs despite ideals of male dominance.

Judgments like these are difficult to evaluate and rest heavily on the eye of the beholder and the kinds of cases observed. But I believe that this generalization does not fit the Nahuat and that both parents have close relationships with their children, albeit relationships of a different kind. To be sure, the father spends most of his day working in the field away from the domicile, and some men do drink heavily and abuse their children. In Huitzilan most fields lie quite a distance from home—as much as a two-hour walk one way. But I personally doubt that the mother generally enjoys a closer relationship with her children than the father if one considers how relationships evolve through the course of the developmental cycle of the household.

The mother most assuredly devotes her exclusive attention to her youngest child by giving it her breast and sleeping with it on a separate straw mat or in a separate bed. But the father assumes a nurturant role with the next youngest child by playing with it on his knee and sleeping with it along with other children on a different mat or bed separate from the mother.

The relationship remains close between both parents and their children, and the Nahuat encourage their children to be dependent through a number of childrearing practices. They swaddle young infants, mothers nurse them as long as possible until the sixth month of the next pregnancy, both parents show considerable affection to young children, teach children the world outside the home is filled with hostile forces, and continually stress filial piety through admonishments for disrespect. Both parents change their relationship with their children as they mature. The mother, as well as the father, is stern with children of school age—six and seven—and they assert that at this time they must not show too much love lest they spoil them and undermine establishing a sense of filial piety. But one is hard pressed to see the father necessarily becoming more aloof with the children than the mother. To some extent the mother is the emotional leader and the father is the taskmaster, perhaps creating greater tension between the father and his children, but this generalization is an oversimplification of

Nahuat family relations. Considerable variation exists among families within the same community—in some the father acts as
a disciplinarian but in others it is the mother—suggesting that
norms regarding emotional and taskmaster leadership by sex are
not rigidly followed.

Sexual segregation is an important factor affecting the relationship between adolescent children and their parents. Adolescent
boys sleep apart from other members of the family in support of
the strict Nahuat incest prohibition between brother and sister.
They generally sleep in separate rooms of the same dwelling, or in
different dwellings than those occupied by other family members if
their parents have erected several structures on the house site.
Adolescent boys work with their fathers in the *milpa*, and adolescent girls help their mother in and around the domicile. The
mother and daughter often develop an exceptionally close relationship, making it painful for Nahuat women when their daughters
marry and go live with their husbands' families of orientation. The
father-son relationship sometimes exhibits tension because the father wants his sons to remain in the household and help work the
family estate. But sons frequently seek their independence shortly
after marriage when they hope to devote their energies to supporting their wives and children. At this time the son may find himself
in the midst of intense conflict between his mother and wife.

If other things were equal—and they seldom are—the Nahuat
practices would tend to create sexual equality. But patrilineal land
inheritance, virilocality, and the age spread between men and women
make the family androcentric concordant with an ideology of male
dominance.

Land inheritance in both communities is patrilineal: while
Yaonáhuac women inherit much more land than their counterparts
in Huitzilan, they acquire less land than men. Chapters 3 and 4
give the statistics on land ownership by sex in the two communities. Patrilineal inheritance is the basis for the oldest male acting
as head of the household. By virtue of his control over land, he
manages the family estate by handling most of the major business
transactions and deciding how the patrimonial land should be uti-
lized. He decides about marketing crops, organizes the temporary
work groups to prepare fields for planting and for harvesting crops,
and generally manages the money obtained from the sale of coffee
or fruit, or from the wage labor of the household members. The
major exceptions to the practice that men manage the purse occur
in households where the father has died. Normally his oldest son
becomes the head of the household or the family, but the mother

keeps the purse and becomes the trustee to the patrimonial land. She generally decides when to divide the land of the family estate, and she frequently follows the wishes the father expresses verbally before his death. The father ostensibly makes decisions about establishing relationships of ritual kinship, gives consent for his daughters' and sons' marriages in close consultation with the mother, grants permission to his sons to divide from the parental family after their marriages, and decides if the family will assume the heavy responsibility of sponsoring a saint's day celebration.

Postmarital residence in Huitzilan and Yaonáhuac is predominantly virilocal in part because of patrilineal inheritance: couples reside more frequently with the family of the husband because he stands to inherit more land. But many also reside virilocally because most work teams are organized among men to perform *milpa* labor and, thus, the Nahuat prefer to live with the male kin on whom they can rely for agricultural help. Virilocality promotes male dominance because it strengthens agnatic male solidarity at the expense of female kin solidarity. The affinally related women in a Nahuat virilocal household have a notoriously tense relationship with each other, from the Nahuat point of view, and they seldom band together to protect their mutual interests in conflicts with men. The Nahuat mother-in-law, like her counterpart elsewhere, is a sharp critic of her daughter-in-law from the time the young bride enters the household. I believe this contributes heavily to men's image of women as sexually voracious, morally weaker, and more threatening to the moral order than men. It is interesting to note that mothers-in-law frequently attack their daughters-in-law, accusing them directly or by implication of illicit sexual behavior. Mothers and daughters and sisters enjoy perhaps the warmest relationships in Nahuat society, but virilocality scatters them in different neighborhoods and communities.

Community endogamy prevails in Huitzilan and Yaonáhuac, and thus most dislocation for women takes place between neighborhoods within the same village. Table 2 describes the comparative rates of community endogamy for men and women and indicates that slightly more married women than men practice intervillage marriage in both communities. This is consistent with the general practice of virilocality found throughout the Sierra Nahuat area. The high rates of community endogamous marriage for both sexes means that men and women remain close enough to their blood kin to permit frequent visits. They can gain their kin's support in times of crises, but virilocality nevertheless places women under more direct control by their husbands' parental families

Table 2. Rates of Village Endogamy, by Sex and Community

Status	Huitzilan		Yaonáhuac	
	Number	Percent	Number	Percent
Married men born in the community	420	93.3	277	94.2
Married women born in the community	402	89.3	266	90.5
Total married couples	450		294	

and puts them at a comparative disadvantage. Mothers try to visit their married daughters frequently, but virilocality cuts down the number of visits and acts to weaken relations between sisters. Women have heavy responsibilities in food processing and child care, and find it difficult to travel even short distances among different neighborhoods to visit their blood kin. The frequencies of virilocal and uxorilocal marriage in Huitzilan and Yaonáhuac appear in the following chapters.

Women marry at a younger age than their husbands and have consequently had less time to learn habits of responsibility and independence, which contributes to their weaker position in the family, particularly during the early years of marriage. Women are from two to five years younger than their husbands (the median difference), depending on the community. The age difference carries special significance for the Nahuat because in both communities, authority is delegated along the lines of age.

The Nahuat storytellers strongly support the value of filial piety—the backbone of the extended family—by describing gruesome consequences for sons who disobey or rebel against their fathers (Taggart 1977). These images of family relations accord with the general pattern of actual Nahuat family life. The Nahuat father delegates responsibility through his sons in order of their ages so that older sons have authority over younger sons, and the oldest son succeeds the father in primogeniture succession to the headship of the household. The authority of the father extends to his brothers and to other members of the community in the father's generation. The Nahuat act out rank by age and generation in ritual and express the principle in kinship terminology.

A witness to a family ceremonial gathering for ritual kinship or the sponsorship of a saint would see the father or the oldest male act as the official host and take a more prominent role in the rituals than other members of his family. He greets the guests as they arrive at his home; he offers or receives bottles of *aguardiente*, which are part of any family celebration; he distributes packages of cigarettes; he spreads incense and initiates or leads prayers; if the family holds a banquet, he formally invites the guests to begin eating and gives orders to women in the kitchen to attend to the needs and the wishes of those present; when the guests share shot glasses of *aguardiente*, they should offer the head of the household the second drink from every bottle (the first goes to the guest of honor); and departing guests express their gratitude and pleasure to the head for his hospitality.

Kinship terminology expresses the importance of rank by age by assigning separate terms of reference to pre- and postpubescent sons and daughters, adult men and women, and the oldest and youngest siblings. The term for a prepubescent son is *okičpil*, an adolescent boy is *telpuč*, and the term for adult man is *tagat*. The term for a prepubescent girl is *siwapil*, an adolescent girl is *ičpuč*, and the term for adult woman is *siwat*. Gender is not a part of the Nahuat language, and despite the sexual segregation in Nahuat society, siblings are terminologically distinguished only by age. The term for first-born sibling is *tayekanke* (Huitzilan) or *tiačkauw* (Yaonáhuac), and those for the last-born are *tašokoyot* (Huitzilan) and *šokoyot* (Yaonáhuac).

In sum, while it is difficult to rule out entirely the possibility that male dominance is more apparent than real, Nahuat men have a stronger basis to take the initiative in family decision making because they generally control more land, virilocality promotes agnatic male solidarity, and husbands are older than their wives. Of course, one can find cases where women have stronger person- alities than their husbands and take charge of affairs normally as- sumed by men, but these make the exceptions rather than the rule. Chapters 8 through 11 discuss how the prevailing patterns of fam- ily relations in Huitzilan and Yaonáhuac are related to the images of men and women that men depict in narratives. It is important to repeat that men tell stories, and one cannot assume that their images of the sexes are the same as those held by women. This applies particularly to the Nahuat because women generally do not appear in large numbers in the storytellers' audience. Men tell stories in bars, when among migrant workers in the hot country, as members of sugarcane processing groups (in Huitzilan), and in cere- monials (particularly wakes). On most of these occasions, men make up the bulk of the audience, and even in ceremonials, where women and men carry out joint activities, the sexes generally sit separately, consistent with the sexual segregation in Nahuat society. Men do not try to conceal the stories like those discussed in this book from women, some of whom know their contents. But women of both communities do not appear to play a prominent part in the social and psychological process that shapes the Nahuat narrative into a group product.

3. Huitzilan de Serdán

The father exhorts his son

Huitzilan is tucked away in the rugged mountains where the Central Mexican Plateau descends to the coastal plains. The *municipio* consists of eight settlements whose total population of 6,995 lives between 1,100 and 900 meters above sea level in the heart of the coffee zone. The study took place in the *cabecera*—the seat of the *municipio* government—where 2,373 Nahuat live in close association with 275 Hispanics.[1] This is the largest concentration of Nahuat I know of in this part of the northern Sierra de Puebla.

The most obvious characteristic of the *cabecera* is its ethnic stratification. The Hispanic minority is an extremely self-conscious ethnic group that refers to itself as people of reason (*gente de razón*). They believe they are culturally and racially different from, and superior to, the Nahuat. They maintain that the two ethnic groups should not intermarry despite the numerous children born to Nahuat women and fathered by Hispanic men. They emphasize their distinctive ethnic identity by asserting they originated from Tetela de Ocampo, the capital of the ex-district which has jurisdiction over Huitzilan, and other communities on the Central Mexican Plateau. They express their feelings of superiority by referring to the Nahuat as *peoncitos* (diminutive for *peón* = laborer) and sometimes *inditos* (diminutive for *indio* = Indian and a word carrying a belittling connotation).

The Nahuat are also a self-conscious group, who regard themselves as culturally different from the Hispanics. They refer to themselves as *macewalme* (peasants), and they call Hispanics *españoles* (Spaniards), *razones* (those of reason), or *koyome* (gentlemen).[2] Despite their weaker position in the ethnic hierarchy, they regard Hispanics as morally inferior, because they believe members of the dominant ethnic group have immoral habits: they marry their cousins, and thus commit incest from the Nahuat point of view; they are sexually promiscuous and polygynous; they fail to support the religious festivals and hence do not maintain a sacred covenant between god and humans; the Nahuat resent the creation of a hierarchical social order that clashes with their own egalitarian ideal.

The dominant position of Hispanics strikes an observer in very obvious ways. The *cabecera* is a compact settlement of 488 families, who live on the floor of a small, narrow valley at the northern end of the *municipio*. One who walks the length of the town along the cobblestone road which extends the full length of the valley will immediately notice the very large, palatial homes of the Hispanic families. If the same observer ventures along the maze of small footpaths which crisscross the valley floor, and extend up the mountain slopes, he will come across the much more numerous, but humble dwellings of the Nahuat hidden in the coffee orchards and shaded by *chalawite* trees.

HISTORY OF HISPANIC SETTLEMENT

Spaniards first moved into the northern Sierra de Puebla during the last decades of the seventeenth century to exploit the mines of gold, silver, and copper. One of the two mining centers in this region was Tetela de Ocampo, one day's walk to the south of Huitzilan. In 1708 the viceroy of New Spain, the duque of Albuquerque, ordered the governing official of the province to grant Indians to work the mines of Francisco de la Zerna, whose hacienda included Tetela (Silva Anraca 1960). After that date, Spanish settlement of Tetela gradually increased, and by the end of the Colonial period, Hispanics completed the construction of the parish church which remains the center for Catholic worship in the community today.

The nineteenth century was a critical period for many Mexican Indians because the federal government put into effect a number of laws and carried out programs that promoted Hispanic penetration into Indian areas (Wolf 1959; Helms 1975). The Reform Laws of the 1857 Constitution and the Colonization Laws of 1883 and 1894 forced Indians who held land communally to adopt fee simple tenure and register their land in the district capitals. This made land a commodity to sell on the open market and laid the foundation for the Hispanic acquisition of Indian land. At the same time, Porfirio Díaz (1876–1910) promoted the production of agricultural goods sold to the international market by building railroads, making trade agreements, and encouraging foreign capital investment in Mexico. One cash crop which became important at this time was coffee, a crop which grows in limited areas between 500 and 1,200 meters above sea level at this latitude.

The government's policies had the effect of thrusting Hispanics who lived in the highlands around Tetela into the Nahuat and Totonac communities lying in the canyons and valleys to the north. Land around Tetela yields very little because winter frosts permit only a summer corn crop. It is near the limit of the low-hanging clouds which moisten the intermediate and low elevations with a steady drizzle during the winter months following the summer rainy season. Hence rainfall around Tetela is lower and the land is less fertile compared to lowland areas. Hispanics descended into previously isolated Nahuat and Totonac communities where they found good land for crops and pasture, cheap labor, and a climate suitable for growing coffee.

Around the turn of the century, Hispanics started moving into the *municipio* of Huitzilan, some settling first in Totutla, a community lying between Tetela and the *cabecera* of Huitzilan. Many of the older Hispanics living in the *cabecera* were born in Tetela or Totutla and describe Huitzilan as a place with almost no Hispanic families when they came.

Nearly all Hispanics developed close ties with the Nahuat, many became bilingual, and some made sincere efforts to bring what from their point of view was progress. Some of the first settlers who became wealthy caciques (political bosses) used their economic and political power to construct governmental buildings, markets, and schools.

The Hispanics who settled in Huitzilan were driven to make their fortunes, and within a short while after their arrival, they acquired the bulk of the arable land, some by legal purchase, and others by fraud and deception. Hispanics established the first stores and sold goods to the Nahuat on credit. The Nahuat complain many Hispanic merchants demanded immediate payment or title to Indian land, and they describe how some confronted them with written documents which they could neither read nor understand and forced them with legal threats to relinquish their property. I found some of the Indians' complaints in petitions submitted to the Department of Agrarian Affairs in Mexico City. The Nahuat practice of holding expensive celebrations to honor their saints forced them to borrow heavily from merchants. Indians who assume a sponsorship of saints must provide a banquet, pay for expensive adornments placed in front of the saint in the church on the eve before mass, and pay for the mass itself, which takes place on the saint's day in the religious calendar. Some paid their debts by pawning or selling their coffee harvests, others by migrating to the lowland plantations, but most relinquished their land to their creditors.

Many Nahuat found themselves completely landless and sought relief in the postrevolutionary land reform program which set aside government land—ejidos—for impoverished small farmers. The Nahuat petitioned the governor of the state in 1936, during the regime of Lázaro Cárdenas and the period of extensive land redistribution in Mexico. In 1943 they obtained a grant of four ejidos with a total of 336.2 hectares, but this grant was insufficient because the largest parcel was only 295 hectares of rocky and comparatively unproductive soil.

ETHNIC HIERARCHY

Huitzilan is now a biethnic community in which Hispanics own the bulk of the strategic resources and control the local government. The Nahuat of Huitzilan live under immediate and direct Hispanic domination. When the Hispanics settled in Huitzilan, they introduced social classes based on ethnic identification, and the Nahuat became the subordinate group. Hispanics make up only 10.4 percent of the cabecera population, but they own over 80 percent of the land and control the economic life of the community. The life blood of Huitzilan is the coffee which Hispanics produce and purchase from the Nahuat who own small orchards. Hispanics export the crop to buyers in the closest major commercial town—Zacapoaxtla—and import manufactured items, medicine, and major food staples including corn. To be sure, Hispanics generally have more wealth than the Nahuat, but much is concentrated in the hands of a dozen Hispanic families who own the largest orchards, have the most cattle and pasture land, buy the most coffee, and transport the bulk of the exported and imported goods.

A number of behaviors manifest the dominant position of the Hispanics over the Nahuat in Huitzilan. First, patronage—a hierarchical relationship in which a person of lower status obtains the political protection and economic support of a higher-status person in return for loyalty and labor—is very asymmetrical. Nahuat have Hispanic patrons, but Hispanics never have Nahuat patrons. A very large number of Nahuat in Huitzilan work on a regular basis with their Hispanic patrons, to whom they owe deference and respect. Several patrons cement the loyalty of their Indian clients by lending them money, providing them with house sites, selling them building materials for homes on credit, selling them corn and bean plots (milpas) on a schedule of deferred payments, and protecting them from punishment by Hispanic authorities. Hispanic patrons

must secure the loyalty of their Indian clients because patrons
compete for Indian labor. The Nahuat express devotion to their
patrons that resembles but does not duplicate their expressions
of filial piety in the family. Nahuat childrearing practices that in-
culcate obedience and respect for parents reinforce the patronage
system. The importance of patronage and the Huitzilan Nahuat expressions of piety toward their patrons are illustrated in the following anecdote.

THE FUNERAL OF R.

*An Hispanic called R. was one of the wealthiest patrons in the
community. He was born in Tetela and came to Huitzilan as a
young man and managed to build up tremendous holdings in
land, cattle, houses, and machinery used to process coffee. He
amassed a large amount of cash which he loaned to businessmen
all over this part of the northern Sierra to finance a wide variety of
enterprises. In the opinion of one of his Hispanic contemporaries,
he functioned as a banker and promoted a number of activities
that otherwise could not take place for want of capital.*

*R. had a large number of Nahuat clients whom he employed
to maintain his vast estate, to whom he lent land to build their
homes, and whom he helped escape punishment for serious
crimes. Some Nahuat bitterly complained that he had a rough and
changeable character, that he tended to jump to conclusions and
blame Indians for petty crimes they did not commit, and that
he beat Indians who did not correctly carry out his orders. The
Nahuat generally agreed that many Indians depended heavily on
him for their support and were very loyal to him.*

*In March 1978, R. was killed by his nephew in a gun battle
over land. R. had sold his nephew a plot of land on credit, and the
nephew was very slow in making the payments. The two quarreled, and under circumstances no one can pin down, they died in
a blaze of gunfire.*

*The Indian response to R.'s death was an astounding expres-
sion of the positive side of Nahuat ambivalence to their Hispanic
patron. A wake was held that evening, and nearly all 450 Nahuat
families or their representatives made an appearance bearing
candles and gifts of bread. Many Nahuat had little connection
with R., and some were clients of other Hispanic patrons whose
wealth and power approached those of R. Nahuat whom I know
well and who had little experience as clients of R. explained they*

felt obligated to pay their respects by attending the wake and bearing generous gifts of bread because of this Hispanic patron's importance in the community.

Even the peasant insurgents attended his wake and accompanied the Nahuat and Hispanics to the cemetery for R.'s burial. Approximately 100 Nahuat men from the cabecera and adjoining settlements organized into an insurgency movement with help from outside leaders. Their avowed aim was to regain land they regarded as unfairly taken from Indians. They expressed this aim by painting numerous slogans on the houses of wealthy Hispanics and in speeches delivered over loudspeakers located in the hills above the community. The Nahuat insurgents appeared in a solemn procession at the dead man's home, attended a mass in the church, and helped bury his remains in the town cemetery.

The burial procession itself was the most massive expression of grief and respect to take place in Huitzilan since I began fieldwork there in 1968. Nahuat men and women and Hispanics formed a huge procession that extended for more than a kilometer on the cobblestone road covering the length of the community. Over 2,000 people formed the procession, the vast majority of whom were from among the 2,373 Nahuat and 275 Hispanics who live in the cabecera.

Other behaviors that manifest the dominant position of the Hispanics over the Nahuat have a close connection to the wealth differences between the two groups. *Compadrazgo*, a relationship of ritual kinship contracted in a rite of Catholic baptism or in a ceremony patterned after that rite (Mintz and Wolf 1950; Nutini 1976a), is also asymmetrical. The Nahuat ask Hispanics to be the ritual co-sponsors but Hispanics never ask the Nahuat. Interethnic sexual relations creating bonds of blood kinship between Hispanics and Nahuat are also asymmetrical. Hispanic men have sexual intercourse and father children with Nahuat women, but few Nahuat men have had sexual relations with Hispanic women.

The Nahuat population has less reproductive success largely because they lack money to pay for adequate medical treatment. The Nahuat sometimes prefer to consult their own curers over those trained in western medicine. But the vast majority of Nahuat show little reluctance to consult western-trained doctors when they can pay for their services. Comparison of the crude rates of natural increase—the difference between the crude birth rate and the crude death rate—reveals the lower reproductive success of the Nahuat. The Hispanic rate of 37.6 is about twice the Nahuat rate of 18.7. For both groups the crude birth rates are about the same— 47.3 for Hispanic and 49.6 for the Nahuat—but the crude death rates contrast sharply, reflecting the harsher living conditions for the Nahuat. The rates for Hispanics are 8.75 for males and 9.7 for females, while comparable rates for the Nahuat are 34.8 for males and 30.9 for females.

The Nahuat of Huitzilan are blocked from gaining control of the secular offices in the civil-religious hierarchy. Hispanics control the nominating process for candidates on the slate of the dominant PRI (Institutional Revolutionary Party). They name Nahuat adolescent boys as messengers (aguaciles) for members of the town council, and they occasionally nominate the Nahuat for seats in the council itself, but Hispanics control all aspects of the municipio government. The Nahuat have little to say about administering Hispanic laws, deciding who will serve as judges to settle disputes and punish the Nahuat for minor crimes, and initiating and collecting funds for public works projects. While the Nahuat have little to say about running the town council, Hispanics make decisions about the religious side of the civil-religious hierarchy. Hispanic presidents have jailed Nahuat dance groups for failing to perform at the patron saint festival in August, Hispanic priests have grouped the days for celebrating major saints into a seven-day period in August, and Hispanic committees have exerted a heavy hand in selecting sponsors for saint's day celebration.[3] The Nahuat generally act as sponsors, and it was mentioned that this contributed to the alienation of land out of the hands of the Indians and into the hands of the Hispanics.

FAMILY STRUCTURE

Men tend to have a stronger position in the social structure throughout the Nahuat area (see Slade 1975), but Huitzilan women have a weaker position in their families than Yaonáhuac women. Huitzilan family structure is strongly male-dominant because of patrilineal inheritance of land, virilocality, and the fact that husbands are generally five years older than their wives.

Men control more land than women because inheritance is almost exclusively patrilineal both as a norm and as practiced in this community. The following two anecdotal cases illustrate that Nahuat men expect land to pass from father to son. The first case exemplifies the fact that men do not consider that their sisters have a right to patrimonial land even if they reside with their parents.

CASE 1

Fulana [a pseudonym] is the daughter of a man who owned considerable land at the northern end of the community. She married a man who received no inheritance and had no place to live, and the couple settled down to live with Fulana's parents. Some time later Fulana and her husband separated from her parental family houehold and built a small dwelling with a straw roof next to her paternal home. Fulana's father died, and then her husband and finally her mother passed away. Fulana had three surviving brothers, one of whom was disinherited by his father for marrying against his wishes. Her three remaining brothers figured she had no right to any of the patrimonial land and so they forced her to leave. When I left in 1970 she was living on one of the ejidos with her children.

The second case illustrates that widows who reside virilocally do not lose rights in their deceased husband's land.

CASE 2

When Mengana [also a pseudonym] married twenty-three years ago she went to live in the home of her husband. When her parents-in-law died, her husband and his brother divided the patrimonial house site and garden. Ten years ago, Mengana's husband died, and although his brother survives him, he has made no move to claim half of the patrimonial house site as his own because he considers that it belongs to the children of his deceased brother.

While anecdotal cases can illustrate that some families have a rule of patrilineal inheritance, they do not establish that the rule is widely held or generally put into practice. Statistics I gathered on land inheritance by sex tally with the cases just presented and reflect a general practice of giving sons land inheritance over daughters. Table 3 shows the proportion of married women who own land relative to all women in marriages where one spouse is a property holder in fee simple.

Table 3. Land Ownership by Spouse in Huitzilan

Status	Number	Percent
Wife owns land, husband has none	20	12.7
Wife and husband own separate plots	14	9.0
Total number of land-owning wives	34	21.7
Husband owns land, wife has none	123	78.3
Total number of couples with land	157	100.0

Nahuat practice is at odds with the edicts of the Puebla Civil Code, which states that daughters as well as sons should inherit shares of their parents' property in the absence of a testament indicating otherwise.[4] Few Nahuat write wills specifying how they want their land divided among their children, but property inheritance is patrilineal rather than bilateral because the Nahuat, fearing extortion by Hispanic *municipio* authorities, do not like to refer cases of land division to the town council, who will enforce the bilateral edict.

It is interesting to speculate about the effects of Hispanic settlement on Nahuat inheritance practices. Historical data are very scarce for Huitzilan inheritances because few Nahuat in this community draw up documents (testaments or bills of sale) when bequeathing land. Thus it is not possible to reconstruct how the Nahuat passed land to their children prior to Hispanic settlement in the community. Collier (1975) suggests that land scarcity in Mayan communities has promoted patrilineality, and it follows from his argument that a shortage of land created by the Hispanic acquisition of Indian land may have promoted patrilineal inheritance in Huitzilan. Many Nahuat who own small plots express reluctance to divide land among their children of both sexes as required by the Puebla Civil Code. When they lack land they generally favor their sons over their daughters in inheritance. A number of Huitzilan Nahuat couples—ninety-six—have rights in ejido land which they can bequeath, but the Agrarian Code specifies that parents who have ejido plots can pass them on to only one child.[5] Most Nahuat consequently give ejido plots to their sons rather than their daughters, following their general preferences about land inheritance.

The lack of land affects the role women play in the civil-religious hierarchy and in the family decision-making process. While Nahuat men are blocked from the secular offices, women rarely hold offices on either side of the civil-religious hierarchy. Because women lack land, they generally cannot act as sponsors of saints, the most important religious offices. The Nahuat have no rule against women assuming sponsorships, and they assert that anyone may act as a sponsor if he or she has the will to do so. But women who lack land cannot assume the expensive responsibilities connected with the office. Sponsors must pay for wax adornments, rockets, *aguardiente*, cigarettes, and huge quantities of pork, corn, beans, tomatoes, and spices for a ceremonial meal offered to a large number of invited guests. The few women I knew who were sponsors were widows who had acquired the trusteeship of land belonging to their former husbands.

It is important to note that assuming the sponsorship of a saint confers prestige on the office holder but no real power or authority. Both sexes lack access to the important formal positions of authority in the community government and thus are comparatively powerless. Moreover, men cannot assume sponsorships without the approval of their wives, because men who assume this office must depend on women to prepare the ceremonial banquet. Thus women's lack of access to religious office probably has a modest effect on the balance between the sexes in the community.

A more important result of patrilineal land inheritance is the power it gives to men in the family decision-making process. The major family decisions hinging on land involve utilizing the family estate, marketing crops, selling or pawning land to meet ceremonial and everyday expenses, initiating marriage negotiations and deciding to hold marriage ceremonies (which may require pawning or selling land), and bequeathing land in inheritance. Women most assuredly can exert influence in family decisions, but men have a stronger structural position to dominate the decision-making process.

The position of men and women in the family depends on other factors, including the degree of male-kin versus female-kin solidarity. As noted by Fischer (1958) and others (Quinn 1977), when male-kin solidarity is stronger than female-kin solidarity, one would expect that women would have a weaker position because they would be at a disadvantage in confrontations with men. Anything that promotes male-kin solidarity at the expense of female-kin solidarity (such as a virilocal residence rule) will tend to weaken the position of women in the kinship system. The predominant postmarital residence practice in Huitzilan is virilocality (married sons reside with or near their parents), which acts to

Table 4. Uxorilocal and Virilocal Residence in Huitzilan

Type of Residence	Number	Percent
Uxorilocality		
Couples live in wife's parental household	28	
Couples live in house owned by wife's family who resides separately	19	
Couples live in house owned by wife: wife's family lives separately or deceased	27	
Subtotal	74	18.4
Virilocalilty		
Couples live in husband's parental household	102	
Couples live in house owned by husband's family who resides separately	26	
Couples live in house owned by husband: husband's family lives separately or is deceased	200	
Subtotal	328	81.6
Grand totals	402	100.0

Ninety-three of the two hundred couples listed as living in houses owned by the husband live on ejido land. The forty-eight couples who live on house sites borrowed from nonfamily members are not included in this table.

cluster agnatically related males and disperse blood-related women and thereby promotes solidarity among the father, sons, and brothers at the expense of solidarity among the mother, daughters, and sisters.[6] Table 4 shows the rates of uxorilocal and virilocal residence in Huitzilan.

4. Santiago Yaonáhuac

The symbols of womanhood

Across two ranges of mountains to the southeast of Huitzilan lies the monoethnic community of Yaonáhuac. This long and narrow *municipio* extends northward from the highlands to the lowland coffee zone. The terrain descends gently at first from an elevation of 1,870 meters, but then drops suddenly in spectacular canyons lined with a patchwork of *milpas* clinging to the abrupt slopes. The quick descent of the land breaks the *municipio* into southern highland and northern lowland halves. This study took place on the southern highlands—the seat of Yaonáhuac's government (the *cabecera*)—where 73 percent of the total *municipio* population lives.

The 2,487 individuals who live in the highland half of Yaonáhuac have a much more egalitarian social structure than many of their counterparts in other communities of the northern Sierra de Puebla.[1] Few Hispanics settled inside this part of the *municipio*, because it lacked desired strategic resources. The first Spaniards came during the last years of the seventeenth century to exploit the mines located below what is now the major industrial and commercial center of Teziutlán. A number of these established the community of Teteles de Ávila Castillo two kilometers south of Yaonáhuac along a major trade route between the mines and a smelter in Tepeyahualco further in on the Mesa Central. Farmers and cattle ranchers trickled into the area during the 1700s and 1800s, and when coffee became an important cash crop in the 1880s some moved into the lowland Yaonáhuac settlements—particularly Atotocoyan—but they did not come in large numbers and they do not dominate the Nahuat who live in the highlands. Although some Hispanics of neighboring communities—especially Teteles—own Yaonáhuac land, they have acquired much less land than Hispanics have obtained in Huitzilan.

While Yaonáhuac is basically a monoethnic community, the Nahuat living there are nevertheless constantly reminded that they are the subordinate group in an ethnically plural society when they venture into the neighboring Hispanic town of Teteles, or carry out their business in one of the regional commercial or political centers

where most Hispanic families congregate. The Nahuat of Yaonáhuac, like their counterparts in Huitzilan, are a self-conscious
group aware of their position in the plural society. They call themselves the poor ones (*los pobres*) or peasants (*masewalme*) and they
refer to Hispanics as the rich ones (*los ricos*) or the gentlemen
(*koyome*).

YAONÁHUAC SOCIAL STRUCTURE

The Nahuat of Yaonáhuac participate fully in both the secular and
the religious offices of the civil-religious hierarchy. Almost all *municipio* presidents and councilmembers during the last fifty years
have been Indians. One resident Hispanic has served as secretary
periodically for several decades and has considerable power by virtue of his ability to deal with government officials and because of
his knowledge of Mexican law. But his influence derives directly
from his collaboration with a group of several Nahuat families who
form a prominent political faction. Members of this faction have,
until recently, controlled the process of nominating the official PRI
candidates, but in the last ten years they have lost their position to
another faction of Nahuat.

There is a much broader base of Nahuat participation in plan-
ning and administrating public works projects, in directing the
activities of the school, and in organizing numerous church committees. Most teachers are Hispanics who do not reside in the
community, and some have acted in heavy-handed ways to impose
Hispanic values on the Indians. But the Nahuat have successfully
curtailed their efforts by having them transferred. I was astounded
at the very large number of Nahuat who attended public meetings
to discuss matters of public policy. The total Nahuat populations of
the highland portion of Yaonáhuac and the *cabecera* settlement of
Huitzilan are very similar—2,487 for Yaonáhuac and 2,648 for
Huitzilan—and yet ten times as many Nahuat attend open meetings concerned with school policy in Yaonáhuac.

Political power and authority probably were more concentrated
in this community in the past. A search of the bills of sale, testaments, and acts of property division in the archives of the *municipio* and former district capital of Tlatlauqui revealed that a landed
aristocracy, albeit a weak one, existed around the turn of the
century. During a ten-year period at the close of the nineteenth
century, for which land records are available, a small number of
individuals made a large number of land acquisitions: two acquired
twenty-seven plots between them. No such concentration has

Table 5. Land Acquisitions in Yaonáhuac, by Historical Period

Number of acquisitions	Prerevolutionary 1887–1889; 1894–1900*		Recent past 1968–1977	
	Number of individuals or couples	Percent	Number of individuals or couples	Percent
1	169	70.4	310	85.6
2	42	17.5	38	10.5
3	14	5.8	11	3.0
4	5	2.1	2	.6
5	4	1.7	1	.3
6	3	1.3	0	0
7	1	.4	0	0
12	1	.4	0	0
15	1	.4	0	0
Total individuals or couples	240	100.0	362	100.0

*Bills of sale and testaments for the years 1890–1893 could not be located in the *municipio* archives.

taken place during a comparable ten-year period in the recent past (see table 5). The small landed aristocracy that existed around the turn of the century was primarily Hispanic. Two ancestors of the Hispanic families who presently live in Yaonáhuac made the largest number of acquisitions. But their descendants sold much of the estate, and today they do not rank among the largest landowners in the *municipio*.

The rates of Nahuat-Spanish bilingualism in Huitzilan and Yaonáhuac reflect the present positions of the two Nahuat groups with respect to Hispanics. Both communities have had schools since the turn of the century or before where Hispanic teachers impart Spanish to Indians, but the Huitzilan Nahuat are much more monolingual than their counterparts from Yaonáhuac. I contracted local Nahuat in both communities to collect statistical data on Spanish proficiency. Census takers were instructed to rate every individual in each household they visited on a four-point scale according to ability to speak Spanish. Census takers came from the local communities to ensure a high rate of response and to take advantage of their knowledge of those who answered their questions and those whom they rated. Table 6 shows the results and illustrates the degree to which the Huitzilan Nahuat have re-

Table 6. Spanish Proficiency, by Community

Knowledge of Spanish	Huitzilan		Yaonáhuac	
	Number	Percent	Number	Percent
None	1598	69.0	152	9.6
Little	219	9.5	187	11.8
Some	326	14.1	326	20.5
Much	172	7.4	924	58.1
Totals	2315	100.0	1589	100.0

No information was obtained for thirty-three individuals in Huitzilan and seventy-four persons in Yaonáhuac, most of whom were infants too young to speak.

mained monolingual, while the Yaonáhuac Nahuat have become markedly bilingual.

A number of factors account for the rates of monolingualism and bilingualism in the two communities, and they are connected to the degree of ethnic hierarchy that prevails in Huitzilan and Yaonáhuac. The comparative poverty of Huitzilan Nahuat families forces parents to keep their children home to help harvest coffee from November through February, during the months when school is in session. Nahuat parents from this community frequently complain that teachers, who are almost entirely Hispanics, punish and occasionally beat Indian children. Hispanics, on the other hand, do not actively enforce the compulsory education laws and have curtailed the efforts of the National Indian Institute (Instituto Nacional Indigenista), which has sent bilingual Nahuat-Spanish instructors into the community to teach Spanish as a second language. It is to the advantage of Hispanics to keep Indians monolingual to retain a cheap source of labor and hold on to their control of the secular *municipio* government.

The Yaonáhuac Nahuat, on the other hand, actively promote school attendance, and some are now sending their daughters as well as their sons to secondary schools in Teteles, the former district capital of Tlatlauqui, and the commercial and industrial center of Teziutlán. These Nahuat have more access to important strategic resources and have prospered more than the Huitzilan Nahuat with the post–World War II economic growth in Mexico. They see the school as one of the avenues by which their children can acquire nonfarming occupations and even enter the middle class. At the same time, they regard the school as less threatening to their traditions because they share in its operation by virtue of their control over the *municipio* government. Schools in this community, like those in many rural *municipios* in the state of Puebla, depend heavily on the community for economic support. In the past thirty years, the Yaonáhuac Nahuat have contributed money, materials, and labor to add new classrooms and administrative offices. The school's director leans heavily on the Indian community for enforcement of the state's compulsory education laws. Consequently local school administrators must fashion a school policy that fits the perceived needs of the Nahuat and avoids offending Indian values and traditions.

MEN AND WOMEN

A pronounced shift in the position of men and women has taken place in Yaonáhuac social structure. Yaonáhuac women have improved their status in the family with a change from patrilineal to bilateral land inheritance, giving them more control over the most important strategic resources and providing a basis for their greater initiative in family decision making. It is possible to reconstruct Nahuat land inheritance practices for the last ninety years in this community because Yaonáhuac Indians generally transfer land to their children with a bill of sale or occasionally a testament. Table 7 is based on a search of land records in Yaonáhuac and the former district land office in Tlatlauqui and shows an increase in the proportion of women who acquired land from 1887 to 1977.

Two factors probably combined to bring about this change which improved the position of women relative to men. The first is the diminished concentration of land, which probably favored bilateral inheritance because it gave women more potential access to land. As mentioned earlier, when the Nahuat lack land, they bequeath it to their sons but not to their daughters. As land becomes more plentiful, the Nahuat appear to pass it on to their children of both sexes.

The Reform Laws administered during the nineteenth century were probably a more important factor. One aspect of these laws aimed to establish fee simple land tenure and thereby abolish corporate or communal land ownership in the Indian areas of Mexico. When these laws were applied for the first time on a widespread and systematic basis, during the regime of Porfirio Díaz (1876–1910), it led to the registration of land titles and the transfer of land through inheritance by testamentary disposition and more frequently through bills of sale (*actas de compra-venta*). Eventually the shift occurred from patrilineal to bilateral land inheritance for the fol-

Table 7. Sex of Those in Yaonáhuac Who Acquired Land, by Historical Period

Sex	1887 to 1905		1962 to 1977		
	Number	Percent	Number	Percent	
Women	37	15.9	141	34.1	
Men	196	84.1	273	65.9	
Totals	233	100.0	414	100.0	N = 647

$x^2 = 23.8$ with 1 df, $p < .001$ (two tailed test).

lowing reason. Under Mexican law of the nineteenth and twentieth centuries, married couples are single legal entities, making the wife a co-owner of her husband's property (bills of sale from the time of Porfirio Díaz frequently specify this fact). Exceptions to this rule occur when the couple marries with a divided property provision, but this practice is exceedingly rare among the Nahuat. Consequently even though a husband may have acquired patrimonial land from his parents, his wife legally must give her consent to its sale if the land passed to the husband with a new land title. This gives the wife a legal basis for influencing how the patrimonial land should be distributed, and over several generations it appears to have led to the practice of giving land to daughters as well as to sons.

Statistical data I gathered to compare land ownership by sex in the two communities reflect the contrast in inheritance practices and illustrate that Huitzilan is now something like what Yaonáhuac was during the latter part of the nineteenth century in terms of land inheritance practices. Table 8 summarizes the different proportions of married women owning land in relation to all married women where at least one spouse owns land. It does not include landless couples, most of whom are young married pairs who have yet to receive their inheritance, or Huitzilan couples with ejido plots but no land in fee simple. The vast majority of married women listed in this table as owning land acquired it through inheritance rather than purchase. Hence this table computes the differences between Huitzilan and Yaonáhuac in their application of inheritance rules by sex. It is important to mention that although Yaonáhuac women own considerably more land than their counterparts in Huitzilan, they generally own less land than men, a factor contributing to male dominance in both communities.

The community property provision promoted more bilateral

Table 8. Married Women Who Own Land, by Community

| | Huitzilan | | Yaonáhuac | |
Status	Number	Percent	Number	Percent
Married women who own land: ejido land included for Huitzilan	34	21.7	108	50.7
Other married women whose husbands own land in fee simple	123	78.3	105	49.3
Totals	157	100.0	213	100.0 $N = 370$

$x^2 = 31.03$ with df 1, $p < .001$ (two tailed test).

Husbands also own land in the case of fourteen couples from Huitzilan and seventy-six couples from Yaonáhuac.

inheritance in Yaonáhuac because more Nahuat of this community adopted the practice of testamentary disposition and bequeathal of land with a bill of sale. The Huitzilan Nahuat have not adopted these practices because to do so would require payment of all back taxes on their land, and many are several decades behind. The responsibility of collecting land taxes rests with the office of the Recaudación de Rentas (Tax Collection) in the former district capital of Tetela de Ocampo, one day's arduous walk or horseback ride from the *cabecera* of Huitzilan. All tax collectors operate out of this office, and most have been residents of Tetela with weak ties to the Nahuat of Huitzilan. Tax collectors who visit this community tend to focus on the larger landowners, most of whom are Hispanics. Because few Nahuat of Huitzilan have drawn up testaments or bills of sale when passing land in inheritance, few wives of landowners are or have been mentioned as co-owners of their husbands' property. Hence they have had no legal basis for influencing decisions on the distribution of land in inheritance, and land generally has passed to sons only following the wishes of the father.

The Nahuat living on the highland half of Yaonáhuac, on the other hand, are a short distance—ten kilometers—from the former district capital of Tlatlauqui, the center of property tax collection. Bus transportation has linked the community with the former district capital since 1944. Tax collectors operating out of the Tlatlauqui office have visited Yaonáhuac on a very frequent basis. Motivated by quotas set by their superiors, they have assiduously worked to collect taxes from the bulk of the Nahuat landowners because land is less concentrated in this community. One tax collector reported to me that he urged the Yaonáhuac Nahuat to pay back taxes so they could bequeath land with a bill of sale or testament to prevent others from filing competing claims of ownership in the former district capital. This ploy apparently worked because of the general Nahuat suspicion that others will attempt to take advantage of their weakness. Hence the Yaonáhuac Nahuat have more frequently bequeathed their land with documents containing a community property provision promoting bilateral land inheritance.

Bilateral inheritance not only strengthened the position of women by giving them access to an important strategic resource, but it also slightly affected the balance between the sexes through its effects on postmarital residence. A few more couples reside uxorilocally in Yaonáhuac than in Huitzilan. Table 9 compares the rates of uxorilocality and virilocality for the two communities and

Table 9. Uxorilocal and Virilocal Residence, by Community

Type of residence	Huitzilan		Yaonáhuac	
	Number	Percent	Number	Percent
Uxorilocality				
Couples who live in wife's parental household	28	7.0	12	4.1
Couples who live in house owned by wife's family who resides separately	19	4.7	10	3.4
Couples who live in house owned by wife: wife's family lives separately or deceased	27	6.7	36	12.4
Subtotals	74	18.4	58	19.9
Virilocality				
Couples who live in husband's parental household	102	25.4	59	20.3
Couples who live in house owned by husband's family who resides separately	26	6.5	19	6.6
Couples who live in house owned by husband: husband's family lives separately or deceased	200	49.8	154	53.1
Subtotals	328	81.7	232	80.0
Grand totals	402	100.1	290	99.9

$x^2 = 11.3$, with df 5, $.05 > p > .02$ (two tailed test) for all categories of uxorilocally and virilocally residing couples. Ninety-three of the two hundred couples from Huitzilan listed as living in houses owned by the husband live on ejido land. The forty-eight couples from Huitzilan and the four couples from Yaonáhuac who live on house sites borrowed from nonfamily members are not included in this table.

Table 10. Age Difference between Spouses, by Community

	Huitzilan	Yaonáhuac	
Married couples below the combined median	158	200	
Married couples above the combined median	207	72	
Totals	365	272	$N = 637*$

$x^2 = 56.68$ with 1 df, $p < .001$ (two tailed test).

*N does not equal the total of 746 married couples reported in the censuses of the two communities because 107 cases falling on the median and 2 cases in which age differences are unknown are excluded.

describes the degree to which more Yaonáhuac couples reside in houses owned by the wife or by her parental family. This probably enhances the status of women in this community because it promotes slightly more female kin solidarity, removes some women from the scrutiny of a potentially hostile and critical mother-in-law, and gives women a stronger position in conflicts with their husbands. The greater rate of uxorilocality in Yaonáhuac reflects more bilateral inheritance in this community, but the difference in residence practices between Huitzilan and Yaonáhuac is smaller than the contrasting proportions of women who have acquired land. Yaonáhuac women inherit much more land than their counterparts in Huitzilan, but most of this land consists of *milpas* and orchards rather than house sites.

A more important difference between Huitzilan and Yaonáhuac that parallels the differences in land inheritance and postmarital residence is the median age spread between spouses. As mentioned earlier, women probably have a stronger position in the family when they are closer in age to their husbands because they have had about equal time to learn habits of independence and responsibility. In both communities, husbands are generally older than their wives, but the median age difference is less for Yaonáhuac (two years) than for Huitzilan (five years). Table 10 compares the median age differences between spouses by community and shows the degree to which it is statistically significant. Because a large number of couples share this difference, it probably has a greater impact on oral tradition than the rates of uxorilocality.

The larger age spread between husbands and wives in Huitzilan is probably because men in this community postpone their marriages while women marry at about the same age in both com-

munities. Table 11 describes the lack of difference between the
ages of women at the birth of their first child in Huitzilan and
Yaonáhuac. This probably reflects the fact that women marry at
about the same age in both communities, although it could reflect
other factors. The data come from the *municipio* birth records and
could reflect the biased judgments on age of the secretaries who
record births and deaths. Hispanics have served as *municipio* secretaries in both communities for the past several decades. Nahuat
fearing punishment for marrying young girls may report false ages
for their wives when they report births. The data could also reflect
differences in diet causing women to reach the age of menarche
later in Huitzilan and hence give birth long after their marriages.
Frisch (1978) has argued that undernutrition, hard physical work,
and difficult living conditions make menarche later and cause
higher pregnancy wastage. Hence Huitzilan women could marry
earlier than Yaonáhuac women without this fact showing up in the
birth records. Therefore the age spread between husbands and
wives could develop because Huitzilan women marry earlier than
Yaonáhuac women.

But despite these possibilities and Hispanic rumors that the
Nahuat betroth their women in infancy, I contend the greater age
spread between husbands and wives is because men marry later in
Huitzilan. First, the Nahuat of this community do not betroth their
daughters until they have reached menarche. To be sure, some who
are good friends talk about the eventual marriages of their children, but very few Nahuat parents can arrange the marriage of their
sons or daughters without their children's consent. Most marriages
originate with the sweethearts themselves. Despite the shy public
behavior of betrothed couples, one can find plenty of evidence that
a strong romantic attachment exists between them during their
engagement period. Several cases came to my attention where

Table 11. Age of Women at Birth of Their First Child, by Community

	Huitzilan (1958–1968)	Yaonáhuac (1968–1978)
Median	19	19
Mode	18	18
Mean	20.3	20.2
Standard deviation	4.40	4.62
N =	386	237

young men adamantly defended their marital choices despite the
advice of friends, relatives, and parents and scandalous gossip.
Young men have ample opportunity to meet young women when
they attend ceremonials and when girls fetch water at springs or
make purchases in stores. Some have remarked to me that many
couples exchange letters during the incipient part of their engagement periods, and they seem fearful this practice will lead to
elopement.

    Second, Huitzilan men probably postpone the age of marriage
to earn money to pay for the bride-price and contribute to the expensive betrothal ceremony. A young man who desires to marry a
particular girl begins marital negotiations by requesting that his
father select an intermediary (siwatanke), who usually is an old
and respected woman. She conveys the wishes of the young man to
the girl's parents, then waits for several days for an answer, and
finally reports success or failure to the boy's parents. If successful,
the groom's family makes repeated visits to the young woman's
parents bearing small gifts of food and aguardiente. During this
period the parents of the couple reach an agreement over the postmarital residence of the couple (usually virilocal) and then set the
date for the formal betrothal ceremony, at which time the groom
and his family will deliver the bride-gift. The gift generally consists
of a leg of pork, two turkeys, corn, beans, spices, aguardiente, and
cash. The delivery of this gift seals the marital contract, although
the couple normally waits to consummate the marriage until after
the ceremony. Marriage by civil and religious authorities follows
and is succeeded by another celebration, this time held in the husband's home in honor of the godparents of marriage. But comparatively few (35 percent) Huitzilan couples own land, and many
men must migrate to work on plantations on the coastal plain to
earn their part of the marriage expenses. Yaonáhuac men marry
earlier because fewer contract their marriage by paying the bride-
gift, and more families (72 percent) own land producing an income
to help defray the costs of the marriages of their children. Table 12
compares the frequency of betrothals in the two communities and
shows the much higher rates in Huitzilan. These statistics even
underestimate the number of negotiated marriages involving a
bride-gift in this community because they represent only those
cases where the betrothal climaxed with a large ceremony attended
by many guests in the bride's home. Many cases where the parents
of the couple agreed to deliver a bride-gift and hold a very modest
celebration with a few very intimate friends, relatives, and compadres because they could not afford an elaborate ceremony are not

Table 12. Frequency of Betrothals (*Siwatalis*) for First Marriages of Men and Women, by Community

	Huitzilan	Yaonáhuac	
Men and women married with a betrothal	554	41	
Men and women married without a betrothal	521	658	N = 1774

$x^2 = 394.2$ with df 1, $p < .001$ (two tailed test).

represented in the table. The statistics in table 12 also reflect the emerging Yaonáhuac practice of living as man and wife in a free union without a betrothal and waiting several years before consecrating the marriage with a religious and civil ceremony.

The marriage ceremonials, to which the Huitzilan Nahuat more tenaciously cling, resemble those of the ancient Aztecs (Soustelle 1970: 180) and probably have some pre-Hispanic antecedents. The most notable parallels are the *siwatanke (cihuatlanque)*, the woman who as intermediary brings the couple together, and the gifts of new clothes to the bride and groom. These rituals, which the Yaonáhuac seem more willing to abandon, serve as boundaries to mark off the Indians from the Hispanics. The Huitzilan Nahuat have resisted the erosion of their cultural tradition, a resistance based on their resentment of Hispanic wealth, power, and influence. But their attitude toward the dominant group is extremely ambivalent: they not only hate the Hispanics but also covet their wealth and power. Thus Hispanic priests and storytellers exert considerable influence over the oral tradition in this community.

SUMMARY

The stories from Huitzilan and Yaonáhuac should fit with the similarities and differences between the two communities. They should exhibit the same poetic style because similar metaphors tend to occur among storytelling populations with common linguistic, historical, and cultural antecedents. The social structural parallels should contribute to similar social metaphors developed to explain the same dilemmas that occur with ethnic and sexual hierarchy.

The following two chapters in part II discuss how these common factors contribute to the similarities in the narratives of the two communities. Chapter 5 analyzes a Yaonáhuac creation myth to identify how the ideas it contains fit into a cosmological system shared by the Nahuat in general. Chapter 6 illustrates how this common cosmology underlies the generation of very different kinds of stories—a myth from Huitzilan and an anecdotal tale from Yaonáhuac—that place ethnic groups in Nahuat conceptions of time and space.

The chapters in part III take an entirely different approach because they aim to demonstrate how stories from Huitzilan and Yaonáhuac differ to fit varying degrees of ethnic and sexual hierarchy in social structure. They compare parallel—sometimes cognate—stories to discover how the two groups of Nahuat re-work the same stories differently according to contrasting aspects of social life.

Part II. A Common Cosmology

Tonatiuh

5. Space and Time

The sun

This chapter describes the common cosmology running through the narratives of Huitzilan and Yaonáhuac. This cosmology comprises the more invariant or structural features of Nahuat thought and is to myth what the skeleton is to the human body. It is the framework according to which ideas, like tissues and organs, are arranged in a common manner. But just as diet can affect the size and shape of different parts of the body attached to the same skeleton, so specific historical experiences can influence the formation of ideas arranged on a common conceptual framework.

Nahuat narratives express a bewildering number of ideas that hang on a framework of concepts about space and time. Narrators develop the plots of their stories by moving characters through a stylized conception of space. They regard the earth (*taltikpak*) as a land mass of undetermined shape surrounded on all sides by a ring of water. The sun, the supreme creator deity, rises out of the sea at dawn, and falls back into the sea at dusk. Above the earth lies a domelike heaven whose shape fits the trajectories of the sun and the moon. The stars, thought by some to be burning candles of the souls of the dead, sprinkle the heavens. Below the earth lies the sinister and dangerous underworld of the devil, who constantly attempts to undo the efforts of the sun to bring order out of chaos. An ambiguous region lies at the extremities of the universe where the earth, the sea, the heavens, and the underworld converge. Gigantic Atlas-like figures stand under the universe to hold it up, and when they shift their weight they cause earthquakes.

The basic metaphorical contrast to which many ideas in narratives are linked is the contraposition of the periphery with the center. The center (*centro*) is represented with words standing for the human community—house (*-čan*), community (*pueblo*), or place where one finds Christians from the earth (*taltikpak cristianos*). The center represents the moral order and stands for safety guaranteed by that order. It is juxtaposed against the periphery, which the Nahuat regard as filled with creative and dangerous forces. The Nahuat identify the periphery with the word *forest* (*kwowta*), or with terms for geographical features of the forest that connote danger—a mountain (*tepet*), a canyon (*atawit*), an abyss (*tepekonko*), or a dangerous and ugly place (*owikan*).

Narrators move characters through space as they develop the messages of their tales. They place encounters with the personified forces of nature and heinous crimes in the periphery. They bring characters into the center as they draw them back into conformity with the rules of the moral order.

Notions of time, like those of space, have moral connotations. Narratives express how the universe evolved from an amoral past to a moral present through two eras of creation—the pre-Christian Era of Darkness and the Christian Era of Light. The first came to an end when a flood destroyed a race of giants (variously referred to as Gentiles and Jews), who grew tall because they did not have to endure heat. The second began with the creation of the sun and the moon to establish the Christian order as they know it today. The Nahuat describe the coming of the sun and the birth of Christ as identical events. The coming of the sun began a division between humans (Christians from the earth—*taltikpak cristianos*) and animals.

There is a metaphorical relationship between space and time in which the present is to the past as the center is to the periphery. Human characters who venture into the periphery encounter creatures who lived during the pre-Christian Era of Darkness, specifically, talking animals.

Key concepts related to space and time unfold in the following creation myth told by Yaonáhuac narrator J. M. The interpretation after the story places these concepts in the context of Nahuat thought and ritual. This story comes from Yaonáhuac, and I did not locate a cognate from Huitzilan, but it does express ideas found in the oral tradition of both communities. Stories from Huitzilan and Yaonáhuac are mentioned in the notes to this chapter to support the contention that this myth expresses ideas generally found in Nahuat belief.

MYTH OF CREATION

1. Then so it was when Jesus Christ, in a moment, made the world where we are. 2. From there, well, what will the earth wear? Well, let her dress with grass. He put the grass on the earth to grow. 3. No, but there must always be a forest. Then he made the forest. It was beautiful. 4. Now so that it would grow, there must be water. Ah, but there must be lightning-bolts. They will thunder

*and bring the water to the earth and the forest and grass will grow.
5. There will be mice. 6. There will be crickets. They'll sing at
night and from there, the devil will be angry. And he said, "The
night belongs to me." 7. He went to speak to Jesus, who used to be
his brother. He said, "The night is to be mine." 8. He said to the
devil, "The night will always be yours, but when the chicken crows,
you'll go to your home in the underworld." 9. And from there, he
won because once the chicken crowed, it marked the time for
night to separate from day. 10. "Well, good, it's just that," the devil
said, "if the chicken is going to win over me, your children will eat
it. They'll eat it for being a gossip." 11. "It isn't a gossip. It tells
the truth," replied Christ. 12. "Fine. Let's make a bet," replied the
devil. 13. It came to be midnight, it came to be one in the morning; "Ki ki kiriki," crowed the chicken. 14. The devil went away.
He lost.*   STORYTELLER J. M.

Line 1. *Then so it was when Jesus Christ, in a moment, made the
world where we are.*

The Nahuat combine the sun and Christ into a composite
personality who is the masculine creative force in the Nahuat universe. The sexual identity of the sun is clear, because narrators
describe how boys become the sun (chapter 7). He is the prime
moving deity who created the world and all things in it. Like the
ancient Aztecs (Carrasco 1979) and other Indian groups in Mexico
(Gossen 1974), the Nahuat regulate much of their religious life
according to the movement of the sun during the annual and 24-
hour solar cycles.

The sun is believed to travel around the earth, a notion expressed by the Nahuat words for *east* and *west*. East is "the place
where the sun comes out [of the water]" (*tonal kisayampa*) and
the west is "the place where the sun goes [into the water]" (*tonal
kalakiyampa*). One narrator metaphorically describes the sun's
descent into the sea with a story about a boy with his head in the
water, who becomes the sun.[1]

The annual movement of the sun toward the north from its
lowest point on the horizon at the winter solstice is concordant
with the annual festival cycle. The major winter solstice ceremony
celebrates the birth of Christ and the annual re-birth of the sun as
it begins to move north bringing more heat and light with gradually
longer and warmer days. The annual movement of the sun along
the horizon is analogous to the movement of the sun during the
24-hour period, so that the winter solstice is to the summer sol-

stice as midnight is to noon. The climactic moment of the Christmas celebration—a procession carrying the Christ child from the house of the *mayordomo* (ritual sponsor) to the church—occurs at the time of the day (midnight) analogous to the corresponding time of the year (winter solstice). Other major festivals fall on or near other major events in the solar year. The Easter celebration occurs near the vernal equinox; the festival in honor of San Juan occurs just after the summer solstice; and All Saints' Day in honor of the dead is near the autumnal equinox.

The association of north with noon and the summer solstice and south with midnight and the winter solstice has ancient Aztec antecedents (Carrasco 1979: 53)[2] and occurs among the contemporary Maya (Gossen 1974: 32–33). The Nahuat, like other groups in Mexico (Gossen 1974: 32–33), assign positive connotations to north and negative connotations to south according to key beliefs, empirical observations, and historical experiences. From the point of view of the sun when it rises at dawn and crosses over the earth in an arc, the south lies to its left and the north lies to its right. The Nahuat attach sinister significance to left, for example, by referring to pneumonia as wind coming from the left (*opočehekat*). By extension they give a sinister connotation to the direction south. It is important that nights get long as the sun moves south from the summer to the winter solstice. South has a relationship with night, the most dangerous time of the day, when the creative powers of the sun are weakest. The sinister connotations connected with the south have a good basis in historical experience because Hispanics, who began to settle in the Nahuat area during the last decades of the seventeenth century, generally migrated from the Central Highlands, which actually lie to the south of the Nahuat communities. Because of the disruption they brought to the Nahuat, narrators represent the devil as an Hispanic person coming from the south (see chapter 6). The Nahuat attach more positive significance to the right, and by extension they give more positive connotations to the north. Days get longer as the sun moves north from the winter to the summer solstice, and thus north has a relationship with day, when the creative powers of the sun are strongest. It also makes sense for the Nahuat to connect the north with the heat and light of the sun because the northern Sierra de Puebla slopes northward toward the warm coastal lowlands.

Line 2. *From there, well, what will the earth wear? Well, let her dress with grass. He put the grass on the earth to grow.* Line 3. *No, but there must always be a forest. Then he made the forest. It was beautiful.*

The earth is the feminine creative force and the counterpart of the masculine sun. The Nahuat personify the earth as a benevolent old woman, or as a beautiful and sensuous young woman whom men in folktales find sweeping or washing her hair in a hollow in the forest. Her creative power is most evident when she assumes the image of the young woman. She gives vast quantities of wealth to men who wander through the forest and find her in this form. An obvious relationship exists in Nahuat thought between the sensuality of women and the bounty of the earth, because some men who receive wealth from the earth personified as the young woman also embrace her in a warm sexual encounter.[3] But some storytellers express fear of her sexuality concordant with the position of women in Nahuat social structure (see chapters 8 through 11).

The sun is to the earth as Nahuat are to their *milpas*, and as husbands are to their wives. Just as the sun is masculine and the earth is feminine, so it is that according to the rules of the sexual division of labor, men plant the *milpas*. Yaonáhuac narrators express a direct connection between the sun and men who plant in a story of a boy who plants a *milpa* in the forest and becomes the sun.[4]

Nahuat experiences and expressions reflect ideas connecting planting and procreation. Men plan their *milpas* with a dibble which they insert rhythmically into the earth's moist surface to make holes for corn and bean seeds. The Nahuat word *to plant* (*tatoka*) connotes sexual intercourse; the Nahuat say that the woman's vagina is her husband's *milpa*, and they refer to a woman's pubic hairs as the plants growing on that *milpa*.

The link between planting and procreation is the basis of a common metaphorical expression that the Nahuat community was created as if it were a *milpa* cut from the forest.[5] The creation of the Nahuat community pushed the forest toward the periphery and created two distinct domains—that of humans and that of animals—at the beginning of the Second Era of Creation. The separation of the two domains did not sever all relations between humans and animals, because humans still have animal companion spirits (*tonalme*), and witches (*nagualme*) can change into animals to punish their enemies and correct immoral behavior (chapter 9). But the distinction between the human and animal domains remains sharp. To be human means to cultivate *milpas*, cook food, eat tortillas, wear clothes, live in houses, talk, and be Christians who live according to the rules of the Nahuat moral order. To live according to moral rules means to control impulses, and those who refuse are regarded as like animals. A number of tales from both communities tell of those who do not exert impulse control and end up living in the forest. Cognate stories from Huitzilan and Yaonáhuac tell how a man who refuses to cultivate his *milpa* (he cannot control his impulse to be lazy) ends up as a bird living beyond the boundaries of the human community.[6]

The creation of Nahuat civilization is regarded as a reversible process. The Nahuat worry that the forest will one day encroach on the human community as it did at the end of the First Era of Creation, when all humanity perished in a flood. A metaphor expressing the fate of humanity as the fate of a *milpa* in the forest describes the end of the First Era of Creation: the story tells of a man at the end of the doomed era who cleared the forest to plant a *milpa* and found the trees re-erected on the following day (chapter 11).

Line 4. Now so that it would grow, there must be water. Ah, but there must be lightning-bolts. They will thunder and bring the water to the earth and the forest and grass will grow.

Lightning-bolts mediate between the masculine sun and the feminine earth to create life, by virtue of their connections with the juxtaposed entities of the sun and the earth, and with water, the medium of creation. Yaonáhuac narrators merge the identities of the sun and lightning-bolts by telling about lightning-bolts who cremate themselves to become the sun. Huitzilan narrators retain only vestiges of this myth, whose roots are in Aztec tradition, and combine what remains of it with the Hispanic story of Christmas (chapter 7). Narrators from both communities link lightning-bolts to the sun in the way they place the home of the lightning-bolt captain—Nanawatzin—in space. They say he lives toward the north, in the direction toward which the sun moves from the winter to the summer solstice. Narrators also link Nanawatzin with the sun's heat and light by baptizing him San Juan, whose day on the Catholic calendar is June 24, which comes very close to June 21, the date of the summer solstice and the hottest time of the year.[7]

The Nahuat associate lightning-bolts with the earth by placing their homes in mountainous caves. Living atop mountains fits their mediating role in several ways: by living at high altitudes, they are closer to the sun; by living inside caves they have a connection with the most feminine part of the earth—her vagina. Undoubtedly because lightning-bolts mediate between masculine and feminine entities, narrators from both communities personify lightning-bolts as women as well as men (see chapter 8): like the ancient Aztecs (Sahagún 1950: 6) they describe lightning-bolts living with a female consort.[8]

A number of things associate lightning-bolts with water—their obvious association with rain, the location of Nanawatzin's home, and his baptized name of San Juan. By placing Nanawatzin's home to the north, the Nahuat place him toward the sea, the source of the water which he and the other lightning-bolts bring to create life. By baptizing Nanawatzin as San Juan, the Nahuat have given him the name of a saint whose day on the Catholic calendar is at the height of the rainy season.

Lightning-bolts mediate to play a creative role and support the Nahuat order. They obtained food for humanity in the Second Era of Creation by breaking open Sustenance Mountain and releasing corn (chapter 7). Nanawatzin taught the knowledge of corn planting to other lightning-bolts, and eventually this knowledge passed to the Nahuat.[9] Lightning-bolts as anthropomorphized snakes give men gold rings that generate huge quantities of wealth (chapter 8). Lightning-bolts are personified as wisemen (*tamatinime*), clairvoyant persons who uphold the moral order by punishing those who refuse to conform to Nahuat rules: they punish humans for abusing their political authority, for swearing at the gods, for adultery, for not paying workers (chapter 9), and for stealing.[10]

Line 5. *There will be mice.*

To mediate between the domain of nature (the forest) and the domain of humans, the Nahuat use animals that have links with both. The mouse is one such animal, because although not domesticated, it is parasitic to humans because it eats corn stored in granaries. Other anomalous animals having similar qualities are the hawk and the opossum, which live by stealing chickens. Narrators from both communities tell a number of stories describing how mice and hawks recover a gold ring obtained from the lightning-bolts but stolen by foreigners who come from across the sea (chapter 8). Because these mediating animals have speech, they act like animals of the First Era of Creation, and human characters in folktales often encounter them in the periphery, the spatial equivalent of the past in the space-time metaphor that runs through Nahuat thought.

Line 6. *There will be crickets. They'll sing at night and from there, the devil will be angry. And he said, "The night belongs to me."*

This line sets up the juxtaposition of night and day by describing how Christ (the sun) created crickets to annoy the devil, who personifies the forces of darkness and cold that work during the night to destroy the order created by the sun. The devil assumes a variety of forms derived from Nahuat experience since the Conquest. He is sometimes the Hispanic gentleman (*koyot*), Pontius Pilate, the crying woman (*la llorona*), a blood-sucking witch (*masakat*), a goat, or a bull. It makes sense the Nahuat would depict the devil as an Hispanic gentleman who represents the wealthy members of the dominant ethnic group who have taken the bulk of the Nahuat land. The system of ethnic stratification created by Hispanic settlement in the northern Sierra de Puebla brought drastic changes to Nahuat social structure (chapters 2 to 4) and thought (chapters 7 through 11). Pontius Pilate is a logical symbol because he crucified Christ (the sun), the personification of the prime moving force in Nahuat belief. The crying woman is the temptress who lures men into her arms and kills them with magical fright by turning into a skeleton during the act of love. She obviously stands for the power of women's sexuality, which threatens some but not all Nahuat men, depending on the position of women in the social structure. Blood-sucking witches (*masakame*) kill their victims and thus belong with the forces that undermine the Nahuat order. The devil takes the form of a goat or bull because the Nahuat associate these particular animals with Hispanics, who brought them to the New World. They regard goats as Hispanic men because they have heavy beards. They associate bulls or cattle with Hispanics because wealthy members of the dominant group acquired large tracts of Nahuat land previously used for *milpa* farming and now converted into pastures for cattle. It is interesting that when the Nahuat feed their workers who help them plant their corn fields they feed them pork but never beef. When the insurgents organized in Huitzilan, they took over tracts of pasture land they regarded as unfairly taken from the Nahuat by the Hispanics.

Line 7. *He went to speak to Jesus, who used to be his brother. He said, "The night is to be mine."*
Just as there was once no dichotomy between the domain of humans and the domain of animals in an earlier era of creation when animals spoke like people, so the devil and Christ were once brothers. The Nahuat believe that Christ, the saints, and their agents (the lightning-bolts) form a tightly knit, unified community whose members speak with one another and arrive at decisions that have vital importance for the human condition. The devil once

belonged to this community, but was banished because he ate
Christians on the earth.[11] The Nahuat term *to eat* (*takwa*) has a
number of different connotations when narratives use it to describe
the devil eating Christians. Storytellers sometimes mean the devil
devours human souls personified as chickens to cause soul loss
resulting in sickness or death. Some narrators give the term a sexual meaning by describing how the devil punishes sexually promiscuous women. One from Huitzilan graphically describes how the
devil, in the guise of an Hispanic gentleman, carried off a sexually
voracious and promiscuous wife, and devoured her in the act of
love, leaving only her heart, which bounced about the floor of
his cave, palpitating and eventually regenerating into a complete
woman, whose destiny is to endure the experience over and over
again.[12]

Line 8. *He said to the devil, "The night will always be yours, but
when the chicken crows, you'll go to your home in the underworld." Line 9. And from there, he won because once the chicken
crowed, it marked the time for night to separate from day.*

The crow of the rooster announces the point of separation
between night and day, the point in time when the balance shifts
from the forces that undermine the moral order to the forces that
maintain it. The Nahuat place the chicken in this role because it is
considered an ally of Christ. Narrators from both communities tell
how the chicken helped Christ escape from his tomb after his
Crucifixion. The Jews buried Jesus and placed a chicken on top of
his grave to warn them if he tried to escape. But Christ persuaded
the chicken not to crow until he had risen to heaven. The chicken
obliged, and Christ rewarded it with eternal life.[13] Because the
chicken represents the souls of Christians, this means that Christians will have eternal life after death. These beliefs rest on a
fundamental opposition between Christians of the Second Era of
Creation and non-Christians (Jews/Gentiles) of the First Era of Creation whose last attempt to exert their control over the universe was
the crucifixion of Christ.

Line 10. *"Well, good, it's just that," said the devil, "if the chicken
is going to win over me, your children will eat it. They'll eat it for
being a gossip."*

This line expresses the widely held Nahuat belief that the
devil causes internal conflict in Nahuat society and is responsible
for human mortality. The devil demanding conditions from Christ
is a recurrent theme in Nahuat thought and metaphorically depicts

the unstable and potentially dangerous tension between the forces of good and evil.

Line 11. *"It isn't a gossip. It tells the truth," replied Christ.*
Line 12. *"Fine. Let's make a bet," replied the devil.*
    Christ and the devil make a wager about whether truth shall prevail over falsehood. Like the ancient Aztecs (Garibay 1970: 108–109), the Nahuat recognize the potentially disrupting effects on their social order of slander and malicious gossip. They assert that gossip directed among ritual kin is a serious offense that brings supernatural punishment.
    A contest or wager between Christ and the devil is a common metaphor to express the tense balance between the forces of darkness and cold and the forces of light and heat. It appears in a number of other tales as a contest to answer a riddle: the devil asks God, or one of his agents, to tell who the devil's parents were. The devil is so primordial that no one remembers having met them, but by putting the devil to sleep, or getting him drunk, God discovers the answer. The devil's parents assume a variety of sinister forms: in one tale, they are black and white dysentery, and in another they are the ash in the middle of the hearth and the thorny heart of the maguey plant.[14] The sinister and bizarre parentage of the devil, of course, serves to emphasize his antithetical and dangerous nature for the human community.

Line 13. *It came to be midnight, it came to be one in the morning;*
"Ki ki kiriki," crowed the chicken.
    The narrator establishes the precise division between night and day. Like others in Mesoamerica (Gossen 1974: 42–43), the Nahuat divide the 24-hour period into two rough halves. The half beginning after midnight and ending sometime around noon is the period of increasing sun and is associated with increasing order. The half from after noon to slightly after midnight is the period of waning sun and is associated with increasing uncertainty and disorder. The Nahuat not only express this idea in their myths, but they also act it out in their marriage rituals, which have the ostensible purpose of creating unity between the bride and the groom and their families. The rituals generally cover a 24-hour period starting around nine or ten o'clock at night. I have witnessed instances in both communities of play-acted anger between representatives of the bride and the groom. It is generally smoothed out by dawn, when the parties hold a climaxing ceremony that expresses the unity they hope will prevail between them. In Huitzilan the inter-

mediary (*siwatanke*) joins the bride and groom and their godparents of marriage and weaves them together in a sacred web of
incense. In Yaonáhuac the bride and groom, their parents, and the
godparents of marriage embrace each other and then dance with
bread images of the children they hope will be born to the couple,
cementing their marriage.

Line 14. *The devil went away. He lost.*

The concept that Christ wins a contest with the devil has
repeated expression in Nahuat oral tradition and ritual. The stake
in the wager is command of the earth, and a number of storytellers
describe how Christ wins to establish his supremacy and banishes
the devil to live in the periphery of the universe. The devil returns
to the center at night, when the power of the sun is weak.[15] The
Nahuat express Christ's supremacy over the devil in their ritual
dramas. In Huitzilan the San Miguel dancers act out a sword fight
with the devil—dressed in black and called the "Chichimeco"—
and win. In Yaonáhuac dancers act out a drama of killing Pontius
Pilate.

SUMMARY

The skeletal structure of Nahuat thought consists of concepts
about space and time, powerful creative and destructive forces,
and personalities expressed in the above myth of creation. The
concepts are arranged in homologous juxtapositions mediated by
entities that bridge the gap between entities that stand in logical
opposition. The juxtaposed elements of space are:

center		periphery
north	: :	south
right		left

The juxtaposed elements of time are:

day (noon)		night (midnight)
summer solstice	: :	winter solstice
present		past

Common threads run through the juxtaposed spatial and temporal
elements, tying them together. All elements in the left-hand column are associated with forces supporting the Nahuat order, and

most of the elements in the right-hand column are associated with things that work to undermine this order. These forces, which stand in a precariously balanced relationship, are:

$$\frac{\text{heat}}{\text{light}} \quad :: \quad \frac{\text{cold}}{\text{darkness}}$$

The corresponding social images are as follows:

$$\frac{\text{Christ}}{\frac{\text{Christians}}{\frac{\text{humans}}{\frac{\text{Nahuat}}{\text{men}}}}} \quad :: \quad \frac{\text{devil}}{\frac{\text{Gentiles/Jews}}{\frac{\text{animals}}{\frac{\text{Hispanics}}{\text{women}}}}}$$

Mediating between juxtaposed elements of space and time, forces and personalities are anomalous entities that combine qualities of logical opposites. In Nahuat stories, lightning-bolts are characters who bridge many polarized elements in the universe and help tie it together into a whole. They have both human and animal identity and thus link the human domain in the center with the animal domain in the periphery. Their images in myth express the underlying relationship the Nahuat perceive between the human and animal domains. They connect other important polarized concepts including the masculine sun and the feminine earth by virtue of their connections with both these creative forces in the Nahuat universe.

6. Nahuat and Hispanics

Spaniards landing on the coast

This chapter describes how narrators place ethnic relations in their coordinates of space and time. To be sure, the Nahuat of Huitzilan and Yaonáhuac have experienced different histories of ethnic relations contributing to different images of Hispanics. But numerous parallels cross-cut the two communities and account for the way narrators place Hispanics into a common spatial and temporal framework in similar fashion.

Although Nahuat in monoethnic communities like Yaonáhuac can escape immediate and direct Hispanic domination, all Nahuat are aware that Hispanics have gained control over the bulk of the stategic resources in the northern Sierra de Puebla. They are keenly aware of the threat Hispanics pose to their order by virtue of Hispanic economic and political control over the region. Thus narrators of Huitzilan and Yaonáhuac juxtapose Hispanics, whom they regard as threatening, against the creative forces that support the Nahuat order. The most important creative force is the sun, whose spatial equivalent is the north and whose temporal equivalent is noon. To explain the threat Hispanics pose to their order, storytellers place the dominant group in coordinates of space and time just the opposite of those associated with the sun. They regard Hispanics as originating from the south, and they describe encounters between Nahuat and Hispanics taking place at night. As mentioned in the previous chapter, this fits with actual Nahuat experience, because many Hispanics who settled in the northern Sierra de Puebla came from communities to the south on the Central Mexican Plateau.

Narrators from both communities place ethnic conflict between the Nahuat and the Hispanics into the realm of religious personalities by depicting it as a struggle between the lightning-bolts and the devil. They maintain a direct link between the supernatural forces assigned ethnic identity and the symbolism of the cardinal directions. The lightning-bolts, who mediate between some polar concepts in the Nahuat view of the universe, stand for the Indians in their struggle with the Hispanics. It makes sense for the Nahuat to represent themselves with lightning-bolts because they connect these personalities with the sun, the creative force in their universe. It was mentioned that the Nahuat place lightning-bolts to their conceptual north by making the home of the head lightning-bolts to the north of their communities. The devil, the personification of the destructive forces of the universe, represents the Hispanics. The Nahuat place the devil to the conceptual south by asserting that he originated from the Central Mexican Highlands to the actual south of Huitzilan and Yaonáhuac.

The stories in this chapter depict Nahuat and Hispanic ethnic relations as a conflict between lightning-bolts and the devil. They were chosen because they illustrate how the Nahuat place the action of the plot in named, easily identifiable places in and around the two communities. The narrators of both use actual localities to the north and south of their communities to place their lightning-bolts and the devil in space to develop the metaphor in which Nahuat : Hispanics : : north : south.

Unlike the stories compared in subsequent chapters, these stories do not have a common historical source. Each is an account of a unique historical event tailored to fit the particular features of the geography of a single community. Moreover, they represent different story types, because one is a mythic account of the Hispanic invasion of Huitzilan, which the Nahuat believed occurred in the remote past of the present era of creation. The second story is an anecdotal account of a Yaonáhuac man who believes he actually encountered the devil in the very recent past. An examination of these tales illustrates how the underlying structure of Nahuat narratives (see chapter 5) acts as a template for generating very different kinds of stories. The tales have a similar structure because narrators develop their plots to fit a common conception of space and time.

THE MONSTER AT IŠTEPEK

The first story by Huitzilan narrator N. A. H. tells in figurative language how Hispanics settled in his community to create a biethnic social order. The central metaphor is that Hispanics threaten the Nahuat as the flood destroyed humanity at the end of the First Era of Creation. The story tells of a monster, a seven-headed serpent, which is the animal companion spirit (*tonal*) of the Hispanics. The monster has a metonymical relationship with water because the monster and water appear together to threaten the Indians in the northern Sierra. They first appear in Ištepek, a Totonac community to the north of Huitzilan, and then come to Huitzilan itself. The story places Hispanics in a spatial framework by asserting that the monster and the water, who represent Hispanics, originated from Tetela de Ocampo, the former district capital to the south of Huitzilan.

The story makes reference to a revitalization movement that took place between 1885 and 1901 in several Totonac communities near Papantla, eighty kilometers to the north of Huitzilan and Ištepek (Velasco Toro 1979). It describes how lightning-bolts chase Hispanics from the Totonac area, much as the Totonacs near Papantla tried to rid their region of Hispanics a century ago. The Nahuat did not take part in the nineteenth-century rebellion, a fact expressed by the storyteller who tells how the monster came to Huitzilan to stay. But in 1977–78, the Nahuat of many communities in this part of the northern Sierra organized a peasant insurgency movement aimed at restoring land the Nahuat believed was unfairly taken from them by Hispanics.

THE MONSTER AT IŠTEPEK

1. They say there was a day in the remote past when water appeared at Ištepek. 2. They say they [who lived at Ištepek] were on top of a ridge, and there wasn't any water. 3. Then they say water appeared at the foot of the church. 4. They say the people liked it. 5. They say the water began to grow and grow. It became a small spring. 6. And they say it became larger there. 7. Afterwards they say children were not to get near it. A child would go to stay. Baby chicks or pigs would go and they would stay. 8. Then no one, not even big people and big animals, went close because they would go to stay. The water swallowed them. 9. There was a big animal there. 10. The people from Ištepek wondered and wondered and asked, "Well, what'll we do? Now there is this animal. There it is. The water is really not a good thing!" 11. It even began to drip water from high inside the church. 12. They decided, "Well, let's go over there to Huitzilan. We know there is someone there who is wise." 13. They decided to go see a woman who lived up here. 14. They said to her, "Now we want you to help us take it out." 15. Those who spoke to the woman were wisemen too. They were probably lightning-bolts. 16. They say that a long time ago they knew about those things. 17. Then that old woman told them, "Well, why not?! Let's go. But go find twelve little girls and twelve little boys, and twelve grown-up girls and twelve grown-up boys, and twelve old ladies and twelve old men." 18. Then they col-

lected them. Then they went to see the water. They say a big rain storm began and there was some thunder. 19. They began to go after it here at Ištepek. Some of the lightning-bolts went into the water. They began striking it and striking it. 20. Then they say some went to wait for it. It was making smoke as it ran to the place from whence it had come. That water went all the way to Tetela. 21. The lightning-bolts went into the water at Ištepek and chased it to where the other lightning-bolts saw it come out at Tetela and there they hit it. 22. Then they killed that animal there. And from there some say they didn't kill it. 23. And one day they say they met him below. A worker went to the lowlands and found a gentleman. They say that gentleman was descending [probably from Ištepek], and he asked the worker, "Where are you going?" 24. The worker replied, "I'm headed to work in the lowlands. And you? Where are you going?" 25. "I'm going back to my home because I was at Ištepek but they wouldn't let me stay there. But whenever I want, I'll pull them in. They're mine," he said. 26. They say a gentleman came here. Well, he was nicely dressed. He asked permission from the municipio *president, "Won't you do me the favor of letting me live here?" 27. They didn't ask him, "Where are you from? Where is your home?" Rather the president just trusted him as if he were his kinsman. He said, "Well, why not? Wherever you'd like to build your house." 28. Then they say they lost sight of him. Fifteen days to a month passed and the president saw water come out of the ground.*   STORYTELLER N. A. H.

Lines 1 to 4. *Water appeared at Ištepek.*

The first lines of the story introduce the central metaphor in which water threatens the people of Ištepek as Hispanics threaten the Totonac and Nahuat Indians of the northern Sierra de Puebla. The conclusion that the water represents the Hispanic invasion gradually becomes apparent through the course of the story. By the end (line 23), the narrator makes the meaning of the metaphor unmistakenly clear by introducing a character whom he calls a gentleman (*koyot*) and whose animal companion spirit (*tonal*) is the monster brought to Ištepek by the water. The Nahuat use the term *gentleman* (*koyot*) to refer to Hispanics and to the devil in their narratives and in ordinary discourse. The storyteller builds up to the meaning of the central metaphor in very interesting ways by drawing on Nahuat beliefs and on the geography and history of his community.

First, water, like the Hispanics, has threatened the Nahuat and the Totonacs. In Nahuat belief, the First Era of Creation came to an end when water destroyed all humanity except Noah. This has a parallel in actual experience, because floods have caused heavy damage in the adjacent community of Zapotitlán, lying just north of Huitzilan, along the tributary flowing into the Zempoala River. Hispanics have threatened Nahuat and Totonacs by taking their land and gaining a monopoly of political power.

Second, obvious parallels exist between the pattern of Hispanic settlement in Huitzilan and surrounding communities including Ištepek and the flow of water from the Central Mexican Highlands to the Gulf Coast. Many Hispanics who settled in Huitzilan and Ištepek came from Tetela de Ocampo and adjacent *municipios* on the Plateau. This directly parallels the flow of water from the highlands to the lowlands. One of the major tributaries that feeds into the Zempoala River just below Ištepek originates near Tetela de Ocampo in the adjacent *municipio* of Aquixtla.

Third, the reaction of the Totonacs in the story to water that appeared in Ištepek is like the initial Nahuat reaction to Hispanics when they first settled in Huitzilan. The Nahuat say they welcomed the first Hispanic families because they provided employment for the Nahuat in their commercial enterprises, they established stores, and they provided medicine. Likewise, the Totonacs of Ištepek welcomed the water when it first appeared in their community because it made their lives much easier. Ištepek lies atop a very high ridge where there are no hills to provide drainage to feed springs near the community. The Totonacs who live there have to make long treks to fetch water for their kitchens by descending the ridge to reach lower ground where water drains from above.

Fourth, water appeared in a part of the community where Hispanics constructed their homes when they settled in Ištepek. The narrator describes how water appeared at the foot of the church which lies in the central plaza. Hispanics generally build their homes around the plazas of Totonac and Nahuat communities, leaving the outlying areas for the Indians. The church is also an important symbol to the Nahuat because it contains images of Christ, the patron Santiago, and other important religious objects. Thus the appearance of water near the church is a poetic device to express the Hispanic threat to Nahuat and Totonacs.

The storyteller develops the central metaphor to fit the Nahuat conceptions of space and time which underlie their narrative tradition. Both elements in the metaphor "water as Hispanics"— the tenor *Hispanics* and the vehicle *water*—originate in the story and in reality from the south, the spatial equivalent of midnight and the winter solstice. It was mentioned that these times of the day and the year occur when the destructive powers of the universe are at their peak according to Nahuat belief.

The narrator utilizes the metaphorical relationship between time and space which runs through Nahuat narratives. It was noted that the modern-day Nahuat, like the ancient Aztecs, regard things of the periphery as things of the past. The narrator uses this device when he asserts that Hispanics, represented by water, came first to Ištepek and then appeared in Huitzilan. The narrator places the appearance of water in Ištepek early in Nahuat chronology with a singular verb suffix indicating ancient time (-ka) which he attaches to the verb stem appear (monešti-) in the first line of the story. He appears to place the event early in the Second Era of Creation. The Nahuat frequently assert that ancient events took place in the primordial periphery of the universe surrounding their community. They place the Totonac area including Ištepek toward the periphery and often attribute to the Totonacs bizarre behaviors they believe took place during earlier eras of creation. I could find no confirmation that Hispanics actually settled in Ištepek before they came to Huitzilan. Hispanics appear to have settled in both communities at about the same time around the turn of the century.

Lines 5–9. *The water grew and a monster appeared.*

The narrator fills out the central metaphor by indicating how the water standing for Hispanics threatens the Totonacs of Ištepek. He describes water growing and swallowing animals and people. The word swallow (kitolowa) used in line 8 is a word the Nahuat use in a variety of contexts to connote devour. They apply it in stories and other speech genres to explain illness by soul loss, to depict the devil killing Christians and to describe metaphorically how a stronger person can take advantage of a weaker one. The narrator develops the central metaphor by describing the water growing from a trickle to a flood and by depicting the water swallowing animals and people of increasing age and size. This fits the Nahuat belief that children have souls less firmly attached to their bodies and thus more easily succumb to soul loss. This belief resonates with the Nahuat because it fits with the high rate of infant mortality in their community and coincides with the principle of rank by age that underlies Nahuat social life.

The storyteller represents the threat posed by water with the monster who is the animal companion spirit of Hispanics. Although he does not say so, he refers to a seven-headed serpent, a frequent animal companion spirit for the dominant ethnic group in Nahuat stories. The seven-headed serpent probably originated from the ancient Aztec deity Chicomecoatl (Seven Serpents), who had charge of human livelihood (Sahagún 1950: 4). But friars and the secular clergy turned this snake into a negative symbol, particularly in Huitzilan.

Lines 10–17. *The people of Ištepek consult the wisemen of Huitzilan to get rid of the monster.*
　　The narrator expands the central metaphor by adding the animal companion spirits of the Nahuat who battle with that of the Hispanics. Lightning-bolts are the companion spirits of the Nahuat as a collectivity. By adding these elements, the narrator expands the central metaphor into a complex external analogy in which Nahuat : Hispanics : : north : south : : lightning-bolts : monster (seven-headed serpent).
　　The storyteller draws a clear connection between lightning-bolts and the Nahuat in several ways. First, he describes the Totonacs going to the Nahuat community of Huitzilan to obtain the advice of the lightning-bolts for expelling the monster. Second, he depicts the Totonacs consulting with wisemen (*tamatinime*), whom the Nahuat consider are those in their communities who have strong blood and powers of clairvoyance and divination. The Nahuat believe they are actual individuals who have lightning-bolt animal companion spirits. Occasionally the Nahuat, particularly of Yaonáhuac, will claim they or their ancestors were wisemen, and they never identify wisemen as Hispanics. The woman whom the Totonacs consult is probably the living counterpart of the female consort of the lightning-bolts of Huitzilan. The Nahuat describe the lightning-bolts living with their mother deep in the forest and high atop mountains where they make the weather.
　　Related beliefs illustrate how the Nahuat regard lightning-bolts as the protectors of their community. They frequently describe how lightning-bolts defend them against threats from outside their community posed by other Indians as well as Hispanics. They believe each Indian community has special protector lightning-bolts who attack other communities. They conceptualize these attacks as violent rain and thunderstorms which can cause floods or landslides, and they cite cracks in church bells as evidence for these attacks. A number of Nahuat narrators express the power of their lightning-bolt protectors by referring to the clarity of their church bells. They argue that their bells ring loud and clear because their protectors have the strength to fight off attack by enemy lightning-

bolts from other communities. The mention how other church bells ring less loudly and less clearly as further testimony for the superior strength of their lightning-bolt protectors, whom—they contend—have penetrated the defenses of other communities and cracked the bells in their parish churches. This narrator expresses his community pride by telling how the Totonacs came to the Huitzilan Nahuat lightning-bolt protectors because of their renowned strength.

Lines 18–20. *The lightning-bolts chase the monster to Tetela, where they kill it.*

The narrator makes a reference to the rebellion of 1885 to 1901, when several Totonac communities near Papantla rose up in armed rebellion against the local Veracruz and federal Mexican governments. The Colonization Laws of the nineteenth century were important factors that triggered the rebellion, because they enabled Hispanics to acquire Totonac land easily (Velasco Toro 1979).

The storyteller's description of lightning-bolts expelling the monster from Ištepek fits the Totonac rebellion in several ways. First, both were organized efforts. Just as the Totonacs organized armed resistance under their leaders, so the Totonacs of Ištepek gathered many different lightning-bolts—twelve little girls and little boys, twelve grown-up girls and boys, and twelve old ladies and old men—who represent all sections of the Nahuat, and by the storyteller's extension, the Totonac community (see line 17). The number twelve has significance to the Nahuat because it is divisible by both three and four, the numbers by which the Nahuat mark important periods of time and units of space. The narrator classifies the lightning-bolts according to three categories of age, and his classification accords with the age categories in Nahuat elementary kinship terms (see chapter 2). The Nahuat also divide the year into three planting periods: 1. the *tonamil* in the late fall and early winter; 2. the *tahkomil* in the early spring; and 3. the *šopamil* in the summer. If one considers the primordial state of the universe as the first stage, then the Nahuat likewise identify three stages of creation: the first or primordial stage when all was water; the creation of the earth during the Era of Darkness; and the Era of Light which began with the appearance of the sun. The Nahuat place particular importance on the four cardinal directions, and they make four divisions in the day: 1. *kwalkan* = dawn; 2. *nepanta* = noon; 3. *tiotak* = nightfall; and 4. *tahkoyowal* = midnight.

Second, just as the actual rebellion between 1885 and 1901 involved Totonacs but no Nahuat, so the storyteller carefully says the Totonacs use their own lightning-bolts, not those of Huitzilan, to expel the monster. To be sure, the Totonacs of Ištepek consult with the wisewoman of Huitzilan, who tells them how to get rid of the threat to their community, but the Nahuat do not take part in the venture themselves. Probably few Totonacs from Ištepek joined the Totonacs of Papantla in their rebellion of the last century, but the Nahuat connect the two groups by virtue of their linguistic and cultural similarities.

By placing the monster's origin at Tetela de Ocampo, the narrator reinforces the central metaphor of the story in which Nahuat : Hispanics : : north : south : : lightning-bolts : monster. As noted, this community lies to the actual south of Huitzilan, and it contributed a large number of Hispanic settlers to Huitzilan, Ištepek, and other communities in this part of the northern Sierra de Puebla.

Lines 23–28. *A gentleman came to live in Huitzilan and after about a month water appeared.*

The narrator completes the central metaphor by firmly establishing the Hispanic identity of the monster. Just as the Totonac rebellion of 1885 to 1901 did not rid the area around Papantla of Hispanics, so the lightning-bolts could not kill the seven-headed serpent. The monster re-appears in human form as a well-dressed gentleman whom a worker encounters on the road, and who eventually comes to live in Huitzilan. As noted, the Nahuat apply the term *gentleman* (*koyot*) to Hispanics and the devil. The narrator specifies that the gentleman is well dressed to express the wealth difference between ethnic groups.

The storyteller has unfolded the central metaphor in a manner consistent with the stages of the creation of the universe mentioned earlier. First, he uses water to represent the Hispanic threat, just as all was water during the primordial stage of creation. Second, he introduces the seven-headed serpent as the animal companion spirit of Hispanics, just as talking animals inhabited the earth during the Era of Darkness. Third, in the final episode he represents the Hispanics as the well-dressed gentleman, just as humans became distinguished from animals in the Era of Light.

THE TIME I MET THE DEVIL

The second story by Yaonáhuac narrator J. M. tells of an incident from the storyteller's own life and carries a much more optimistic message. J. M. describes how he found refuge from Hispanics by

returning to his monoethnic Nahuat community. Despite differences, this story has a number of similarities with the preceding
tale. First, the narrator contraposes the world of the Nahuat and
the world of Hispanics. Second, he describes this contraposition as
a battle between a lightning-bolt standing for the Nahuat and the
devil representing the Hispanics. Third, he connects the Nahuat
with the north and the Hispanics with the south. In this case he
does it by placing his encounter with the devil in Teteles de Ávila
Castillo, an Hispanic *municipio* that borders Yaonáhuac on the
south. As the story unfolds he walks north to Yaonáhuac, where he
frees himself from the devil. The narrator adds a temporal dimen-
sion not included in the preceding tale. He places his encounter
with the devil at night and describes his escape from the devil at
dawn, when the balance shifts from the sinister forces of darkness
and cold to the creative forces of light and heat.

THE TIME I MET THE DEVIL

1. *One time I went to Tecolutla, which is past Gutiérrez Zamora.*
2. *And there in my head the devil was dancing. He was dancing,
dancing, and dancing. He didn't let me sleep. 3. Well, then I came
home. I took the 6:00 P.M. bus for Teziutlán. I arrived at 11:30
P.M. 4. I came. I came. I came, and I came home. I got off in Teteles at
the house of Don Joaquín Ortega, north of Rodolfo's house. There
I stood, and the devil spoke to me. He said, "Don't be afraid. I'll
come along and talk to you." 5. "And what do you want?" I asked.
"Nothing more than to have you work with me," the devil replied.
6. "I won't work with you. I work with Jesus Christ," I replied.
7. He said, "Then Jesus Christ buys souls? I buy souls—bodies
and souls. Jesus Christ is poorer than I am." 8. That's when I said,
"I won't." Then I went down to where the road makes a turn—
where they fix machinery, cars, and trucks. 9. Then the devil said
to me, he said, "Do you want to see me—the way I dress—my
clothes?" I said, "Fine." 10. He was dressed in black. His cape was
black. And then he had a flat hat. 11. He said, "Do you want to
see me another way?" I said, "As you like." 12. He pulled. He pulled
on his hat. It grew big like Pedro Infante's. It was a big hat like a
mariachi's. And I saw it get bigger. Whore, his teeth, they were
like those of a horse! 13. "Well, do you want to see me another
way?" I said, "Well, as you like." 14. He rolled up his big hat. He
formed big horns. 15. "Do you want to see me another way? Do
you want to see me mount my horse?" I said, "Whatever you want."
16. There on this side of the house of Rafael Ortega, he mounted*

his horse, but it was a big horse, a black horse that threw sparks.
17. He disappeared with each car that passed by the road. 18. Here,
below the crossroads, there I entered [Yaonáhuac] and yes, the
rain came. I thought, "Well, I'm going to see if he'll pass by the
Calvary." Ah, he didn't pass. He turned. 19. But now I'm going to
where our little patron Sr. Santiago is because he came from Mér-
ida, the little father Sr. Santiago did. 20. I passed the church. Well,
I went on down by the house of Isidro Morelos. The devil didn't
bring his horse. Down here he was Pontius Pilate. 21. He said,
"Now just give me two chickens every month." 22. And they weren't
chickens. He wanted Christians—people. 23. Then I arrived out-
side the kitchen of my house and there stood the devil as Pontius
Pilate. 24. And then the chickens would be frightened. For that
reason I know if the chickens are frightened, I know what is hap-
pening. 25. Then I turned and came into the house. 26. "I've come,
little mother," I said. 27. "O son, and what are you doing? It's
night!" she said. 28. The chickens were frightened. They said,
"Masakat." 29. I left. I went to the Red Bridge there by the water. I
passed twenty blows of the machete through him and beat him.

STORYTELLER J. M.

Lines 1–4. *The narrator encounters the devil in Teteles.*

According to Nahuat belief, one would expect to encounter the
devil around midnight, when the creative powers of the sun are
weakest. One would expect the encounter to take place in an Hispanic community because the Nahuat, like others in Mesoamerica
(Warren 1978), generally regard the devil as an Hispanic person. So
it is that this narrator fixes his meeting with the devil in this story.

He describes how he left his monoethnic Nahuat community
and entered the world of Hispanics. He tells about his trip to the hot
country as a migrant laborer, where he worked on an Hispanic plantation. Like many in his community he often works on the migratory work team in Veracruz. The places he mentions—Tecolutla
and Gutiérrez Zamora—are large towns along one of the main
highways to the large Veracruz city of Poza Rica. He tells how he
returned to Teteles, a *municipio* consisting predominantly of Hispanics that lies to the south of Yaonáhuac. His encounter takes
place in this community near the house of Joaquín Ortega Peña, a
descendant of one of the founding Spanish families that came to
Teteles in the late seventeenth century.

The narrator places the encounter around midnight by giving
details of his times of arrival at various easily recognized points

along the road from Poza Rica to his home in Yaonáhuac. He carefully recounts how he reached Teziutlán, the point of embarkation for many migrant workers headed to and from the coastal plantation, at about 11:30 P.M. He describes how he takes the bus from Teziutlán to Teteles, a twenty-kilometer bus ride that takes about forty-five minutes. This would place his arrival in Teteles somewhere between 12:15 and 12:45, a time of night when the sun's power is weak and the destructive force of the devil is strong.

The encounter between the narrator and the devil is another example of how the Nahuat represent ethnic groups with lightning-bolts and the devil. The narrator has asserted many times that he has a lightning-bolt animal companion spirit and is a wiseman with clairvoyant powers. Others of his community scoff at his particular claim, but they firmly hold the belief that some among them actually are wisemen. Several critics of this particular narrator's claim declared their deceased relatives or compadres were actual wisemen. The narrator makes clear the ethnic identification of the devil by making him appear near obvious markers of the Hispanic presence in the area around Yaonáhuac.

Thus in the first four lines of the story, the narrator sets up the central metaphor in which Nahuat : Hispanics : : lightning-bolts : devil : : north (Yaonáhuac) : south (Teteles) : : noon (by extension) : midnight. The remainder of the story fills out the skeleton established in the first episode.

Lines 5–8. *The devil offers to buy souls, but the narrator refuses.*
The narrator expresses the relationship between himself and the devil in a way that fits with the actual ethnic relations in this part of the northern Sierra de Puebla. The Yaonáhuac Nahuat have a comparatively strong position relative to Hispanics, a fact this narrator expresses by saying he refused the devil's offer. Yet these Nahuat are clearly aware that Hispanics have more wealth and power and thus stand in a superordinate position in the ethnic hierarchy. This narrator expresses the hierarchy of ethnic groups by having the devil say he is richer than Christ.

Lines 9–17. *The devil takes many different forms.*
The narrator fills in the details in the central metaphor by developing the Hispanic identity and sinister nature of the devil. He further establishes the Hispanic identity of the devil by associating him with Spanish items of dress and animals the Nahuat connect with Hispanics. The storyteller depicts the devil wearing a cape and flat hat to resemble the garb of the Colonial Spaniards

who settled in Teteles in the late seventeenth century. The devil changes his hat to look like that of the famous Mexican singer Pedro Infante, and the players in a mariachi band, both considered by the Nahuat as part of the Hispanic world. The narrator associates the devil with horses and cattle, animals the Nahuat frequently use when depicting Hispanics in other stories of their oral tradition. He gives the devil the teeth of a horse and describes the devil mounted on a horse near an Hispanic landmark (the house of Rafael Ortega, a descendant of a founding Spanish family). He describes the devil rolling up his hat to form the horns of a bull. The Nahuat have adopted the biblical association of cattle with Satan and extended it to Hispanics. They associate the bull with Hispanics because Spaniards introduced cattle to the northern Sierra and acquired much Nahuat farmland to convert into pasture. He develops the sinister nature of the devil a step further by associating him with the destructive forces of darkness and cold, describing the devil dressed in black mounted on a black horse. He illustrates how the devil is the antithesis of heat and light by having him disappear in the headlights of the cars passing along the highway. Just as the sun forces the devil to disappear from the Nahuat community at dawn, so the headlights of the cars temporarily make the devil disappear from view.

Lines 18–29. *The narrator enters Yaonáhuac, where he kills the devil.*

In Nahuat belief, one would expect to elude the devil in the safety of the Nahuat community and away from the dangerous and threatening world of Hispanics personified by the devil. One would place the Nahuat world to the north of the world of Hispanics to reflect the actual geographical alignment of communities by ethnic composition in the northern Sierra, and because the Nahuat regard the north as the spatial equivalent of noon and the summer solstice, the times when the sun's powers are greatest and the devil's powers are weakest. One might also expect to elude the devil toward dawn, the time of day when the balance shifts from the destructive powers of darkness and cold to the creative powers of heat and light.

This narrator fulfills these expectations in the way he completes the central metaphor in the final episode of his story. He rounds out his account of how he eluded the devil by tracing his progress from Teteles in the south to his home deep in the *municipio* of Yaonáhuac to the north. He uses place markers recognized by any member of the Yaonáhuac community who might be in his audience. He mentions the crossroads where the main highway from Teteles intersects with the dirt road into Yaonáhuac. He describes the Calvary chapel, which lies further north between the crossroads and the central plaza of his community.

The Nahuat believe one can elude the devil in sacred places in their community like the Calvary chapel. This is a sacred and safe place because it contains an image of the patron Santiago and other religious personalities, who are allies of the sun. The narrator mentions that the devil does not pass by the Calvary chapel, and most Nahuat would understand that this is because it contains personifications of the forces antithetical to the destructive powers of darkness and cold which the devil represents.

The narrator continues his journey northward and marks his progress by mentioning the parish church near the plaza housing a second image of the patron saint. It is interesting that at this point the devil takes the form of Pontius Pilate, who is one of the players in a ritual drama of the crucifixion which the Nahuat of this community enact during the patron saint celebration in July around the Calvary and in the plaza. The storyteller mentions next the house of Isidro Morelos, just north of the plaza. He marks his progress northward by his phrase "down here" (*tanipa*; line 20), which the Nahuat of the northern Sierra generally use to indicate north. "Down" means north, because northern Sierra villages slope northward from the Central Mexican Highlands to the Gulf Coast Lowlands.

The narrator reaches his home north of the plaza and deep in his community. Here he encounters the safety of his home, which a priest blessed when he laid the foundation, and which saints on the family altar guard against the destructive forces represented by the devil. He indicates the safety of his home by depicting his wife addressing him with the term *son*, which, when used between spouses, connotes affection. Husbands and wives endearingly address each other with terms for children: just as women address their husbands as *son*, men sometimes call their wives *daughter*. The Nahuat, perhaps like many others, attribute safety to positive affect, and they connect danger with negative affect. Thus this narrator has created an interesting juxtaposition in which he describes himself entering his home, a symbol narrators frequently use to represent the center of the universe, where he finds love in a sanctified environment. He also evades the devil, who represents hatred (the Nahuat attribute heinous crimes to the work of the devil) and the destructive forces of the periphery.

The narrator mentions that chickens warn of the devil's presence by pronouncing the Nahuat word *masakat* (blood-sucking witch). In Nahuat belief they are those who, with diabolical intervention, sustain themselves by drinking the blood of their neighbors. The storyteller's use of chickens fits the Nahuat belief that chickens were the allies of the sun-Christ because they helped him escape from those who crucified him.

The story concludes with the narrator's account of how he killed the devil near the Red Bridge by the water. This poetic ending draws together a number of elements in the story and fits with Nahuat belief and experience. The narrator has chosen to say he killed the devil in a locality near the midline of his long and narrow *municipio*, far from the world of Hispanics where the initial encounter took place. He selected a spot near water because he believes he is a lightning-bolt and has recounted in other stories (see chapter 5) how God created lightning-bolts to bring water from the sea to make things grow. The narrator says he killed the devil, who now appears as Pontius Pilate, with a machete and thus has painted an image of himself that reminds his listeners of the ritual drama of the Santiago dancers, who perform during the patron saint celebration in July. They too use their swords to slay the devil, and they too represent the devil as Pontius Pilate, the slayer of Christ. The narrator slays the devil well after midnight, at a point in time when the devil's destructive powers have weakened, and the narrator's creative powers have grown stronger with the approach of dawn.

SUMMARY

These chapters have emphasized how a common structure underlies the formation of Nahuat narratives. They illustrate how the same conceptions of space and time play an important role in the generation of very different, nonparallel, and noncognate stories. The common structure that underlies different narratives derives from the similar linguistic, historical, and cultural antecedents of the Nahuat communities in the northern Sierra de Puebla.

The following chapters emphasize differences between narratives from Huitzilan and Yaonáhuac that coincide with variations in social structure created by the checkerboard pattern of Hispanic settlement in the northern Sierra. To illustrate these differences, I used other techniques of story comparison. I compared stories with a large number of parallel themes to discover how the Nahuat rework common ideas differently according to contrasting patterns of social relations. The following chapters focus particularly on cognate narratives from the two communities to control for differences attributable to the historical source of narratives and the random factors in story collection. They aim to identify the differences in constructs underlying both social life and the formation of Nahuat narrative tradition by controlling for as many contaminating variables as possible.

Part III. Differences in Parallel Stories

Ehecatl-Quetzalcoatl

7. Narrative Acculturation

Quetzalcoatl

This chapter describes the injection of Spanish beliefs and religious personalities into Nahuat oral tradition. This is the most obvious effect of Hispanic domination of Indian narrative thought. The Spanish introduced Christian personalities and beliefs which fused with parallel Indian ones, eradicated or drastically altered Indian beliefs antithetical to Spanish Catholicism, introduced entirely new concepts with few parallels in the pre-Spanish tradition, and ignored pre-Hispanic notions that do not clash with Spanish Catholicism and lie beyond the range of concepts central to Spanish culture. Comparison of modern Nahuat and sixteenth-century Aztec cognate myths can reveal several aspects of this process of narrative change. As one might expect, the degree of change brought to Indian narratives depends on the particular nature of Hispanic-Indian relations.

The introduction of Spanish motifs into Indian narratives is a special case of religious acculturation that takes many forms. The personalities of modern Mexican saints such as the Virgin of Guadalupe, the Virgin of Ocotlán, Santiago, and Christ are composites of pre-Spanish and Spanish deities (Wolf 1958; Nutini 1976b). Ritual dramas that frequently take place during religious festivals in honor of modern saints derive from Indian and Spanish antecedents (Bricker 1977). The civil-religious hierarchy which developed to govern Mexican Indian communities is a fusion of pre-Hispanic, and Colonial Spanish practices (Carrasco 1961). The bewildering number of beliefs associated with illness and witchcraft probably derive from peninsular Spanish as well as Indian culture (Foster 1952).

Narratives, of course, do not reflect every aspect of this acculturative process, which scholars must consequently approach through a variety of avenues. But stories, particularly those of Nahuat oral tradition, frequently contain the key ideas and personalities in Indian religious thought and act as barometers of the pressures the Hispanics exert on Indians to change their beliefs. Comparison of sixteenth-century Aztec and modern Nahuat narratives reveals two aspects of the religious acculturative process. First, it illustrates what aspects of Indian thought Hispanics have changed and what aspects they have ignored. Second, with respect to those aspects changed by Hispanics, it reveals how the degree of change varies with the nature of Hispanic-Indian relations.

Contemporary Nahuat narratives reflect the acculturative process because Spanish friars, clergy, and settlers directly affected Indian oral tradition. The friars and secular clergy converted and continue to convert Indians by enacting religious dramas, and I suspect many of these became Nahuat stories. The tales of the birth of Christ (considered below) and the crucifixion contain numerous elements that correspond to ritual dramas carried out today in Huitzilan and Yaonáhuac. Priests in the northern Sierra have taught and continue to teach Indian prayer leaders the Catholic beliefs and biblical stories now repeated as myths by a number of storytellers in both Nahuat communities (see chapters 10 and 11). Prayer leaders are generally bilingual Nahuat who form a crucial link between Indians and Hispanic priests, particularly in communities like Huitzilan and Yaonáhuac where priests do not maintain their residence. Finally, the Spanish who settled in the northern Sierra were and are great storytellers and contributed many Spanish tales to Nahuat oral tradition through their intimate associations with the Indians. Spaniards who established plantations and businesses developed ties of patronage with the Nahuat, and they cemented these ties with ritual kinship to create a loyal labor force. Hispanic men fathered many children with their Nahuat mistresses, creating complex webs of kinship with the Indian community. These ties encouraged Hispanics and Nahuat to become bilingual and promoted the exchange of stories, poetry, and songs between the two ethnic groups. Hispanic patrons earned the loyalty of their Indian clients by entertaining them with stories, and Hispanic labor recruiters continue the practice today. Hispanic and Indian musicians translated Spanish songs into Nahuat to perform at Indian family festivals, further contributing to the Indian oral tradition.

The Nahuat and the Hispanics undoubtedly exchanged stories with each other, but Hispanics donated more stories and motifs to the Indian oral tradition because they are the dominant ethnic group. Hispanics are in a particularly strong position to censure, criticize, ridicule Nahuat beliefs, and reinforce the teachings of the friars and priests because of their control over strategic resources.

Indian ambivalence toward Hispanics contributes heavily to the flow of motifs from Hispanic to Nahuat oral tradition. The Indians generally both covet and resent Hispanic wealth and political power. Nahuat stories discussed in chapter 9 clearly express this ambivalence by describing how Indians both identify with and resent characters who stand for the Hispanic landed aristocracy. The Nahuat identification with Hispanics, which is based on the positive side of the Indians' ambivalence toward the dominant group, sets the stage for the Nahuat acquisition of Spanish stories and motifs.

AZTEC ANTECEDENTS OF NAHUAT ORAL TRADITION

To gauge the effects of Hispanic pressure on religious acculturation in narratives, I compared sixteenth-century Aztec myths with modern stories from Huitzilan and Yaonáhuac. Two stories are cognate in all three traditions—the sixteenth-century Aztec, the Huitzilan Nahuat, and the Yaonáhuac Nahuat. The first is a myth about the Origin of Corn which describes how the gods obtained human sustenance. The second is the Origin of the Sun and the Moon, which describes the appearance of the Fifth Sun for the ancient Aztecs, and tells how heat and light appeared for the first time for the modern Nahuat.

I make no claim that the sixteenth-century Aztec tales in these sources are the exact prototypes for the modern Nahuat stories. Considerable distance separated the northern Sierra de Puebla and Tenochtitlán, where the chroniclers collected the ancient texts. The Aztec tales and the Nahuat stories probably shared a third, and unidentified, prototype. I contend the sixteenth-century Aztec stories from the Valley of Mexico probably resembled the unidentified prototype on the grounds that a common folktale and cultural base existed in the Aztec-speaking part of the Central Mexican Highlands in the years immediately preceding the Conquest (see Hunt 1977).

The myth of the Origin of Corn illustrates that some pre-Hispanic religious personalities remain comparatively intact in modern Nahuat oral tradition, despite heavy pressure to adopt the religious beliefs of the dominant ethnic group. The story of the Origin of the Sun and the Moon illustrates how other deities, central to Aztec religious thought, fused with personalities central to Spanish Catholicism.

THE ORIGIN OF CORN

The central characters in the ancient Aztec story are two closely linked deities, Quetzalcoatl and his lightning-bolt counterpart,

Nanahuatl. Comparison with the Nahuat stories reveals that Nanahuatl (for the Aztecs) or Nanawatzin (for the modern Nahuat) continues to play a role in the contemporary mythic tradition highly
parallel to the one he played in the sixteenth-century Aztec thought.
Storytellers from Huitzilan and Yaonáhuac, like their ancient counterparts, tell how Nanawatzin (the Old Lightning-bolt), together with
his lightning-bolt companions, obtained corn for humans in the
Second Era of Creation by breaking open Sustenance Mountain. The
modern Nahuat stories clearly derive from a pre-Hispanic prototype
resembling an Aztec myth in the *Leyenda de los Soles* (Paso y Troncoso 1903; Lehmann 1906; Feliciano Velázquez 1975).

It was mentioned in the preceding chapters that lightning-bolts
play an important role in Nahuat cosmology, and they have become important symbols of Nahuat ethnic identity. They mediate
between the masculine sun and the feminine earth to create life.
They have both human and animal identities and thus link the
human domain in the center with the animal domain in the periphery. They take the side of the Nahuat in the competitive ethnic
struggle by doing battle with Satan, who represents the Hispanic
threat to the Nahuat.

Three narrative texts follow to illustrate the parallels between
the Aztec account of the Origin of Corn and the modern Nahuat
versions from Yaonáhuac and Huitzilan. The sixteenth-century
Aztec version appears first so the reader can use it as a baseline of
comparison with the contemporary tales. It is a free English translation based primarily on Paso y Troncoso's (1903: 14, 30) Nahuatl
and Spanish versions of this myth. Where Paso y Troncoso's Spanish translation does not appear to fit the Nahuatl original, I have
made corrections that accord with the accounts of Lehmann (1906:
245–257) and Feliciano Velásquez (1975: 119–121). The numbers
appearing in the texts refer to the pre-Hispanic elements appearing
in the modern Nahuat tales.

SIXTEENTH-CENTURY AZTEC VERSION

*After the flood destroyed the Fourth Creation, Nata [My Father]
and his wife Nene [Vulva] were sent to earth with specific instructions to eat no more than a single ear of corn each. But they dis-
obeyed orders and roasted fish. The smoke rose up to the heavens
and angered the gods. 1. Titlacahuan and Tezcatlipoca descended
and turned the couple into dogs as punishment. Quetzalcoatl
traveled to the world of the dead and brought back to Tamoan-*

chan the precious bone.[1] He and his wife used it to bring humans to life.

2. Then the gods asked, "What will they eat, O gods? Look for sustenance." 3. An ant went to fetch corn inside Tonakatepetl [Sustenance Mountain]. 4. The ant abruptly came upon Quetzal-coatl, 5. who asked, "Where did you fetch it? Tell me!" 6. But the ant did not want to tell. 7. Quetzalcoatl spent effort asking him and 8. finally the ant told where he found the corn.

9. Quetzalcoatl turned into a black ant and quickly went to bring the corn. He went into Sustenance Mountain, and 10. fetched some corn and seized the red ant. 11. He brought the corn to Tamo-anchan, where the gods ate it. One of them said, "Our Lord Quet-zalcoatl placed it in our mouths so we could nourish ourselves. What are we to do with Sustenance Mountain?"

12. Quetzalcoatl, who wished to carry it off, tied a rope around it, but he could not lift it. 13. So then Ošomoko quickly drew lots with maize and Cipaktonal, the woman who was the wife of Ošo-moko, quickly foretold the calendrical signs. They said, "Nana-huatl will strike Sustenance Mountain, scattering the grain." It would happen because they divined it. 14. The rain gods quickly came to earth—the blue rain gods, the white rain gods, the yellow rain gods, [and] the red rain gods. 15. Nanahuatl immediately broke open Sustenance Mountain 16. and the rain gods snatched the sustenance—the white corn, the dark corn, the yellow corn, the turquoise corn, the beans, and the amaranth seeds.

YAONÁHUAC VERSION

Once there was a boy who planted a big milpa in the forest with the help of animals. The boy and the animals built a big house, and then they harvested the corn and put it into the house. One day the boy told the animals that he had been called away, but they would see him come with the light. He told them to meet him. 1. The animals came to see him shine as he came. From that day on, the animals could no longer talk.

2. All the corn was in the granary, and there was nothing to eat. The lightning-bolts walked about asking where the corn was because there was nothing for them to eat. 3. And one day a mule-teer ant went for a walk. He took [a kernel of corn that he had spotted] because he carried off everything he found. He cut a small path. 4. A lightning-bolt found him and saw him carrying the kernel of corn. The lightning-bolt wondered, "But where does

he fetch it?" 5. So he decided to let the ant go, and he waited [to see what would happen]. He sat down and then he saw the ant come out [of the granary or mountain].

9. The lightning-bolt decided to follow the ant to discover where he fetched the corn. He pondered about how he would follow the ant: he saw how small the ant was and how he could pass through small spaces. He wondered how he, who was so big, could go where the ant went. He decided to tie himself to the ant with a cord. The ant's body was not slender then, and when the ant tugged on the string, he pulled on the lightning-bolt, who was too large to enter, and he cut himself in the middle. The muleteer ant escaped, but the lightning-bolt felt [inside the mountain] with his fingers until he found the ant again. The lightning-bolt tied himself to the ant a second time, but he couldn't enter the granary, which had turned into a mountain.

So the lightning-bolt decided to wait, and he waited at the mouth [the entrance], and the ant came out bringing a kernel of corn. He waited for the ant to leave the kernel and return to fetch another. 10. Then the lightning-bolt grabbed the sample the ant left behind. 11. He took it to where his companions [the other lightning-bolts] were, and he told them, "I went for a walk and I found the corn. There is corn, but we cannot remove it. I tried, but I couldn't do it." His companions replied, "We'll go see it. We'll go tomorrow."

14. The next day the lightning-bolts all came together and went to the mountain. They watched the muleteer ant, and then they were happy! 12. They said, "We'll break it open." So they gathered to strike [the mountain]. They thundered to break it open, and they made a loud noise. They struck a blow, but they wore themselves out, and they couldnt break it open. 13. So then they said, "Let's tell the Old Thunder-bolt [Nanawatzin] right now. He's stronger and let's see if he can help." They found him and told him, "That granary is sealed and we couldn't break it open." They invited him to join them. "Good," he said. "If you want to, let's go. Get your mules ready. We'll go tomorrow."

The next day they brought their mules. They gathered around him, and he said, "When we make the strike, let's thunder together. I'll spend myself. I'll sleep [from exhaustion] for a little while [after breaking the mountain open] and you wait for me to divide [the corn] for you." They agreed, and he added, "We'll go as a single force."

15. They thundered together and broke open the mountain. A mouse, which was inside the granary, ran out bringing the corn. Nothing happened to the other lightning-bolts, but the old thunder-bolt had fallen. He had spent himself. He slept. He rested. He said, "I'm tired. Wait for me so that we'll divide the corn together." 16. But those lightning-bolts couldn't wait. They saw the mountain was full of corn and they filled their sacks. They brought their mules and loaded them on top [pressing the corn]. That is the reason [kernels of corn] are flat. And they say the kernels of corn were also flattened by the mouse's teeth. When the older thunder-bolt awoke, there was no one. He was alone. They left him only the debris.   STORYTELLER F. J.

HUITZILAN VERSION

When it dawned for the first time, the muleteer ants were cutting a path. 2. There was no corn and [the lightning-bolts] asked [where the corn was]. 3. Ants were carrying [the corn] into a mountain—a very big mountain. 4. [The lightning-bolts] saw one of the ants and 5. [one of the lightning-bolts] asked him, "Where do you fetch the corn? We're hungry. There isn't any corn here."

6. [The ant replied], "Over there, but there isn't any more." 7. [The lightning-bolt] said, "But there is [more]!" The ant insisted that there wasn't any [more]. [The lightning-bolt] asked, "But how is it that you were carrying it?" The ant replied, "We have finished carrying it. It's all gone." [The lightning-bolt insisted], "It isn't true that it's all gone!" "It is all gone," reaffirmed [the ant]. "Bring a rope," commanded [the first lightning-bolt]. They grabbed the first in command of the muleteer ants, and they tied a rope here [around his waist]. One stood here, and another stood there, and they squeezed. Now you'll talk! Tell us the truth!" [demanded the first lightning-bolt]. 8. "Don't squeeze me so much. Loosen me, and I'll tell you," [pleaded the ant]. "There is corn. There is a lot of it," [confessed the ant]. "Oh good," said [the first lightning-bolt]. "Now we'll loosen you." [The ant] said, "There is a lot of corn, but no one can remove it. It's in a big mountain."

14. Then, as for what they did, all [the lightning-bolts] conversed. Many came together up there. 13. The captain of the lightning-bolts came and announced, "I'm going to break open this mountain. But you wait for me. Don't gather up the corn [before I rejoin you]. I'm going to break it open with a blow from my head." 15. There were a lot of people [Christians] who saw him break open the rock. 16. They charged forward, stepping on

*the corn, and they carried it off. That's the reason all the kernels
of corn are flat. He who broke open the mountain was lying un-
conscious. He almost died. His head was clouded.*

STORYTELLER M. F.

Interpretation

The modern Nahuat stories of the Origin of Corn are examples of
the analogy between creation and procreation described in chapter 5.
They describe how Nanawatzin and the other lightning-bolts break
open Sustenance Mountain much as a man penetrates a woman in
the act of love. The narrator of the Yaonáhuac version, who has a
reputation for stressing sexual themes in his tales, develops this
analogy more explicitly than his Huitzilan counterpart, but the
basic elements of the metaphor appear in both Nahuat stories.

The analogy between creation and procreation developed by all
Nahuat narrators of the story has lightning-bolts standing to Sustenance Mountain as the penis stands to the vagina and womb. It is
based on the masculine identity of Nanawatzin and the feminine
identity of the earth, and it rests on numerous parallels the Nahuat
draw between planting corn and sexual intercourse.

The Yaonáhuac narrator develops this metaphor more than his
Huitzilan counterpart by including the following elements in his
story. He describes the lightning-bolt feeling inside the orifice in
the mountain to find the corn, much as a man plays with a woman
during the prelude to the act of love (item 9). He describes the Old
Lightning-bolt spending himself and sleeping after breaking open
the mountain much as a man and woman relax after reaching a
sexual climax (item 15).

Aztec Antecedents

On first glance, it would appear that the ancient Aztec myth is
based on a metaphor very different from the one in the modern
Nahuat stories. The sixteenth-century account describes Nanahuatl breaking open Sustenance Mountain as one threshes corn,
thereby drawing an analogy between the mountain and an ear of
corn. The original Nahuatl verb, which I translated as "break open
[Sustenance Mountain]" (items 13 and 15), is *kiwiteki*, which liter-
ally means "shake out grain with sticks" (Paso y Troncoso 1903:
14, 30; Lehmann 1906: 256; Feliciano Velázquez 1975: 121). To be
sure, one modern Nahuat narrator (F. J.) uses a related verb (*kwite-
kiliya* = strike a blow with sticks) and thus he may have a similar

metaphor in mind. But he and his Huitzilan counterpart (M. F.) generally describe how Nanawatzin and the other lightning-bolts split open (*kitapana*) Sustenance Mountain as one splits wood with an axe.

However, the modern Nahuat, like the ancient Aztecs, tend to create double metaphors, and on a second level of meaning, one can see the metaphor in which lightning-bolts : Sustenance Mountain : : penis : vagina and womb in the sixteenth-century account by placing the ancient characters in the context of Aztec belief. First, there is the right sexual symbolism in pre-Hispanic as well as modern Nahuat thought. Nanahuatl (Aztec) and Nanawatzin (Nahuat), the lightning-bolts who broke open Sustenance Mountain, are males. The earth, which has an obvious relationship with the mountain, is female. Like the modern Nahuat, the Aztecs personified the earth as an old woman (Our Grandmother—Toci) and as the sensuous Goddess of Spring Xochiquetzal (Sahagún 1950: 4; Caso 1967: 52–54; Nicholson 1971: 421–431). Second, one can find a clear expression in ancient Aztec thought of the relationship between sex and the creation of maize in the myth about Xochiquetzal, who slept with Piltzintecuhtli, and gave birth to Tzenteotl (Cinteotl), the God of Maize (Krickerberg 1971: 121).

To be sure, the modern Nahuat stories of the Origin of Corn reflect changes in the Indian society that took place following the Spanish Conquest. During the Colonial period, independent Indian kingdoms changed into communities of peasants, and the Indian class system collapsed with the formation of an ethnically stratified society of Indians and Hispanics. The highly complex religion of the ancient Aztecs, which reflected in many ways their stratified and centralized society, broke down (Carrasco 1975, 1976a). Comparison of the ancient Aztec and the contemporary Nahuat stories reveals the results of this process. Relative to the sixteenth-century account, the contemporary narratives have fewer religious personalities organized in a hierarchy, and they lack mention of divination by calendrical signs. The Aztecs assigned colors to the four cardinal directions, and in the sixteenth-century account, the narrator categorizes the rain gods by four colors to place them precisely in space (item 14). The modern Nahuat have lost the color symbolism, along with other key beliefs including the five Aztec eras of creation (also identified by the same colors), and the twenty-day-per-month calendar. These changes undoubtedly stem from the loss of specialists highly trained in esoteric belief. But the Nahuat stories still retain a very large number of pre-Hispanic elements, as is evident by comparing them with the ancient Aztec text. More-

Table 13. Aztec Ideas in Origin of Corn Tales, by Community and Storyteller

Aztecs Anonymous	Yaonáhuac F. J.	Huitzilan M. F.
1. After the deluge, Nata and Nene are changed into dogs.	Animals become mute with the coming of the sun.	
2. The gods look for human sustenance.	After the boy's corn granary becomes a mountain and there is no more corn, the lightning-bolts walk about asking where the corn is.	When there is hunger, the lightning-bolts ask where the corn is.
3. An ant goes to fetch corn from inside Sustenance Mountain.	An ant carries a kernel of corn from inside a mountain.	Ants carry corn into a mountain.
4. The ant meets Quetzalcoatl.	A lightning-bolt sees the ant carrying the kernel of corn.	Lightning-bolts spot an ant carrying corn.
5. Quetzalcoatl asks the ant where he fetches the corn.	The lightning-bolt resolves to watch the ant to find where he fetches the corn.	Someone (probably a lightning-bolt) asks the ant where he is taking the corn.
6. The ant does not want to tell.		The ant says where he is taking the corn, but he adds that there is no more.
7. Quetzalcoatl must work hard asking him.		Someone (probably a lightning-bolt) insists there is more corn. The ant denies it, and the first lightning-bolt directs others to tie a rope around the ant and squeeze him to make him talk.
8. The ant tells where he fetches the corn.		The ant tells where the corn is.
9. Quetzalcoatl turns into a black ant and enters the mountain.	The lightning-bolt tries to follow the ant into the mountain by tying himself to the ant with a string. The lightning-bolt is too large to enter.	
10. Quetzalcoatl seizes some corn.	The lightning-bolt seizes a kernel of corn the ant removes from the mountain.	
11. Quetzalcoatl takes the corn to Tamoanchan, where the gods eat it.	The lightning-bolt takes the corn to his companions.	

Table 13 (*continued*)

Aztecs Anonymous	Yaonáhuac F. J.	Huitzilan M. F.
12. Quetzalcoatl ties a rope around Sustenance Mountain and tries to lift it. He fails.	All the lightning-bolts try to open the mountain, but they fail. A rope is mentioned in item 9.	A rope is mentioned in item 7.
13. Ošomoko and Cipaktonal divine that the kernels of corn will be released by Nanahuatl breaking open Sustenance Mountain.	The lightning-bolts invite the old lightning-bolt (Nanawatzin) to join them when they try to break open the mountain.	The first lightning-bolt (Nanawatzin) decides to break open the mountain.
14. The rain gods come to earth.	The lightning-bolts gather and watch the ant.	Many (lightning-bolts) gather up above.
15. Nanahuatl immediately breaks open Sustenance Mountain.	The lightning-bolts, this time accompanied by Nanawatzin, break open the mountain.	The first lightning-bolt breaks open the mountain.
16. The rain gods snatch the sustenance.	The lightning-bolts snatch the corn.	Christians snatch the corn.

over, the Huitzilan and Yaonáhuac accounts share about the same number of ancient Aztec ideas. An examination of table 13 will reveal that the two modern Nahuat versions resemble the sixteenth-century text to about the same degree. Thus Hispanic Christian personalities have not superseded the role of lightning-bolts (particularly Nanahuatl) in obtaining human sustenance in the oral tradition of either community.

Pre-Hispanic tales like the Origin of Corn probably had a good chance for survival because they deal with themes peripheral to those in Hispanic religious thought of the sixteenth and seventeenth centuries. It is plausible to argue that they have retained a large number of indigenous elements, despite heavy Hispanic pressure, because they revolve around corn, which is a New World crop. The Nahuat have generally retained practices and beliefs concerning corn because they are associated with a technique of subsistence adopted by, rather than radically modified by, the dominant ethnic group. The Spanish adopted corn and made it the staple crop, particularly in the northern Spanish provinces of Galicia, Astúrias, and the Basque region. The Spanish cultivate corn in Mexican *milpa* fashion by interspersing it with beans, squash, and other crops (Foster 1952: 298).

Lightning-bolt personalities have changed considerably during the four centuries since the Conquest. They appear in modern Nahuat stories as clairvoyant figures called wisemen (*tamatinime*), who differ from the ancient Aztec wisemen (*tlamatinime*), who were philosophers or people of wisdom (León-Portilla 1974: 391–392). They have retained some of the characteristics of the clairvoyant personalities like Tezcatlipoca in ancient Aztec myth, but they also share qualities with the wisemen (*sabios*) found in Spanish oral tradition. Moreover, the modern Nahuat have taken these synthetic characters and placed them into a number of post-Conquest dramas they recount in their stories (see chapter 8).

DIFFERENCES CONNECTED TO SOCIAL STRUCTURE

The Origin of Corn tales are clear examples of cognate stories told in different ways concordant with the social structure of Huitzilan and Yaonáhuac. These two Nahuat communities evolved in opposite directions owing to patterns of Hispanic-Nahuat competition for land. Huitzilan has developed a more hierarchical social order because Hispanics have settled in the community, creating a system of ethnic stratification, and they have taken much Nahuat land, promoting the development of Hispanic-Indian patronage. Relations between men and women remain or possibly have become more androcentric because of more pronounced patrilineal land inheritance. Yaonáhuac, by contrast, has become more egalitarian with the breakdown of a landed aristocracy and the shift from patrilineal to bilateral inheritance and changes in other factors promoting more equality between men and women.

Storytellers of each community re-tell the same story of the Origin of Corn differently to fit the way their social systems have changed. Huitzilan storyteller M. F. expresses the hierarchical nature of his community in the way he describes the relations among Nanawatzin and the other lightning-bolts. Nanawatzin is the captain or leader of the lightning-bolts according to Nahuat belief in both communities (see chapter 5). But this narrator depicts a much more hierarchical relationship among Nanawatzin and his lightning-bolt companions. He describes how Nanawatzin barks orders to the others to tie a rope around the ant and squeeze him to make him confess the location of the hidden corn (item 7). He has Nanawatzin deciding by himself to break open the mountain (item 13) and he has him succeed by acting entirely alone (item 15).

Yaonáhuac narrator F. J., on the other hand, expresses the egalitarianism of his community in his account of parallel events. In his version Nanawatzin is invited by the other lightning-bolts to join them when they try to break open the mountain (item 13) and he acts in unison with them rather than taking it upon himself to do it alone (item 15).

It is possible to connect the differences between the Huitzilan and Yaonáhuac versions to a number of aspects of social organization in the two communities. The characters are composite personalities or multivocal symbols who stand for a variety of persons in real life. The Nahuat of Huitzilan can easily connect the authoritarian relations between Nanawatzin and other lightning-bolts to relations among Hispanic patrons and Indian clients, or between the Nahuat father and the subordinate members of his household. Likewise the Yaonáhuac Nahuat can easily relate Nanawatzin's more egalitarian relationship with his lightning-bolt companions to the more diffuse pattern of community decision making, the economic independence of *milpa* farmers who do not depend heavily on Hispanic patronage, and the more egalitarian family decision-making process between husband and wife.

THE ORIGIN OF THE SUN AND THE MOON

When the friars and secular clergy established Catholicism in the northern Sierra de Puebla, they probably converted by stressing parallels between their religion and that of the Nahuat. Pre-Spanish tales with themes running parallel to Hispanic religious belief were probably superseded by Christian ones. By stressing a link between the origin of the sun and the birth of Christ, the friars linked the principal deities in the two religions and set the stage for the eventual replacement of the Aztec gods by the Spanish Catholic religious figures.

The flow of Hispanic motifs into Indian oral tradition varies among the Nahuat communities according to different patterns of ethnic relations in the northern Sierra de Puebla. Where Hispanics directly dominate Indians in the biethnic community of Huitzilan, Nahuat stories contain fewer pre-Hispanic and more Spanish elements, primarily because of the greater pressures on Indians to change their beliefs in conformity with those of the dominant group. Comparison of stories of the Origin of the Sun and the Moon from ancient Aztec and modern Nahuat tradition reveals how the retention of pre-Hispanic ideas varies with the degree of Hispanic domination.

In both communities, the stories are fused to some degree with the Spanish story of Christmas, but the degree of fusion differs dra-

matically between Yaonáhuac and Huitzilan. The Huitzilan Nahuat, who have experienced more domination by a large resident
Hispanic group, have submerged the Aztec personalities and replaced
them with Christian ones. The Yaonáhuac Nahuat, who live under
indirect rather than direct domination by Hispanics, depict much
more clearly defined Aztec personalities in their stories.

The following five texts—an ancient Aztec version and four
Nahuat ones—illustrate the different degrees to which Yaonáhuac
and Huitzilan narrators develop Aztec or Hispanic Christian personalities in their stories. The first text is a pre-Hispanic Aztec
account which appears in the *Florentine Codex* (Sahagún 1953:
3–8) and the 1558 anonymous manuscript known as the *Leyenda
de los Soles* (Paso y Troncoso 1930: 30).

The sixteenth-century Aztec story describes two gods—the
humble and pustuled Nanahuatzin and the aristocratic Tecuciztecatl—cremating themselves at Teotihuacan to become the sun
and the moon. On first glance it appears that the Yaonáhuac, but
not the Huitzilan, accounts are derived from a prototype something
like the Aztec story that appears below. Only the Yaonáhuac tales
specifically describe the creation of the sun and the moon through
the important event of self-cremation. But I contend both the modern Nahuat versions derive, at least in part, from this prototype,
although the accounts from Huitzilan are now basically Spanish.
The coming of the sun equates with the birth of Christ in both
communities. Huitzilan narrator M. A. (Huitzilan version 1 below)
says that when he (Christ) was born in a stable, it dawned (for the
first time). Yaonáhuac narrator L. V. (Yaonáhuac version 2) makes a
similar point when he says that the sun is called God Jesus Christ.
These are not obscure points incidentally mentioned in the stories,
but are basic tenets of belief in Nahuat thought. Thus the Huitzilan Christmas stories can be considered highly Hispanicized versions of the Aztec Origin of the Sun and the Moon tales. The Aztec
ideas in the Huitzilan stories are less evident because these Nahuat
have more radically re-worked them to fit Catholic doctrine in
response to intense pressure for religious acculturation.

The Aztec and Nahuat stories appear below with numbers
inserted in the text to identify the items shared among the sixteenth-century Aztec, the Huitzilan, and the Yaonáhuac versions.
The pre-Spanish myth appears first because it serves as a baseline of
comparison with the four Nahuat stories that follow in an approxi-
mate acculturational sequence. The ancient Aztec tale is a composite of the accounts from the 1558 manuscript and the *Florentine
Codex*. The bulk of the sixteenth-century story is paraphrased from

Anderson and Dibble's excellent translation of Sahagún's Nahuatl version (Sahagún 1953: 3–8).

SIXTEENTH-CENTURY AZTEC VERSION

1. *The fourth sun ended in a deluge, and all the inhabitants of the earth were turned into fish [Paso y Troncoso 1903: 28]. 2. When all was in darkness, the gods gathered at Teotihuacan, where they asked who would take it upon himself to be the sun. One of them, Tecuciztecatl, said, "O gods, I shall be the one." Again the gods spoke, "And who else?" No one else came forward, because everyone was afraid. Nanahuatzin stood among the others listening, and then the gods called to him, "Thou shalt be the one, O Nanahuatzin." He eagerly accepted, saying, "It is well, O gods; you have been good to me."*

3. *Then they began doing penance. Tecuciztecatl and Nanahuatzin fasted for four days, and then at this time a fire was laid. It burned in a hearth they called the* teotexcalli. *Tecuciztecatl did penance with costly things. His fir branches were quetzal feathers, and his grass balls were of gold. His maguey spines were of green stone, and the reddened, bloodied spines were of coral. His incense was very good incense. As for Nanahuatzin, his fir branches were made of green water rushes—green reeds bound in threes, making nine bundles. His grass balls were aromatic reeds, and his maguey spines were just maguey spines. The blood covering them was his own blood, and the incense was the scabs from his sores.*

4. *For each of them, a hill was made. There they performed penance for four nights. The hills are now called the pyramid of the sun and the moon. When they ended their penance, each threw down and cast away his fir branches and all with which he did penance.*

5. *When midnight came, they readied them. They adorned them and they gave Tecuciztecatl his round, forked heron feather headdress and his sleeveless jacket. But as for Nanahuatzin, they gave him a headdress of mere paper and tied on his paper hair. They gave him his paper stole and his paper breech cloth. When midnight came, the gods encircled the hearth called the* teotexcalli, *where, for four days, a fire had burned. The gods arranged themselves on both sides, in a line, and they set Tecuciztecatl and Nanahuatzin standing in the middle. The gods spoke, saying, "Take courage, O Tecuciztecatl; fall—cast thyself—into the fire!" Upon this he prepared to cast himself into the flames, but when the heat reached him, it was insufferable, intolerable, and un-*

bearable. The hearth had blazed up a great deal, a great heap of coals burned, and flames flared up high. He was terrified. He stopped in fear, turned about, and went back. Once more he set out, but he could not do it. Four times he tried, but he could not do it.

6. Thereupon the gods cried, "Onward, thou O Nanahuatzin! Take heart!" And Nanahuatzin hardened his heart and firmly shut his eyes. He had no fear; he did not stop short; he did not falter in fright; he did not turn back. 7. All at once, he quickly threw and cast himself into the fire. Thereupon, he burned; his body cracked and sizzled. 8. And when Tecuciztecatl saw that he had burned, then he cast himself upon the fire and also burned [Sahagún 1953: 3–6]. 9. Nanahuatl [Nanahuatzin] fell into the fire, 10. and Four Flint [Tecuciztecatl] fell upon the ashes [Paso y Troncoso 1903: 31].

11. And afterwards, the gods sat waiting to see where Nanahuatzin would rise—he who first fell into the fire—in order that he might shine [as the sun]; in order that dawn might break. When the gods had been waiting for a long time, the reddening [of the dawn] began in all directions; the dawn light extended all around. And, so they say, thereupon the gods fell upon their knees in order to await where he who had become the sun would rise. They looked in all directions. They could not agree on any place. There was dissension. Some thought it would be from the north and looked there; some to the west; some placed themselves to look to the south. They expected that he might rise in all directions because light was everywhere. 12. And some placed themselves so that they would watch toward the east. They said, "For there, in that place, the sun already will come to rise." True indeed were the words of those who looked there and pointed with their fingers in that direction. They say that those who looked there were Quetzalcoatl, Ecatl, and Totec or Anauatl itecu, and red Tezcatlipoca. And there were those who were called Mimixcoa, who were without number, and four women: Tiacapan, Teicuo, Tlacoyehua, and Xocoyotl.

13. And when the sun rose, he appeared to be red; he kept swaying from side to side. It was impossible to look into his face; he blinded one with his light. He shined intensely. He issued rays of light from himself. His rays reached in all directions; his brilliant rays penetrated everywhere. And afterwards Tecuciztecatl rose, following behind him from the same place—the east—near where the sun had come bursting forth. In the same manner they had fallen into the fire, so they came forth following each other. They had become exactly equal in their appearance, as they shone.

When the gods saw them to be exactly the same, they issued a judgment: "Thus will this be; thus will this be done." Then one of the gods came running. He wounded the face of Tecuciztecatl with a rabbit. He darkened his face. He killed its brilliance. Thus doth it appear today.

14. When both appeared over the earth, they could not move. They remained motionless. So once again the gods spoke: "How shall we live? The sun cannot move. Shall we perchance live among common folk? Let this be, that through us the sun may be revived. Let all of us die."

15. Then it became the office of Ecatl to slay the gods. But they say that Xolotl wished not to die. And when death approached, he fled from its presence; he ran; he quickly entered a field of green maize, and took the form of two corn stalks growing from a single root which the workers in the field named xolotl. But he was seen in the field of green maize. Once again he fled and quickly entered into a maguey field. There he quickly changed himself into a maguey plant consisting of two parts called mexolotl. Once more he was seen, and once more he went into the water, where he became an amphibious animal called an axolotl. There they could seize him to slay him.

16. And they say that although all the gods died, the sun still could not move. Thus it became the charge of Ecatl, the wind, who arose and exerted himself fiercely and violently. And he moved him, and he went on his way. And when he had followed his course, only the moon remained there. When the sun entered the place where he set, then the moon moved. Thus the sun comes forth and spends the whole day in his work; and the moon undertakes the night's task; he works all night; he does his labors at night (Sahagún 1953: 6–8).

YAONÁHUAC VERSION 1

2. A woman gave birth to a child who did not grow up, and so she tossed it into the water, and the child floated away. The mother of the dwarfs went to fetch water for her kitchen, and she spotted the child floating in the water and rescued it. After the child grew up [matured], he told his mother he was going out for a walk. He went on for some distance and found a lot of dwarfs.

3. There was a very big fire. 2. It was dark then. 5. The dwarfs made a wager that he who could put out the fire would be king of the world. But no one jumped into the fire to put it out. 6. The boy said perhaps he could put out the fire.

4. *So he climbed a hill, and 7. jumped from the top, with the wind. 9. He took most of the fire; a little remained. He went forever to stay at the mouth of the sea. Now he is the sun, and he is the heat, and he is the light. 8. His mother came looking for him, and she found the dwarfs, who told her that the boy had gone. They said he had taken the light and now circles the earth as the hands go round a clock. So she decided to follow him. 10. A little fire remained for her to take.*

16. *So it is that the sun and the moon chase each other. The moon is less bright because she took the little fire that remained.*

STORYTELLER J. M.

YAONÁHUAC VERSION 2

1. *Father Noah survived the flood and had a family. A new world was made again. 2. Then there were two orphan children, a brother and a sister.*

3. *A big fire was made for them. 7. They threw the orphans into the fire. 9. The boy was the more burned, but 10. as for the girl, they did not burn her so much. After they charred the boy well, after he wallowed around in the fire, he became the sun. The girl, who was less burned, became the moon. Then he put the moon in the world. God decided he should come, and they called him God Jesus Christ.*

11. *All the people, all the animals—the seeds—who remained from the ark, they asked where the sun would come. A bird, a turkey, a chicken, horses, and pigs all asked, "Where will the sun come?" 12. Only the dog knew. He asked God where he would come, and the dog went about telling the others where the sun would rise. The dog told them they should go meet the sun. Some had no clothes, so the birds borrowed pieces of clothing, and the armadillo was weaving her clothes for the debut. The dog ran about telling everyone the sun would come from the east.*

15. *In those days the dog spoke, but at that moment, God slapped him so that he would stay mute. 14. Then all the animals went to meet the sun. The armadillo had not finished her skirt. Now the armadillo looks as if half of her skin is woven and half is striped. The stripes are the weaving sticks she carried. When they went to meet him, God blessed them, and they remained wearing their clothes ever since. The armadillo and the birds could no longer remove their clothing.*

STORYTELLER L. V.

HUITZILAN VERSION 1

*2. When he [Jesus] was born, it was dark in the stable. 11. Many
came together and began looking for him.*

*13. It was dark, very dark. And why did it dawn? He was
appearing. It was dawning. He was appearing beautifully; he was
shining as he came. 12. But he appeared down there, and they
said, here is where he is. There he came, rising. They all saw him.
Many had gathered, and they all saw him. Behold it was dawning,
it was dawning, it was dawning until it dawned completely.*

*15. From there they began looking for him. Many looked
for him and they were angry. The Jews knew: they were angry.
14. They killed many children, thinking perhaps he would be
among them.* STORYTELLER M. A.

HUITZILAN VERSION 2

*Our Little Mother [the Virgin of the Conception] told her father
that his clothes were dirty. He took them off, and she took them
to the river to wash them. There she met St. Joseph, who tried to
persuade her to leave St. Peter and marry him because St. Peter
had a heavy beard. Our Little Mother replied that she could not
go now because her father had nothing to wear; she agreed to go
away with St. Joseph in a week.*

*Our Little Mother went again to wash, and she did not return
home because St. Joseph took her away to his home. Our Little
Mother went off on his donkey, and St. Joseph walked. Within a
half a year she had a child. The child was born on a road in the
forest. [Our Little Mother and St. Joseph] came to a house and
asked for lodging. But they were denied because the house was
too small. So the child was born on the porch. Ice fell on the child
when he was born; it was cold.*

*When the child arrived, the opossum went to see it. The
opossum was also a Christian [then]. 3. St. Joseph asked if the
opossum knew where there was a fire, and the opossum said he
would look for one. There was a woman who lived alone, who was
making a fire. The opossum asked her if he could warm himself,
and the woman said yes. So while toasting himself, the opossum
wrapped his tail around a piece of burning wood and took it to
the child so that he could warm himself. At that moment, the
opossum said, "Ah, Jesus. Ah, Jesus" [while noticing that the fur
on his tail had burned off]. And that is why the opossum's tail has*

*no fur. St. Joseph told the opossum to make a big fire with wood
shavings to warm the child.*

*Our Little Mother fed him milk. 14. When she finished, she
asked the opossum to bring a little chicken. She said her father
would not give her one because she eloped and made him angry.
He would beat her with a piece of wood. The opossum said he
would do what she requested. He fetched a chicken as big as this
[narrator gestures to indicate a large chicken] and dragged it with
his mouth and brought it to the child. Our Little Mother asked for
another one, but this time they caught the opossum and shot him.
He went there to stay.* STORYTELLER J. H.

Interpretation

Yaonáhuac narrators express the metaphor men : women : : sun :
moon by depicting how a son and his mother, or a brother and his
sister, cremate themselves to become the sun and the moon. Narrators from both communities maintain the same sexual symbolism when they identify the sun with Christ. The Nahuat also link
Mary with the moon although no narrator mentions this in these
texts. Other narratives not cognate with these stories clearly identify the moon as Mary,[2] and the Nahuat generally assert the connection in ordinary discourse.

The Yaonáhuac narrators clearly express the primacy of men
in the way they describe the creation of the sun and the moon.
They depict the boy cremating himself first, indicate how he takes
most of the fire, assert that he has more heat and light (is brighter)
than the woman who becomes the moon, and describe the moon
following the sun. The light and heat of the sun are the prime
moving forces that bring moral order out of chaos; hence making
the sun masculine expresses the moral strength of men. The light
and heat emanating from the moon are much weaker than those of
the sun and cannot hold back the darkness and cold—symbols for
the forces that undermine the Nahuat moral order. By making the
moon feminine, they express the idea that women have less moral
strength than men.

Aztec and Hispanic Antecedents

The sexual symbolism expressed in the modern Nahuat tales could
easily derive from sixteenth-century Aztec thought. To be sure, the
gods who became the sun and the moon—Nanahuatzin and Tecu-

ciztecatl—in the ancient Aztec text are both masculine. But the sexual identities of the sun and the moon as man and woman are expressed elsewhere. The Aztec text describes how the moon works at night (item 16), a time of the day associated with women. The Aztecs connected nightfall with women by making the west, the place where the sun sets, the domain of women (León-Portilla 1974: 120–123). It would be an easy step to assign the moon feminine identity, a step the Aztecs took in other expressions of belief. Some regarded the moon as Coyolxauhqui, the sister of Huitzilopochtli (Hummingbird on the Left), the fifth Aztec sun (Caso 1967: 13).

The sexual images expressed in the metaphor men : women : : sun : moon in both Aztec and modern Nahuat thought could easily derive from the positions of the sexes in the social structure. Women had a weaker position than men in ancient Aztec as well as modern Nahuat society. The Aztecs, like the Nahuat, practiced virilocality, which promoted agnatic male solidarity and weakened the ties between blood-related women (Carrasco 1964, 1976b). Aztec women had fewer legal rights than men: women, but not men, had to be chaste before marriage, and women had to be faithful to their husbands, but they could not demand their husbands' fidelity (Vaillant 1966: 125–126).

The Nahuat accounts of the Origin of the Sun and the Moon have changed with alterations brought to Indian society by the Spanish Conquest of Mexico. The modern Nahuat mention far fewer religious personalities, and they no longer place those that remain neatly in the four cardinal directions by using color symbolism. While the ancient Aztec narrator mentions red Tezcatlipoca to place this god to the east (item 12), the modern Nahuat narrators do not categorize lightning-bolts or other religious personalities by colors to place them in space.

The modern Nahuat stories contain a number of ancient Aztec personalities and beliefs fused with parallel Spanish ones. As mentioned, the sun became Christ, and the moon became the Virgin Mary, but the stories contain more subtle instances of fusion. Yaonáhuac narrator J. M. combined the Aztec-derived story with the biblical account of Moses: he describes the mother of the dwarfs fetching the baby out of the water (item 2) much as the Pharoah's daughter in Exodus 2 rescues Moses. Narrators L. V. (Yaonáhuac) and M. A. and J. H. (Huitzilan) merge the Aztec story with the biblical account of Christmas, and L. V. tacks his story to an account of Noah's Ark. The Jews' search for Jesus in M. A.'s tale (Huitzilan version 1) could be derived from Ecatl's chase of Xolotl

Table 14. Aztec Ideas in Origin of the Sun and Moon Stories, by Community and Storyteller

Aztecs	Yaonáhuac J. M.	Yaonáhuac L. V.	Huitzilan M. A.	Huitzilan J. H.
1. The Fourth Creation ends with a flood.		Father Noah survives the flood and has a family.		
2. When all is darkness, the gods gather in Teotihuacan and ask who will be the sun. Tecuciztecatl offers himself, and the gods name Nanahuatzin.	A boy who never grows up takes a stroll and comes upon many dwarfs. It was dark then.	There are two orphan children, a brother and a sister.	It is dark in the stable where Jesus is born.	
3. A fire is laid in the hearth called the *teotexcalli*.	The dwarfs have made a big fire.	A big fire is made for the orphan children.		The opossum steals fire from an old woman to warm the infant Jesus. He brings the fire to Joseph, who tells him to make a big fire with wood shavings to warm the child.
4. The gods build two hills—one for Tecuciztecatl and one for Nanahuatzin—where they do penance.	The boy climbs a hill.			
5. When midnight comes, the gods tell Tecuciztecatl to cast himself into the fire. He tries, but he turns back four times.	The dwarfs make a wager that he who puts out the fire will be king of the world. No one jumps into the fire to put it out.			
6. The gods call Nanahuatzin and tell him to take heart.	The boy says perhaps he can put out the fire.			

Table 14 (continued)

| Aztecs | Yaonáhuac | | Huitzilan | |
	J. M.	L. V.	M. A.	J. H.
7. Nanahuatzin throws himself into the fire.	The boy jumps from the hill, with the wind, into the fire.	They throw the orphans into the fire.		
8. Tecuciztecatl then casts himself into the fire.	The boy's adopted mother, who is also the mother of the dwarfs, takes the rest of the fire.			
9. Nanahuatzin falls on the fire when it is hotter.	The boy takes most of the fire.	The boy is the more burned.		
10. Four Flint falls into the ashes.	Only a little fire remains for her to take.	The girl is burned less than the boy.		
11. The gods wait to see where Nanahuatzin will rise. They look in all directions. Some think he will come from the north, others think he will come from the west, and still others think he will come from the south.		The people and the animals— the seeds from the ark—ask where the sun will rise.	Many gather and begin looking for him.	
12. Some look toward the east and say the sun will come there.		Only the dog knows where the sun will rise because he asked God. The dog runs about saying the sun will rise from the east.	They say, here is where he is. They all see him.	
13. When the sun comes, he blinds everyone with his light. He shines intensely.			He appears beautifully. He shines as he comes.	

Table 14 (*continued*)

Aztecs	*Yaonáhuac* J. M.	L. V.	*Huitzilan* M. A.	J. H.
14. The gods sacrifice themselves.		The other animals run to meet the sun. When he blesses them, they remain with their clothes on forever.	The Jews kill many children, thinking one is he.	The opossum is shot when he tries to steal a second chicken.
15. Ecatl chases Xolotl, who escapes by changing into a twin corn stalk, a maguey plant, and an amphibious animal. But Ecatl finally slays him.		God slaps the dog, making him mute.	The Jews begin looking for him.	
16. When the sun follows his course, the moon moves.	So it is that the sun and the moon chase each other.			

(item 15 in the sixteenth-century Aztec version) and from the biblical account of Herod's search for the Christ child in Matthew 2.

While there is no question that biblical themes exist in the versions from both communities, the Yaonáhuac narrators emphasize Aztec themes, and their Huitzilan counterparts emphasize biblical ones. Table 14 presents sixteen Aztec ideas appearing in the Nahuat tales and reveals that over twice as many occur in the Yaonáhuac stories. But the aggregate statistics conceal the fact that events in the Yaonáhuac stories are closer to the sixteenth-century Aztec account than similar events in the Huitzilan tales.

The most important elements in the stories are the identities of the central characters and how they create the sun and the moon. The central characters in the Aztec tales are Nanahuatzin and Tecuciztecatl, and the former has obvious parallels with the boy who never grew up and the orphan boy and girl in the Yaonáhuac stories (see item 2). Nanahuatzin, the character who became the sun, often assumed the form of a lightning-bolt in Aztec tradition.

In the sixteenth-century myth of the Origin of Corn discussed earlier in this chapter, Nanahuatzin as a lightning-bolt broke open Sustenance Mountain to release corn for the inhabitants of the world in the Fifth Creation (see Paso y Troncoso 1903: 30). The modern Nahuat frequently depict lightning-bolts as dwarfs or children who live with a female consort. To be sure, the central characters in the Huitzilan tales are also deities—Christ, Mary, and Joseph —but they have little in common with the Aztec god Nanahuatzin. One of the most important events in the Aztec story occurs when Nanahuatzin and Tecuciztecatl cremate themselves to become the sun and the moon (items 5 through 10). This event occurs only in the Yaonáhuac tales, and while fire appears in one Huitzilan story (version 2), it is used to warm the infant Jesus.

Compared to the Yaonáhuac stories, which share several key ideas with the ancient Aztec account, the Huitzilan versions are basically Spanish. Intermediate accounts may have existed at one time in Huitzilan oral tradition, and I suspect they looked something like the contemporary Yaonáhuac stories. The Huitzilan storytellers now relate accounts which conform closely to the biblical story of Christmas. Narrator J. H.'s story (version 2) resembles a ritual drama of the birth of Jesus acted out in Huitzilan, Yaonáhuac, and many other communities in the northern Sierra de Puebla.

The ritual drama in Huitzilan, which takes place during the nine nights before Christmas day, may have influenced the way narrators from this community re-worked the myth of the Origin of the Sun and the Moon. On each of the nine nights, the drama is the same: at about eight o'clock in the evening, a procession bearing images of Joseph and Mary and the infant Jesus arrives at the home designated for enacting the drama. The house is decorated inside and out with pine boughs and poinsettias. The pilgrims in the procession ask for shelter for Mary and Joseph. Those inside the house answer that they are afraid to open the door because of the late hour. But the pilgrims insist, and the occupants repeatedly deny them until the pilgrims explain that Mary carries the son of God in her womb. The door opens, the procession enters, and the pilgrims place the images on the altar of the house. The pilgrims, their hosts, and guests in the procession say the rosary and then everyone is invited to partake of bread, bean tamales, and coffee. If musicians are present, the participants dance to the tunes of *huapangos*, music typical of the neighboring state of Veracruz. The procession repeats this drama every night at a different house, and on Christmas eve, the drama is enacted a final time at the house of the ritual sponsor, who provides lavish pork tamales and generous amounts of *aguardiente*. At midnight, the procession departs for the church, bearing the images and announcing the birth of Christ by shooting off rockets that brighten the December darkness.

To be sure, the Nahuat of both communities have witnessed the ritual drama. But I contend that the Nahuat whose position is weaker in the plural society have taken this ritual drama and other Spanish accounts of the Christmas story as models for replacing the Aztec story of the Origin of the Sun and the Moon.

It was mentioned that a number of Hispanic agents promoted the acculturation of Nahuat narratives—priests, Nahuat prayer leaders who work with the priest and lay religious committees, and Hispanic patrons who have the power to change the Indian beliefs underlying narrative tradition. Because Huitzilan and Yaonáhuac are basically similar in their contact with some of these agents, and different in their contact with others, one can isolate the aspects of ethnic relations that contribute most to the acculturation of Nahuat narratives.

The relationship between the Nahuat and Hispanic priests is similar in the two communities. No priest lives in either one: the parish church and the priests' residences lie in neighboring *municipios*. Priests visit Huitzilan and Yaonáhuac with about equal frequency and depend heavily in both cases on local Nahuat prayer leaders to provide religious instruction to children. Comparatively few parents send their children to catechism classes in either community. The most important difference in the Nahuat-priest relationship is that more people from Yaonáhuac are bilingual and can communicate more easily with priests in Spanish. But the church's practice of sending Nahuatl-speaking priests from Tlaxcala to the Huitzilan area partially compensates for the Nahuat monolingualism in this community.

By far the most important difference in ethnic relations between Huitzilan and Yaonáhuac is patronage. The Nahuat of Huitzilan heavily depend on their Hispanic patrons for economic support and political protection. Hispanic patrons in Huitzilan are bilingual, and some are renowned storytellers and undoubtedly contributed directly to changing the Nahuat oral tradition. I contend that patronage has contributed heavily to the Hispanization of narratives from this community because it promotes the identification of Indians with members of the dominant ethnic group. The comparative economic and political independence of the Yaonáhuac Nahuat from Hispanic patronage has contributed to the retention of Aztec motifs and a slower rate of absorbing Spanish ones in the oral tradition of this community. Yaonáhuac Nahuat encounters with Hispanics occur primarily outside the community and are less frequent. A few Yaonáhuac Nahuat have Hispanic patrons, but far fewer depend on daily wage labor with Hispanic employers. A much larger number of these Nahuat can support themselves with *milpa* farming and the cultivation of orchards and are consequently much more economically independent of Hispanics than the Nahuat of Huitzilan. The Nahuat of Yaonáhuac thus covet the wealth and power of the dominant ethnic group less and can more easily resist the erosion of pre-Hispanic beliefs from their oral tradition.

Despite the obvious predominance of Spanish elements in the Huitzilan stories, they, like that of the ancient Aztecs, express a critical attitude toward persons of high status. Huitzilan narrator J. H. (version 2) has re-worked Spanish symbols adopted from the biblical story of Christmas to express the negative side of his ambivalence toward Hispanics. He describes St. Joseph persuading the Virgin Mary to break her betrothal agreement with St. Peter because he has a heavy beard. This means she should abandon St. Peter because he is an Hispanic (Indians have very light beards) and, by implication, this makes Joseph, Mary, and Christ Nahuat rather than Hispanic persons. This fits with the frequent Nahuat assertion that they are the better Catholics because they more strongly support the church. The ancient Aztec account tells how Tecuciztecatl, a person whose dress was regal, lacked the courage to cast himself into the fire and become the sun (item 5). It remained for the more humble Nanahuatzin, who adorned himself only with paper, to do the job Tecuciztecatl was unable to do (items 6 and 7). Of course these parallel feelings toward higher-status persons reflect generally ambivalent attitudes that develop in hierarchical relationships and probably do not stem from common historical antecedents.

OTHER SIXTEENTH-CENTURY AZTEC MOTIFS IN NAHUAT NARRATIVES

A number of the pre-Hispanic motifs are sprinkled throughout contemporary Nahuat oral tradition. Their distribution parallels the distribution of Aztec motifs in the set of cognate tales just discussed: more Aztec motifs appear in Yaonáhuac tales than in those of Huitzilan. This supports the conclusion that highly specific differences in cognate narratives are diagnostic of other differences in oral tradition for the variable of the Hispanization of Nahuat thought.

The fusion of Aztec and Hispanic themes makes the identification of pre-Hispanic motifs and themes in modern Nahuat oral tradition difficult and hazardous. I place little importance on indigenous motifs appearing in Nahuat narratives completely out of their pre-Hispanic context and stripped entirely of their meaning. Thus, the motifs discussed in this section appear in the Nahuat tales in contexts roughly similar to those in which they appeared according to the accounts of the sixteenth-century chroniclers. With these factors in mind, Aztec themes retained in Yaonáhuac, but not Huitzilan, narratives are as follows.

1. *Giants who lived during an earlier creation*: the Yaonáhuac Nahuat tell of giants who lived during the Era of Darkness. One narrator explains that men were tall then because they did not have to endure heat.[3] In conversation, the Nahuat explain that giants constructed the small pre-Hispanic ceremonial center on the border of their community. Whether this stems primarily from Aztec or biblical tradition cannot be determined with absolute certainty. One can argue it is a biblical motif, because Genesis 6 describes a race of giants produced by sexual intercourse between gods and women. This was one example of the moral depravity of ancient times which led to the destruction of the world by flood in Judeo-Christian thought. Yaonáhuac narrator L. V. likewise describes giants perishing in a flood.[4]

But one may also argue it is an Aztec motif (possibly fused with a Judeo-Christian one), because giants populated the earth during one of the four Aztec eras of creation preceding the Fifth Sun. Accounts vary as to which was the era of giants—the *Historia de los Mexicanos por sus pinturas* describes them living during the era of the First Sun (León-Portilla 1974: 105) while the *Anales de Cuauhtitlan* places them in the Second Sun (Krickerberg 1971: 23). Although some of the Aztec sources describe jaguars devouring giants to end one era of creation, and a deluge ending another, the Sierra Nahuat could easily have mixed events of earlier creations when they telescoped the five Aztec eras into the two eras that run through their contemporary thought. Moreover, the Yaonáhuac Nahuat, who describe giants building the ceremonial center lying on the border of their community, parallel the Aztecs, who asserted that giants made the pyramids of the sun and the moon at Teotihuacan (Sahagún 1961: 192).

2. *Motifs connected with lightning-bolts*: storytellers from both communities express numerous ideas of pre-Hispanic origin about lightning-bolts and the production of rain. They tell of dwarfs,

living with a female consort, who produce rain.[5] The notion of dwarfs probably derives from the Aztec belief that Tlalocs created priests with small bodies to produce rain.[6] The female consort in Nahuat tradition probably comes from the Aztec belief that the rain gods had an elder sister (Chalchiuhtliycue = Jade Skirt) (Sahagún 1950: 6). But storytellers from Yaonáhuac have retained more esoteric knowledge of the production of rain from Aztec tradition. Only Yaonáhuac narrators specify that lightning-bolts have pots in their homes containing rain, wind, and hail and describe them removing the lids to produce the kind of weather desired.[7] This closely parallels the Aztec belief that the priests of Tlaloc lived in a home with a patio containing four large jars of water, each with a different kind of weather: the first contained water to make things grow; the second had water to cause corn to mildew; the third sent freezing rain; and the fourth caused corn to dry up.[8] A Yaonáhuac narrator describes the lightning-bolts carrying whips to tame and control storms created by opening the pots.[9] This probably stems from the Aztec belief that the priests of Tlaloc carried sticks to break open the pots of water to produce rain.[10] Finally, a Yaonáhuac narrator describes the lightning-bolts having curly hair,[11] an idea that parallels the Aztec belief that the rain gods had long hair.[12]

Only one Aztec motif appears in Huitzilan, but not Yaonáhuac, oral tradition.

1. *Dog who transports people across water in the underworld*: a Huitzilan narrator describes a man crossing a body of water on the back of a dog to reach the home of the devil, deep in the underworld. This motif probably derives from the Aztec belief that the deceased crossed a river on the backs of dogs to reach the places of the dead (Sahagún 1978: 43–44). It is absent in the Yaonáhuac cognate version of the tale.[13]

It is interesting that intense Hispanic domination over the Nahuat results in more complete ideological change but promotes the retention of indigenous language and rituals that remain as markers of ethnic identity. The Huitzilan Nahuat, who have more completely replaced Aztec with Spanish religious personalities and have lost more of their pre-Hispanic beliefs, are the more monolingual speakers of Nahuat and cling more tenaciously to their Aztec-derived betrothal rituals. On the other hand, the Yaonáhuac Nahuat, who have retained more Aztec religious personalities and beliefs, are more bilingual speakers of Nahuat and Spanish and have more completely abandoned their Aztec-derived betrothal ceremonies (see chapter 4).

8. Men Who Enter the Forest

Some of the most popular Nahuat stories tell of men who venture into the forest, where they come upon a personified force of nature (a lightning-bolt or an earth mother). The men grant a favor, or fulfill a request, they become wealthy, and then they lose the wealth under different circumstances. These stories are eloquent and complex statements of how the Nahuat see their current human condition now that Hispanics have settled in the northern Sierra de Puebla.

Lightning-bolt

Comparison of the lightning-bolt and earth mother characters in the versions from the two communities gives insight into the process by which the Huitzilan Nahuat have more completely replaced their Aztec derived gods with Hispanic religious figures. Lightning-bolt and earth mother characters in modern Nahuat stories have direct parallels with personalities in ancient Aztec mythic tradition. Nahuat storytellers express their identification with these gods by attributing to them Nahuat rather than Hispanic traits in the modern oral tradition. But the stories discussed in this chapter illustrate that the Nahuat identification with these gods varies according to the Indians' position in the ethnic hierarchy. The Huitzilan Nahuat identify less strongly than the Yaonáhuac Nahuat with characters in stories who represent deified and personified forces of nature. They anthropomorphize them less completely, and they express less intimacy between them and human characters. They have consequently pushed them further toward the wild, amoral, and dangerous periphery of their universe, away from the human center. By placing these characters out of the center and in the periphery, the Huitzilan Nahuat express a highly dichotomized view of space in which they sharply separate the domains of humans and animals.

The Yaonáhuac Nahuat image of lightning-bolt and earth mother characters contrasts sharply with corresponding images in parallel stories from Huitzilan. Storytellers from Yaonáhuac, where the Nahuat have more autonomy relative to the dominant ethnic group, more completely anthropomorphize lightning-bolt and earth mother characters, depict more intimacy between them and humans, and have them uphold the moral order. Relative to their counterparts in Huitzilan, narrators from Yaonáhuac present a much more integrated view of the human and animal relationship.

These sharply contrasting images of lightning-bolt and earth mother characters in parallel stories have a clear link with the different images of women held by men in the two communities. Huitzilan storytellers generally depict women as dangerous and threatening to their moral order. Their conception of women conforms to the sexual ideologies of other cultures in different parts of the world. Like the African Bakweri (Ardener 1977a, 1977b), they place their women in the wild, a nonsocial place, and they attribute to them qualities that threaten orderly social life. What is particularly interesting for the northern Sierra is that not all Nahuat hold this view. Those of Yaonáhuac clearly depict lightning-bolt women and earth mothers as less threatening and more supportive of the moral order.

Men's images of women in Nahuat stories hinge on ethnic relations for a number of reasons. It was mentioned that Nahuat men, heavily dependent on Hispanic patronage, develop a sexual ideology that compensates men for their weak position relative to the dominant ethnic group. They depict women as the morally weaker and more dangerous sex, who should submit to control by men. This chapter presents the support for this hypothesis by illustrating how the Nahuat men's images of themselves as a class, relative to the dominant ethnic group, vary with their sexual ideology. It describers how the Nahuat, with the most androcentric view of women, also depict their male as well as female lightning-bolt gods as weak and powerless because they themselves are comparatively powerless and weak relative to the Hispanics.

The male-dominant ideology that came about because of Nahuat dependence on Hispanic patronage undoubtedly justified patrilineal land inheritance in Huitzilan, and thereby weakened the position of women in the family by restricting their access to strategic resources. But Hispanics have changed Nahuat family structure in other ways, affecting the prevailing patterns of husband and wife relations and contributing the different images of men and women in narrative tradition.

Hispanics promoted patrilineal inheritance in Huitzilan by acquiring the bulk of the arable land and by forcing the Nahuat selectively to pass what little land remains in their possession to their sons, but not to their daughters. The application of Hispanic land laws containing a community property provision promoted bilateral inheritance and strengthened the position of women in Yaonáhuac. Hispanics also affected the relative age at marriage of Nahuat men and women, affecting the degree of egalitarianism or hierarchy between husbands and wives.

THE STORIES

I collected eight stories of men who encountered personified forces of nature in the forest. All eight share some cognate episodes, but some share more common elements than others. It is important to emphasize that, while all contain characters who resemble Aztec gods and goddesses, all are post-Conquest creations. The stories deal with the problem of the Nahuat destiny now that Hispanics have invaded the northern Sierra and taken the bulk of Nahuat land. Some stories contain episodes borrowed from Spanish tales and re-worked to express the Nahuat point of view. Taken together, the eight versions express fascinating transformations of key ideas connected with Nahuat men's view of themselves relative to Hispanics, and their view of women.

The eight stories—four from Huitzilan and four from Yaoná-huac—share most of the following sixteen items.

1. A man ventures into the forest.
2. He comes upon a lightning-bolt or an earth mother.
3. The lightning-bolt or earth mother is anthropomorphized.
4. The man helps the lightning-bolt or earth mother.
5. The man accompanies it to its home in the forest.
6. The man is given wealth as a reward.
7. The man receives precise instructions for keeping the wealth.
8. The man loses the wealth.
9. A hawk or mouse offers to help recover the wealth.
10. The hawk gives the mouse directions for recovering the wealth.
11. The mouse carries the wealth (usually in the form of a gold ring) and the hawk carries the mouse across the sea.
12. The mouse drops the ring into the water.
13. A fish swallows the ring.
14. The fish is caught.
15. The hawk or the mouse (or both) opens the fish and removes the ring.
16. The animals return the ring and the man rewards them.

Two of the Yaonáhuac stories depart from the others because they contain more radical transformations of ideas common to the first six versions. They are particularly important because they round out the range of Nahuat ideas about their gods, who personify forces of nature (see Yaonáhuac versions 3 and 4).

The stories appear below, followed by a discussion of their similarities and succeeded by an analysis of their differences.

Numbers inserted in the texts identify their common items (refer to the above list). The analysis of differences focuses on the three major elements: 1. The anthropomorphization of the forces of nature (item 3); 2. the loss of wealth (item 8); and 3. the recovery of the wealth by the hawk and other animals (items 9 through 16).

HUITZILAN VERSION 1

1. There was a boy who grew up to be lazy. His mother supported him by weaving blankets for him to sell. The boy took the blankets down the road and found two hunters, who were about to shoot a hawk in a tree. The lazy boy told the hunters, "Don't shoot. Let it alone." They didn't shoot the hawk, and the boy gave each one a blanket. The boy followed the hunters, who found a fox and ran to shoot it. But the boy shouted again, "Don't shoot, and I'll give you each another blanket." The hunters let the fox go, and the boy gave each another blanket. The hunters went on and came across a badger. "Let it go. It's not attacking you. If you don't shoot it, I'll give you still another blanket," said the boy. So the hunters let the badger go, and the boy gave each one another blanket. 2. Then the hunters made a turn and found a snake. This time the lazy boy was not following them as closely as before, and when he came to the animal, he found that the hunters had already killed it. They had cut it to pieces. 4. The boy spoke to the snake, saying, "They've killed you. Why did you wander into the road?" Then he stuck the pieces of the snake back together and went on his way. 3. When he came to the top of a hill, he found a girl standing there. She was very ill, and the boy asked her, "What are you doing here?" She replied, "I can't go any farther. I'm ill. If you hadn't helped me, they would have killed me."

5. The girl asked the boy, "Would you take me home? I can't go on by myself." So the boy carried the girl in his arms. The girl told the boy as they went along, "My mother will ask you what you want for a reward. She'll ask you if you want chile seeds, or sugarcane cuttings, or kernels of corn, or squash seeds. Don't take any of them because you're lazy and you don't want to work in the milpa. Ask her to give you the middle of a gold ring." 6. When they arrived at the girl's house, the mother asked the boy what he wanted for a reward. He asked for the inside of a gold ring, and she gave it to him with some instructions. 7. She said, "Get a box five meters long and cut it into two sections, each two and a half meters long, two and a half meters wide, and two meters high."

He took the middle of the gold ring home and made the box

*just as told. It produced a lot of money. The boy built a big house
and asked for the hand of a girl in marriage. The girl's father asked
him, "How will you support her? Do you really have a house? If so,
then show it to me." The box was in the middle of the house, and
the house was filled with gold. The house had many rooms, and
each corner of every room was filled with gold as if it were corn.
The lazy boy said to the girl's father, "Well, I want you to give me
your youngest daughter." That is just what the girl's father did.*

*8. One day some foreigners came selling clothes, and they
found the boy's wife sitting alone in front of the house. The boy
had gone to his milpa, and so the foreigners asked the girl to buy
some dresses and pants. But she refused, saying, "There isn't any
money. The man of the house isn't here. He has the money. I
don't." But the foreigners saw the money, and when they went
away, the girl heard a "clink." She realized they had taken the
gold. She saw it wasn't there anymore, and went outside to cry.
The boy returned and asked her what had happened. She said,
"Well, it wasn't a good thing that you went away because they
took what you had inside the house." The lazy boy saw for himself and was angry. He just started walking and walking.*

*9. A hawk in a tree screeched to him, saying, "Let me bring
it." The boy angrily retorted, "What do you mean, 'Let me bring
it'?! Son of the f—— mother! You don't know what makes me
sad." The bird insisted, saying, "I know what you lost. I really
will fetch it for you. Just convince the mouse to help me." The boy
spoke to the mouse, who protested at first, saying, "He [the hawk]
will just eat me." But finally the mouse agreed, and the hawk
carried the mouse to another land. 10. The hawk told the mouse
what to do, saying, "They're sleeping after their party. Go quietly
into the house, and cut into the box that holds the ring." But the
mouse climbed up onto the table and drank what remained in the
foreigners' glasses. The gentlemen awoke to find the mouse lying
drunk on the table, and they thought the cat had brought the
mouse to eat. The mouse heard everything, and when he saw the
gentlemen fall asleep again, he scurried up the wall to the attic to
cut open the box and remove the ring. But as he ran up the face of
the wall, he knocked against a violin, and it fell to the floor. The
mouse fled to the roof, where he met up again with the hawk, who
threatened him, "If you come without the ring, I'll eat you." So he
went back into the house, and this time he did remove the ring
from the box. But as he climbed up the wall, he dropped the ring,
and one of the gentlemen awoke and picked it up and put it into
his mouth. When the man fell asleep again, the mouse cautiously*

walked over the man's blanket, turned around, and stuck his tail into the man's nose. The man sneezed, and out came the ring. The mouse grabbed it and ran up the wall and escaped with the treasure. 11. The hawk grabbed him, and the two animals flew across the sea.

12. But the mouse let go of the heavy ring as the hawk carried him over the water. 13. When the two animals reached the other side of the sea, the hawk wondered aloud, "How shall we get it? It fell into the water and a fish swallowed it!" 14. As they talked, along came a fisherman, who caught a fish and tossed it onto the shore. The hawk asked, "Could it be that fish?" 15. The hawk and the mouse ran over to the fish, and the mouse began cutting it open while the hawk picked at it with its beak.

16. The mouse picked up the ring and the two animals brought it back to the lazy boy's house. The boy asked the hawk what he wanted for a reward, and the hawk replied, "Just a chicken." "Grab one," said the boy, and the hawk did just that. "Now you, mouse, what do you want?" asked the boy. "A bit of corn," was the mouse's reply. "Go ahead and eat," said the boy, and so the mouse climbed into the corn bin and made his home there.   STORYTELLER A. V.

HUITZILAN VERSION 2

1. A man went into the forest and 2. came across a snake with its head chopped off. 4. The man found a chaca *tree and peeled off its bark. He felt sorry for the snake, so he put it back together and patched it with the bark. He told the snake, "Now go. Don't stay around here, or they'll cut you up again." The man left and went home, but later on he returned to the spot to see if the snake had healed. He saw it wasn't there anymore. 3. He heard a boy coming toward him making noise with his shoes. His shoes came up to his knees. The boy greeted him and said, "My father wants to talk to you. He wants to thank you. You cured me that day they struck me down." The man didn't want to go, but the boy insisted, saying, "He'll pay you."*

5. So the man decided to go, and, as the two of them were going along, the boy gave the man some advice. "Soon you'll arrive there and you'll find my sisters very attractive. They'll invite you to eat, but if you accept you'll stay there forever. My father will offer you a plot of land, an axe, a hoe, a machete, or a tumpline for a reward. But don't accept any of these things, or you'll stay forever working with them. My father has a gold ring and a gourd dish. Ask for them and he'll give them to you. Don't be attracted to my sisters. My father will invite you to eat, but tell him you're not hungry because if you eat you'll stay there forever." They arrived at the boy's house, where the boy's father offered him a machete, a hoe, and a tumpline as a reward. 6. But the man took the boy's advice and asked for a gold ring and a gourd dish. The boy's father gave it to him. 7. The boy had told the man to make a wooden box three varas [one vara is 33 inches] deep, three varas wide, and two varas high to store the ring and the gourd dish. The man did as he was told, and money piled up in the box. The man worked with the money, building a huge house and putting in a store.

8. One day he went to his milpa and left his wife alone in the house. Some foreigners came selling clothes and asked her to buy them, but she said, "There isn't any money." They insisted that she did have money, but she protested that she did not. The foreigners looked at everything in the store and insisted again, but the woman said no. So the foreigners went away, and the woman heard a noise, and everything in the house shook. She heard a clang like that of a bell, and the house was emptied. The foreigners had taken the ring and the gourd dish. The man came home and asked his wife what had happened, and when she told him, he was saddened.

9. A hawk was flying above, and the bird tried to cheer the man up, but this only made the man angry. The hawk said he knew where the ring was, and the man demanded that the bird perch on the ground. The hawk did as the man wanted, but with reluctance because he feared the man would hit him. The hawk offered to recover the ring, and he told the man to find a mouse to help with the recovery. The man obliged, and the hawk flew off carrying the mouse. 10. As the two animals traveled, the hawk told the mouse how to recover the ring. "We'll land on top of the house and you go inside because he who has the ring is there. He'll be an old man with his eyes closed," said the hawk. They landed on top of the old man's house, and the mouse went inside and saw the man. But there was a cat, and the mouse, who was frightened, went back to tell the hawk it would be impossible to recover the ring. But the hawk told the mouse to frighten the cat away by cutting down a jarana [small guitar] hanging on the wall. He added, "Put your tail into the old man's nose to make him sneeze to release the ring." The mouse followed the hawk's instructions and recovered the ring. He took it back to the hawk, 11. who carried the mouse, holding the ring in his mouth, back across the sea.

12. At about midway across, the hawk felt the mouse growing

tired. The ring was too heavy for him, and the mouse dropped it into the sea. 13. The two of them watched it fall and be swallowed by a fish. The hawk decided, "Right now, let's go wait at the water's edge. The fish will surface because the ring will get the better of it. I'll quickly grab it." 14. The fish did come to the surface, and the hawk caught it. 15. "Right now," said the hawk, "we're going to rip open its stomach and remove the ring. Help me." The mouse helped, but, as he cut the flesh of the fish, he ate it. But the hawk ate nothing. They found the ring, and they started on their journey again. While flying, the hawk felt heavy and accused the mouse of eating the flesh of the fish, but the mouse denied it.

16. They arrived at the man's house, and the hawk gave him the ring. Later on, the hawk felt hungry and asked for something to eat. The man offered him his chickens. Then the mouse declared he too was hungry, and the man sent him into his corn granary. So the mouse was to eat corn, but the hawk got the better deal.   STORYTELLER N. A. H.

HUITZILAN VERSION 3

Juan Tonto [Dumb John] didn't like to work. He had been lazy for so long that his brothers grew tired of him, and so one day they asked themselves, "What are we going to do with that lazy brother of ours?" 1. They decided to take him into the forest and leave him there. They bought him a carbine, took him into the forest, and said, "You wait here for us." But after a while, Juan grew tired of waiting. His brothers hadn't come, and it was getting dark. 2. He ventured down the road looking for them, and he came upon a tree with a tiger lying at its foot. The tiger was cut into three pieces, and Juan asked the tiger what had happened. 3. "They attacked me, your brothers did," replied the tiger. Juan's brothers had found the tiger sleeping and cut it up. 4. Juan offered to help the tiger, and he grabbed its head and joined it to one of the parts of its body. Then he joined the two body parts together. The tiger said gratefully, "You've saved me." It stood up, but it couldn't walk very well. "You carry me and my father will pay you," the tiger requested.

5. Juan obliged and carried it to its home. "Here is your child," said Juan as he delivered the tiger to the animal's father. "What will you take for a reward?" asked the father. At first Juan said he didn't know, and he declared that he had not done this favor to earn money. 6. But the father insisted, and Juan asked for

his ring. The tiger's father gave it to him, and Juan went home. Juan began working with the money produced by the ring. He built a big house, he bought a sewing machine, and he planted a crop. He kept the ring on the altar of the house.

8. One day when Juan was away, two clothes merchants came and greeted his wife. She invited them into the house, and they said, "Buy all the clothes we have." The wife protested, "But I don't have any money now because my husband isn't here." The merchants insisted that she did have money, and they told her she must buy their clothes. They argued, "You can re-sell them for a profit." The woman repeatedly refused. The merchants went away, then they returned, and they offered again to sell her their clothes, but this time for the ring, instead of money. They had seen the ring on the altar. At first the woman said no, but then she believed what they said about selling the clothes for a profit, and she made the exchange. Juan Tonto came home and tried to find the ring, but he could not.

9. He set out to look for it and came upon a hawk perched in a tree. The hawk asked, "Where are you going?" Juan told the bird what happened, and the hawk said he knew all about it. "Can you bring it?" asked Juan. "It's possible," replied the hawk. The bird sent Juan to look for the hawk's brother, the mouse, to help in the ring's recovery. The two animals knew all about the theft of the ring because they had seen the foreigners steal it. Juan offered to pay them for bringing it back. The hawk had the mouse climb onto his back, and the two flew across the sea. The merchants who took the ring were holding a celebration. 10. The hawk and mouse landed on the merchants' house, and the hawk gave the mouse instructions, "Go look around first. If you come upon a trunk, go inside it right away. Cut through it." The mouse did as told and cut through the trunk while the musicians played so they wouldn't discover him. He went into the trunk, but he couldn't find the ring. The hawk sent him back to look again, this time telling him, "It's way down below." The mouse went again and cut through all the papers in the trunk and found the ring. He removed it and carried it back to the hawk. 11. The two animals flew back across the sea. "You hold the ring in your mouth," said the hawk to the mouse.

12. As they approached the shore, the mouse dropped the ring into the water. 13. A fish swallowed it, and 14. the hawk announced, "We'll catch that fish." When the fish came to the surface, the hawk did just that. He grabbed it in mid-air. 15. The mouse started cutting the fish with its teeth and ate it. The mouse found the ring inside of the fish, and the hawk warned, "Don't drop it again." The mouse replied, "No [I won't]. I dropped it [before] because I was sleepy."

16. They brought the ring back to Juan Tonto, who asked the hawk, "What do you want for a reward?" At first the hawk said, "I don't ask for anything." But Juan insisted, and the hawk said, "I don't want money. I want chickens." Then Juan asked the mouse, who replied, "I don't want money either. I want you to let me into your corn bin." Juan gave them both the rewards they wanted.

STORYTELLER M. A.

HUITZILAN VERSION 4

Once there was basketmaker who decided to marry, and he told his mother, "Ask for that girl for me." His mother was reluctant because she and her son were poor, and the girl's father was rich. But the basketmaker insisted, saying to his mother, "Even so, but I'll support her." So the mother went to the girl's father and announced her son's intentions. The girl's father asked, "How'll he support her?" The mother returned to her son and told him of the man's reply. The man had asked the basketmaker to come see him. The boy obliged, and the girl's father told him to talk to the girl directly. The boy went into the house and spoke to the girl, and, of course, she said she wanted to marry him because they were already sweethearts. When her father realized this, he consented to the marriage with the condition that the boy hold a big wedding celebration in the church and in the presidential palace and celebrate for fifteen days with a banquet three times a day. "That's fine," consented the boy. 1. So the basketmaker went home and worked to make baskets for about two weeks. He took a load of baskets to sell, and while traveling down the road, he heard someone call to him. He didn't pay any attention, but he heard the call again. He went on his way and heard a call for the third time. 2. He looked down and saw a wounded snake. "It's you," said the basketmaker. 3. The snake pleaded to him, saying, "Yes. I want you to drop me off at my house. They injured me here." But the boy said, "No. Perhaps you'll bite me."

5. The snake finally persuaded the basketmaker to carry him in one of his baskets. The snake fainted and came to again while the boy carried it along the road. It gave the boy some instructions, saying, "Don't accept what my father will want to give you. He'll offer you an axe, a hoe, a tumpline, or a machete, but if you take one of those things, you'll stay there working with it. Just

take a ring and a dish. Don't eat either, because if you do you'll stay there for a long time. Also I have some sisters who'll be pleasing to you. But don't eat. Say you're not hungry." They arrived at the snake's home, and the animal's father offered the boy tools. But the boy heeded the snake's advice and asked for a ring and dish. 6. His request was granted, and the boy put the ring in his basket and took it home. He was tired by the time he got there because the ring had filled the basket with money. Later, the boy decided to see his father-in-law, and asked, *"Tell me if this money won't do for getting married!"* The girl's father admitted that the boy had more money than he did. The father said, *"It won't be necessary to do what I told you. A three-day banquet, rather than one for fifteen days, is fine."* Then came the day when the basketmaker and his bride were married. That boy who found the money came out fine.   STORYTELLER N. A. H.

YAONÁHUAC VERSION 1

1. A traveler was walking along the road and heard someone call to him from under a rock. 2. He looked around and found a snake. 3. *"I want to say something,"* said the snake. But the man protested, *"I'll get close [to you], and you'll bite me."* The snake convinced the man that it would not bite him and requested, *"I want someone to come help me."* The snake offered to pay the man, [and] 4. the man agreed to remove the snake from the rock that was crushing it. He straightened it out and put it back together again. Then the snake asked to be carried home, but again the man protested out of fear of being bitten.

5. But the snake convinced the man, and he carried it. The snake gave him directions, and while on their journey, the snake warned the man about his big brothers. The man anxiously said, *"Perhaps they'll eat me."* But the snake replied, *"No. I'll tell them not to."* When they reached their destination, huge snakes rushed out to meet them. The wounded snake shouted to his brothers not to eat the man, and he reported how the man had saved him. The snake then asked his brothers to bring a basket so it could reward the man for doing the favor. 6. The snake removed a ring and gave it to the man, 7. telling him, *"Look, my good man, take the ring and keep it in your house. Empty a drawer and you'll see that you'll have money the next day. But you carry the key. Don't let your wife have it because she'll sell the ring to anyone."* The man did as told and he became rich.

8. But foreigners saw the ring through a telescope. It shone

brightly. The foreigners came in a ship guided by the brilliance of the ring. They came to the man's house, where they found his wife alone. They offered to sell her one of their rings and told her that it would produce money. But she told them, "My husband also has one." The foreigners replied, "Ours are better. Let's see yours." The man left the key, and so the woman opened the drawer and showed them the ring. The foreigners had a lot of rings, and they mixed the real one with the fake ones. The gave the woman a fake one and took the real one for themselves. The fake one was just ordinary metal and didn't produce any money. The man returned home and opened the drawer just as he did every day, but this time there was no money. His wife explained what happened, and the husband was furious. He left the house, fetched some firewood, sunk his axe into a piece of it, and stood there with his arms crossed.

9. Along came a hawk whistling and flapping its wings, and it asked, "What happened?" The man explained, and the hawk replied, "I'm going to speak to my companion, and we'll fetch it for you." This made the man very happy. The hawk spoke to the mouse to get him to help recover the ring. "Is he a good person?" inquired the mouse. "Uh huh. He's always happy. I'm around where they eat and I help myself to what's left over," said the hawk. The mouse agreed to help, and the next day the hawk flew the mouse across the sea, stopping in the middle to perch on a rock and rest. 10. When they reached the other side of the sea, the hawk instructed the mouse, "Now we're going to wait for it to get dark before I drop you off on the roof of the house of the foreigners. Don't do anything foolish because there is a cat who'll eat you." The mouse went into the house, but returned because he saw a cat tied to a trunk containing the ring. The mouse told the hawk to take him to the other side of the house, where he said, "I'm going to go in through a hole I'm going to make. I'm going to come out at the foot of the trunk." The mouse made the hole and went into the house and drilled into the trunk, where he found the ring. He put it into his mouth and rejoined the hawk. It was dawning when the mouse came back out of the house bringing the ring. 11. The hawk offered to take the ring, but the mouse said, "No. I went to fetch it." The hawk cautioned, "Don't drop it."

12. As they flew back over the water, the mouse dropped the ring when he told the hawk to grab a fish. 13. A fish swallowed the ring, and the hawk decided, "We're going to watch from there." He perched on a rock and then circled about. 14. Finally, a fish appeared with the ring shining in its stomach. The hawk quickly

jumped and 15. *split open the fish's stomach, removed the ring,
and carried it back to the rock, holding it in his claws. This time
the hawk said, "I'm going to take it. I went to fetch it." The hawk
carried the mouse to the edge of the sea. When they landed, he
scolded the mouse, "Don't you see, man, I'm very tired. You're a
rascal for not wanting to give me the ring to carry in the first place."
The two argued at the water's edge.*

16. *They found the traveler again in the forest, and they gave
him back the ring. The man invited the hawk and the mouse to
his home for a reward, but the hawk protested, "Won't your wife
be angry?" "No," replied the traveler. "But do you have cats?"
asked the mouse. "Uh huh. But nothing will happen," persuaded
the man. When they arrived, the man asked, "Now what do you
want for your reward? I have no money." The hawk replied, "I
want your chicken coop." The man granted the request, and then
the mouse said, "I want the corn bin." This request was granted
too, and then the man's wife asked, "But what shall I eat?" Her
husband replied, "Well, you have money, but the key stays with
me. I won't leave it with you because you're very untrustworthy.
You'll sell it from me again." But she replied, "Well, if you don't
want to leave it with me, I'm going to leave you. Let it stay here
because my animals are gone." Then they quarreled. Who knows
what happened from there.*   STORYTELLER M. I.

YAONÁHUAC VERSION 2

1. *Once there was a hunter who often went into the forest to kill
animals. But one day the wisemen didn't give him permission to
hunt anymore. The wisemen are lightning-bolts.* 2. *One day the
hunter went to kill one more animal of the forest, and he found a
snake. It was lying off to one side of him, and so he didn't see it at
first.* 3. *The snake said, "Shhh . . . come here. I'm calling you." The
hunter turned his head, but he saw nothing and walked on. He came
upon a deer and prepared to shoot it, but whoever had called him
said, "Let that animal go. Don't kill it because it belongs to me."
Again he turned to see who spoke and saw nothing. Again he aimed
his carbine, and the snake spoke again, saying, "Don't kill it. I'm
going to talk to you." Then the hunter saw the snake, who said,
"Come over to me and I'll tell you what I want, and I'll help you.
Get this rock off me. I can't go home because it's crushing me."*
4. *The hunter obliged.*

5. *Then the snake asked, "Do me the favor of taking me home."
When the hunter first saw the snake, it seemed small, but after he*

removed the rock, it got larger. The hunter protested, "I can't carry you. You're so big." The snake replied, "I'm not heavy." The hunter protested, "I don't have anything for carrying you." The snake said, "Lay down your serape. I'll fit on it. Try lifting me and you'll feel how you'll be able to." So the hunter did as he was told and it was true that the snake didn't seem to weigh much. He tied the serape around his neck to carry it, and the snake said, "Hang your carbine up in that tree. When you pass by here after dropping me off, don't pick it up. You're killing my animals with it. I'll help you make a living, but don't take my animals any more." The hunter protested, "I ought to be afraid of you. You're so ugly." The snake assured him saying, "I'm not very frightening. It's just that you see my clothes which are spotted this way. I'll guide you to the entrance of my home. You'll collect your reward when you drop me off. You just go where I point my tongue. When we arrive, some animals will tear out toward us. We have cats, dogs, horses, cattle, turkeys, and chickens like those where you live, only ours are bigger. If they jump on you, don't be afraid. I know how to calm them. We'll meet my parents, who'll be in front of the house warming themselves. Don't be afraid of my mother or my father or my grandfather because they are spotted like me. My grandfather is a little more spotted and a little larger. My father is larger still. My brother is larger. I'm the youngest. They're larger because they're older." The hunter took heart, and because he was brave, he would win out. The snake's mouth rested on the hunter's shoulder and felt heavy. 3. The hunter looked back and saw he was carrying a beautiful girl. She had beautiful blonde hair and was very beautiful. The hunter no longer feared her, and he carried her with greater pleasure than before because she wasn't an animal anymore. She was a girl. They talked gaily as they traveled and grew attracted to each other. The girl said, "When you arrive, the animals will jump on you, but they won't do anything to you. You'll meet my parents, but don't fear them. They'll be happy. My sisters, too, will jump on you. My siblings will dash about. One will dash about sweeping so there won't be any clutter where you'll sit. Another will dash to put down a stool for you to sit on. They'll give you a beautiful new stool because they'll be ashamed. But you take an ugly broken stool. Get it for yourself. You tell them not to bother sweeping. You sit down in a cluttered place. They'll give you a big plate, but you take an earthen bowl. Be sure not to put many tortillas on it. You'll be hungry, but don't take a lot of tortillas as you do at home. Take only one, two, or three and after a little while, you'll feel very, very full. After you eat, they'll say, 'We're grateful

you brought us our girl. We'll give you whatever will be your reward.' Say you don't want anything. They'll offer you corn, beans,
a chicken, a horse, a cow, turkeys, money, silver, gold, or a pig.
You tell them you brought me because I asked you to, and you did
not want to get anything out of it. They'll insist on paying you,
and then you say, 'Well, if you want to reward me, give me what
you have on your altar.' On the altar is a gold ring, and they'll give
it to you. Up there is the entrance to my home."

The hunter looked up and saw a precipice. No one could walk
up that mountain, but the girl showed him the way. The hunter
was afraid, and he protested, "I'm not going here. I'll fall." But the
girl insisted, telling him, "Close your eyes, and then you'll see."
He did as she told him, and when he opened his eyes again, it was
fine where they went. "We won't perish because we put these steps
here," said the girl. She was a wiseperson and was powerful. They
reached her house, and things were really just as she said they
would be. Huge dogs and cats—man-eating tigers—tore out to
greet them. There were also turkeys and wild pigs from the forest
who eat people. But their mistress calmed them down. Her grand-
parents met them, and the girl told the hunter not to fear them
lest he find them in the form of snakes. Because she told him to be
brave, he found them in the form of Christians. He took the battered stool, he sat in a cluttered place, he took the earthen bowl,
and he ate just a little bit of bean soup and took only a few tortillas. 6. They gave him the gold ring 7. with some instructions,
"Don't let your wife touch it. Keep it on your altar. Adorn it with
lots of flowers. Every day at noon you'll see the cup fill up with
money. Guard the money in some boxes. Make a lot of boxes, and
every day spread incense around the cup." The wisemen helped
him get down from the mountain. He passed by where he had hung
his carbine, but he didn't pick it up. He arrived home and followed
the instructions on how to care for the ring and the money it
produced. He saw the money fill the cup and the boxes. He built
houses.

8. Later on, he remembered his days as a hunter. "I'm getting
bored because I don't go hunting anymore," he said. So he decided
to take a walk in the forest, even though he wouldn't do any hunting. He just went without telling his wife where he was going. But
the woman pondered, "I don't know where he goes to get this money.
He locks it up in the house. I'm going to watch where he leaves
the keys." One time the hunter was careless, and his wife saw him
put the keys under a rock. When the hunter went into the forest,
the little woman took the keys and put them into the locks. She

*put the wrong keys into the locks and broke some of the locks and
some of the keys. She went all over and found the ring on the
altar. "He's probably saving it for his sweetheart. Well now, he's
going to see. I'll put it on. When he comes, I'll ask him why he has
it, and whose it is. If it'd been for me, he would have given it to
me by now," the wife concluded. She put it on her finger and then
decided to wash her children's clothes in the river.*

*The ring was on her finger in the water, and it glistened all the
way to foreign lands. It shone brightly because it was hot, and a
foreigner saw it and flew here in his airplane. He found the woman
and asked her, "Would you sell us two servings of tortillas?" He
offered her a lot of money, and she fetched the tortillas and gave
them to him. When he paid her the money, he removed the ring
from her finger, declaring, "This ring is ours." The foreigners [more
than one came] mounted their airplane and flew away. "These
gentlemen took this ring! Where did my husband get it?" she
wondered. She was angry when she returned from the river. Her
husband was there when she came home. He had returned at noon
and found the locks broken open. He discovered the ring was missing from the altar and he was frantic. When the woman came from
the river, he confronted her, "You've opened it!" "No," she denied.
He angrily declared, "You've destroyed me. There was a gold ring
here. That was how I lived. The money has gone. The seed has
gone. I didn't keep the ring for one of my sweethearts. It was for
you. It wasn't a ring to wear. It was a flower, a treasure." The wife
told him what happened. The man hit her, left the house, and took
a road into the forest, crying as he went.*

*9. Along came a mouse in the debris, who asked, "What hap-
pened to you, my good friend?" The man snapped, "What business
is it of yours?!" The mouse replied, "I'll tell you what happened,"
and the mouse related to the man what had happened and then
offered to help. The mouse said, "I know where they took the money.
I can tunnel to where the money is because it's in a house. It's in
a chest in the corner, and I'll fetch it. It's in a foreign land." The
mouse went to the house of the foreigners and drilled a hole. He
found the chest and drilled a hole into it and removed the ring.
But the mouse dashed away quickly because he was afraid, and
the ring struck something and made a noise. The dogs and cats
and other animals in the yard surrounded the house. The dogs
barked when they heard the noise, and the cats awoke with the
noise and chased the mouse.*

*12. Fearful the cat would eat him, the mouse jumped into the
water, where he dropped the ring. 13. A fish swallowed it, and*

there the mouse was, standing on a branch feeling sad. The ring glistened in the stomach of the fish. Meanwhile, the hunter waited for the mouse to return. Along came a hawk and asked the hunter, "What happened to you, good friend?" The man refused to tell, and so the hawk related to the man the whole story of the loss of the ring. The hawk knew the mouse had dropped the ring into the water and told the man, "I'm going to bring the money and fetch the mouse because the mouse is my good friend and you are my good friend." 14. and 15. The hawk found the mouse and assured his friend by saying, "The fish will come up at noon to eat. One can see the ring shimmering inside its stomach. I'll grab it when it surfaces and I'll open its stomach and remove the ring. When I fly by to fetch you, you grab onto me immediately." The hawk did as he said he would. The hawk fetched the ring, and 11. flew the mouse and the ring back to the hunter.

16. The hawk [probably] presented the ring to the hunter, showing him where it was scratched on the rocks in the river. The hawk [probably] said, "You talk to your wife. Take her to where you keep the cup and tell her, 'Don't think I have this ring either for my sweetheart, or for you, or for me. This is a treasure they gave me. Next time we'll go to see the money in the cup on the altar.' Take your wife to see it. Don't go there anymore alone to see how much money of yours you [plural] have. This is your seed." The hunter thanked the animals and asked, "What do you [plural] want for a reward? You, mouse?" The mouse replied, "I don't want anything. I did you this favor because I'm your good friend." But the hunter insisted, and the mouse finally said, "I only want your granary." The mouse went to stay in the granary, and although we get angry now, the mouse earned the right to live in the granary. The hunter asked the hawk, "What'll be your reward?" At first the hawk said, "I don't want anything." But the hunter insisted, and so the hawk said, "Give me your chicken coop." For that reason the hawk never stops eating chickens. They belong to him. We get angry now, but he earned them.　　　　STORYTELLER L. V.

YAONÁHUAC VERSION 3

1. There was a hunter who liked to hunt deer, badgers, quail, and pheasants. He felt at home in the forest. One time he went to the forest, and his dogs chased a deer into a hollow. The dogs stopped barking, and he went to see what had happened. 2. and 3. He found a girl washing and combing her hair at the edge of the water. She was very, very beautiful. "What are you doing, María?"

he asked. "Nothing, my good hunter," she replied. He remarked that he hadn't seen her, and she replied, "I've seen you. I live here." The hunter asked, "Will you go away with me?" She agreed, "I'll go. Sure. Come back here in a week. Bring two blankets because I'll appear as a spotted cow. Try not to flee. When you see me getting close, put down one of the blankets. When I step onto the blanket, throw a cord onto me, and I'll fall down. Then cover me with the other blanket, and I'll got to sleep." The hunter went home and anxiously awaited the day to return. He went back to where he had found the girl washing, and he whistled. He heard a loud noise in the mountain and saw a spotted cow come running toward him, tumbling rocks and cracking branches as she came. He fled, thinking the cow would kill him.

He told his older brother. "Stupid! Where?" he asked. The older brother went to the spot where his younger brother had encountered the spotted cow. This time the older brother found the girl washing. She was angry because she thought he was the younger brother, and said, "I should be angry for the joke you played on me." 4. "But it wasn't I. I've come to patch things up and take you to my house," he said. "Really? Because if you don't, my parents will kill me. Come back here in a week at eleven o'clock," she said. Her golden hair was so beautiful. He went home to his wife, but he didn't say anything to her. On the appointed day he went back, and this time a snake came toward him. It was horribly spotted, and it stuck its tongue out at him. He quickly threw down one blanket, and when the snake was upon it, he threw a cord down on top of it, and there it fell. He covered the snake with another blanket, and after a while the girl popped up. All her shining clothes were gold and silver.

6. "You prepare satchels with the blankets, and you take one load and I'll take the other," she said. He prepared the satchels, and yes, they played [they had sex] and then they went off. When they approached the man's village, he said, "I'm going to chase my wife away." But the girl protested, "No, man! Why? That's betrayal. I'll go as the servant. I'll do what you want. I'll make your meals and I'll do your clothes. My poor sister!" The man went to his wife, and said, "There is a girl over there who is looking for her destiny." The wife replied, "But there isn't enough work for me." He brought the girl, who asked for a job. The wife took her husband outside the house and said to him, "We don't have any corn or beans." The girl rose to her feet and asked, "Lend me two of your cooking pots." She removed a kernel of corn from a little gourd, and she broke it with her teeth, and then she put it in a

cooking pot. Then she removed a bean from another little gourd, she broke it in half, and then she put it in another pot. She put the pots on the fire to boil, and a lot of corn and beans came from those single seeds. She ground the tortilla dough and called out, "Let's eat." 7. Later, she told the man, "Go see a carpenter so that he'll make me five trunks, each one meter square." He brought them the next day. Gold went into one. Silver went into another. Her ring went into a third. One of her gourds went into a fourth. The other gourd went into the fifth. "Go to the forest to select land where I'll plant. Get me fifty men to clear a field," she said. When that was done, she gave the men seeds to plant the land. She fed all fifty men from one small dinner pot. Then there came along a boy who liked the girl. "My patron has a wife and I don't. I'm going to take his servant girl from him," the boy said to himself. Meanwhile, the men harvested the crop. They built a shed 50 brazas [one braza is about 1.7 meters] long, and put the seeds into it. Afterwards, they made the harvest mole, and the girl said, "Bring your mothers, your wives, and even bring your little children. I'm going to give you a little taco." They killed turkeys and made mole sauce that you wouldn't believe. "Shuck the corn and open the bean pods. Clean these chiles," the girl told the workers, their parents, and their wives who came. The man became rich.

It was going to be seven years. Meanwhile, the boy who liked the servant girl decided to act. "I'm going to talk to her. At noon she'll come to feed us," he said to himself. He tried to intercept her, pretending to urinate in the road where she came bringing the dishes for the meal. But instead he saw a snake coming toward him. The snake was as wide as the road and its tongue stuck out to here [the narrator gestures to indicate a long distance]. The boy threw off his hat and tore out of there. The girl came to feed the men as if nothing had happened.

7. When the harvest came, the girl told the man, "We're doing fine. Do us a favor and don't get drunk. Let the others get drunk, but don't get drunk yourself." 8. They served the harvest mole, and the man ignored the request and got drunk. He went crazy. He grabbed his wife and hit her with his fist. The servant girl came, saying, "Look, sir, don't hit my lady! You're hitting her for no reason. What has she done to you? She's just here as God wishes her to be." But the man replied, "You shut up!" And he struck her on the nose, making her bleed. The servant girl said no more. She just went to the back of the house, and the man went to lie down. At noon two old people came, asking, "Where do you have our

*daughter!" One added, "She told me you hit her for no reason.
Well now, we brought this potion made from the blood you shed.
Drink it." The man protested, saying, "I won't." But one of the old
people said, "If you don't, then she won't come back." The man
agreed, "I'll drink it so she'll return." He put his head back and
drank it and after he finished, his stomach immediately burst,
and everything in the shed and the trunks disappeared.*

STORYTELLER M. I.

YAONÁHUAC VERSION 4

*1. Once there was a boy who went hunting. He took his carbine
and his cartridge belt, and he came upon a big lake. He looked up
and spotted a bird in a tree. He raised his carbine and shot it, and
the bird fell into the lake. He decided to roll up his trousers, and
he went into the lake to fetch the bird. Instead of finding water
in the lake, he found a doorway. 2. and 3. He opened the door and
cautiously went in and found a beautiful girl sweeping. "Come in
and rest," she said. 4. "Look at my orchard. I'm looking for a companion to look after it because I'm here alone. There are fresh corn,
papayas, melons, and chiles," she said. The boy replied, "Fine. Let
me walk around." The girl said, "Return to eat at twelve." The boy
walked around and returned to find a bench and table ready with a
meal. He dug into it. After he finished the meal, the girl said, "Go
take care of the orchard for me, and come back in the afternoon and
we'll talk." He returned, and she fixed him supper. She told him, "If
you're sleepy, there is my bed. I'll be right there after I wash the
dishes. We'll sleep together." He lay down and went to sleep. He
awoke during the night and found her embracing him tightly all
the way. He was alone when the sun came up, and the girl was in
another room. She told him to wash his hands and take a look at
the crops before breakfast. He went out and returned.*

*6. The girl said, "Go see my mother-in-law. Take her a basket
of money. Take another basket to buy a house. We're going to live
there. Your clothes, your hat, and shoes are over there." The boy
did as she said. He went home and told his mother, "I have a girl."
The mother replied, "Uh huh. That's good. By the way, your aunt
is coming." When the aunt came, she asked, "And how beautiful
is the girl!" The boy replied, "I only saw her sweeping. She was
very beautiful then." The aunt said, "Well, so that you'll see if
she'll stay beautiful as when you saw her, I'll give you a lamp and
matches. When the girl falls soundly asleep, light a match so you*

can see her face. If the matches won't work, there is the lamp with a wick." The boy walked about the center of town and found a house. He bought it and received the papers and the keys. He left the keys with his mother, and he went to fetch the girl. At noon he arrived at where she was. 7. "My good hunter, what do you bring in your pocket?" asked the girl. "Nothing," was the hunter's reply. But the girl said, "Yes, you do bring something. Your aunt gave it to you. Throw away everything you brought because if you don't, you'll lose me. I won't be easy to find. If something does happen, just write me and toss the letter into the wind."

8. The boy discarded the lamp but he kept the matches. He ate supper that night and then lay down. He awoke during the night to find the girl embracing him warmly. He carefully disengaged himself, took out a match, and lit it. He saw she was very beautiful. She pleased him. He enjoyed it when they embraced, but when the sun came up, he found he was embracing a tree trunk. He was kissing her, but she had turned into wood. He discovered he was no longer dressed like a gentleman, and there was no longer a house. He was lying in a pasture. The boy decided to see his mother, but she didn't recognize him and said, "You're trash. Get out of here right now. My son is a gentleman." The boy went for a walk to the center of town, where he came across a doorway where there was a photograph of a rich man's daughter. "That's my wife," exclaimed the hunter. But the girl's father had him put in jail. There he cried in desperation until he remembered what the girl had said. He sent for a piece of paper and an envelope and a pencil. He wrote a note and tossed his letter between the bars and into the wind. At twelve o'clock, they were going to kill him, but at eleven o'clock he heard a car coming. It was his wife, and she said, "I've come to see the prisoner." The boy exclaimed, "María! Where were you?" The girl replied, "You're a fool. Why did you go putting things into your pockets?" She spoke to the authorities so they would release him. "Now I'll go with you," said the boy. But the girl said, "No, you won't. You go to the house you bought." And so that is where the boy stayed.

10. But then along came the hawk, who asked, "What's happened to you, my good hunter?" The boy replied, "My wife abandoned me." The hawk said, "You're to blame. But we want to help you. There are four of us." Then the hawk went to see the ant, the tiger, and the lion. The hawk returned and told the boy, "To find that María you lost, you'll have to fly until the sun rises. Fly, fly, fly until the sun comes up. You'll see a tower with two spigots of fire. The two spigots of fire are the bells, but they aren't really

burning. They are bathed in the sun's rays, and the bells are pure gold. We'll help you. We'll be there." So the boy went to sleep in the forest. At three in the morning, he rose and said, "God and the good hawk." He changed into a hawk and flew away. The sun came out, and he came upon the tower. He arrived at five in the afternoon and was hungry. The girl was feeding the chickens, who flapped their wings when he arrived [in the form of a hawk]. The girl called to her father, "Papa, a bird came. It's very beautiful." The father replied, "I'll shoot it." But the girl said, "Let's catch it." She tossed out some corn, and the bird alighted and ate it. She grabbed the hawk while it was eating, and she locked it in a cage and took the cage to the last room in the house. At night the hawk said, "God and the good ant," and he turned into a tiny ant. He climbed out of the cage and went into the girl's room through the key hole. He changed into a man and fondled her. She screamed, "Papa, a man has come in here!" Her father replied, "I'm coming." He grabbed his gun. Then the boy said, "God and the good ant," and snuggled under the bed. The father found nothing and locked the daughter in her room again and left. "God and the good man," said the boy, and he changed into a man again and fondled his wife a second time. The girl called out to her father, who came but found nothing. So he warned the girl, "If you call me again, I'll kill you." Again the boy said, "God and the good man," and he assumed human form. He snuggled up against the girl and grabbed her, and she asked, "Who are you?" He replied, "I'm the good hunter." She warned, "If my father catches me, he'll kill me. My father has three lives. Right now he's a man, but he'll turn into a wild boar. To-morrow he goes to wash in the mud of the lake. From a wild boar he'll turn into a dove, and only if you kill him in his three forms will you reign here and will we be able to live together."

The next day the boy went to the lake, where he found the girl's father sitting in the water amidst a big battle. The hunter had a fine horse, a fine rope, and a fine sword. He tore off his clothes and threw himself into the mud, saying, "God and the good tiger," and "God and the good lion." He tore the wild boar to pieces, but the wild boar turned into a dove. The boy then said, "God and the good hawk," and he grabbed and ate the dove. He returned to the girl and said, "I've killed your father." She replied, "Well now, we'll live together here. You won't go anywhere. You'll be in command here. Go bring your horse and mount it. Bring my father's clothes and put them on so they'll respect you."

STORYTELLER L. V.

SIMILARITIES

All eight stories develop around parallel themes, although some share more similarities than others. They have common central characters and similar plots, although narrators embellish them in very different ways. One cannot, however, determine the precise common historical sources and consequently fix with precision the exact cognate status of the eight stories. Indeed there is no way to know if these stories had a single common source, had several common sources, or exhibit parallels largely because they express common experiences.

With these factors in mind, the stories appear, on the basis of the number of their shared items, to fall into two groups (see table 15). First are all the stories from Huitzilan and the first two stories from Yaonáhuac, which share the greatest number of common ideas and develop these ideas in highly parallel ways. These stories probably share common historical antecedents and have closer cognate status with each other than with the other two tales. The last Yaonáhuac story has interestingly mixed Aztec and peninsular Spanish antecedents. On the one hand, the sweeping woman whom the hunter comes upon in the lake suggests Coatlicue (Skirt of Serpents), the mother of the gods who became pregnant with Huitzilopochtli while sweeping (Krickerberg 1971: 69). The man's Orpheus-like search for her may derive from an Aztec myth, only hints of which remain in the works of the chroniclers, about Piltzintecuhtli, who apparently pursued Xochiquetzal (Precious Flower) into the land of corruption (Sahagún 1951:210).[1] The evidence for the ancient Aztec myth is very weak, making the precise identification of the pre-Hispanic antecedents for this part of the Yaonáhuac story very difficult. On the other hand, the image of the man sleeping with a beautiful woman, striking match to see her, and then seeking her in an Orpheus-like quest appears in peninsular Spanish oral tradition (Boggs 1930: 42). Regardless of their particular antecedents, all eight stories are especially important for comparative purposes because they reveal the range of ideas held by the Sierra Nahuat about personified forces of nature.

The common ideas in these stories develop in all versions in conformity with the structural similarities in Nahuat narrative thought discussed in chapters 5 and 6. It was mentioned that this structure is to a group of stories what the skeleton is to the human body. It acts as a framework on which specific embellishments of common ideas are arranged according to a pattern much as the organs and tissues of the human body are supported on a skeleton.

Table 15. Shared Items in Lightning-bolt and Earth Mother Stories

Item	H1	H2	H3	H4	Y1	Y2	Y3	Y4
1. A man ventures into the forest	x	x	x	x	x	x	x	x
2. Man comes upon a lightning-bolt or earth mother	x	x	x	x	x	x	x	x
3. The lightning-bolt or earth mother is anthropomorphized	x	x	x	x	x	x	x	x
4. Man helps the lightning-bolt or earth mother	x	x	x	o	x	x	x	x
5. Man accompanies it to its home in the forest	x	x	x	x	x	x	o	o
6. Man is given wealth as a reward	x	x	x	x	x	x	x	x
7. Man receives precise instructions for keeping the wealth	x	x	o	o	x	x	x	x
8. Man loses the wealth	x	x	x	o	x	x	x	x
9. A hawk or mouse offers to help recover the wealth	x	x	x	o	x	x	o	o
10. Hawk gives the mouse directions for recovering the wealth	x	x	x	o	x	o	o	x
11. Mouse carries the wealth, and the hawk carries the mouse across the sea	x	x	x	o	x	o	o	o
12. Mouse drops the ring into the sea	x	x	x	o	x	x	o	o
13. A fish swallows the ring	x	x	x	o	x	x	o	o
14. The fish is caught	x	x	x	o	x	x	o	o
15. Hawk or the mouse (or both) opens the fish and removes the ring	x	x	x	o	x	x	o	o
16. The animals return the ring and the man rewards them	x	x	x	o	x	x	o	o
Total number of items present	16	16	15	5	16	14	7	8

x = item present
o = item absent

This section describes the structural similarities in the eight stories by illustrating how they contain common ideas that fit the invariant features of narrative thought. The succeeding section of this chapter discusses how and why narrators from the two communities have developed parallel ideas differently according to the social structures of their communities.

All eight stories describe a man entering a forest, where he comes upon an anthropomorphized force of nature (items 1–3). The stories build on a common spatial juxtaposition in Nahuat thought between the center and the periphery of the universe. It was mentioned earlier (chapter 5) that the Nahuat conceive of the earth as a landmass of undetermined shape. They regard the center of this mass as the domain of humans, marked in stories by words describing or connoting human communities. To this they contrapose concentric rings of stylized space that connote increasing degrees of wilderness. Cultivated *milpas* appear in the first ring, followed by the forest, surrounded in turn by a wild and amorphous area where the earth, sea, sky, and underworld converge.

By describing how the man moved from the center to the periphery, the narrators place him where he most likely will encounter a powerful force. The lightning-bolts whom he encounters stand for the powerfully creative forces in the Nahuat universe. The Nahuat assign to them the role of mediators between the masculine sun and the feminine earth in the process of creation. Their most important creative role is to bring water from the sea to make things grow. Lightning-bolts stand in direct opposition to the destructive forces in the universe which the Nahuat personify as Satan, whom they also place in the periphery.

The narrators make clear, in a variety of ways, the lightning-bolt identity of the characters the man encounters in the forest. First, one narrator (Y2) describes this character as a wiseperson (*tamatini*), an unmistakable reference for a Nahuat to a lightning-bolt. Second, all describe them producing vast quantities of wealth, and the Nahuat believe lightning-bolts live in the periphery in places containing vast treasures. It is interesting that the Huitzilan Nahuat apply the word *teyot* to this treasure, a term which closely parallels the Classical Nahuatl word *teotl*, meaning *god* (Molina 1966: 487). This probably stems from the obvious association between lightning-bolts in modern Nahuat stories and the ancient Aztec serpent gods, particularly Quetzalcoatl, who helped obtain sustenance for humans (see chapter 7).

Third, most narrators describe these characters taking the form of animals the Nahuat identify in other contexts as lightning-bolt animal companion spirits. A number of storytellers (H1, H2, H4, Y1, Y2, and Y3) make the animal a snake, a very clear reference to lightning-bolts. The Nahuat of both communities describe bolts of lightning and lightning-bolt characters in stories as burning or glowing snakes (*tikowame*). One narrator (H3) identifies the animal as a tiger, which most Nahuat would also connect with lightning-bolts, because they often describe them changing into tigers.

Fourth, two narrators (Y2 and Y3) describe them satisfying

a huge appetite with a small amount of food, or producing vast amounts of food from a single bean or kernel of corn. The Nahuat describe in other contexts how lightning-bolts have this miraculous ability, which coincidentally fits with the important role they play in creating and in obtaining human sustenance.

Fifth, narrators who describe these characters as women emphasize their beautiful, blonde gleaming hair (Y2 and Y3). As mentioned in the previous chapter, the Nahuat describe lightning-bolts having gleaming or curly hair, much as the ancient Aztecs believed their rain gods had special hair.

Lightning-bolts in Nahuat belief have connections with the sun and the earth, the masculine and feminine creative forces in the universe, and their ability to produce vast quantities of wealth derives from these connections. It is interesting that one narrator (Y4) describes the man meeting a woman in the forest, who possibly derives from the ancient Aztec earth mother. The Aztecs personified the earth as Xochiquetzal (Quetzal Flower), the Goddess of Spring, and as Coatlicue (Skirt of Serpents), the goddess who gave birth to the other gods in the pantheon (Nicholson 1971: 421–431). The woman in the modern story has qualities of both: she is beautiful and sensual like Xochiquetzal (Brundage 1979: 160), and she appears sweeping like Coatlicue, who, while sweeping, found a ball of down which made her pregnant with Huitzilopochtli (Krickerberg 1971: 69).

The modern Nahuat tend to fuse together closely related religious personalities who appear to derive from different but also related Aztec gods. The narrators of the stories of the Man Who Entered the Forest assign lightning-bolt identities to all characters representing personified forces of nature, including earth mothers. Thus I shall apply the term *lightning-bolt* to cover all personified forces of nature appearing in the eight stories discussed in this chapter.

Most stories depict the man assisting the lightning-bolt, although the particular manner of assistance varies considerably from story to story (see items 4–6). Narrators from both communities describe, in a way that resonates clearly with the Nahuat, how the man comes to acquire wealth from the lightning-bolt: a reciprocal exchange of favors takes place that accords with the principle of reciprocity that permeates Nahuat social life. Indians of both communities establish and maintain numerous social relationships with the ceremonial exchange of goods and services. The most conspicuous examples are the respect relationships of ritual kinship (*compadrazgo*), where co-parents (compadres) reciprocally exchange a large number of ceremonial and utilitarian objects of high monetary value. Reciprocal exchange occurs between blood kin and friends, and between humans and the supernatural. The Nahuat sense of obligation to return a favor is particularly apparent in these exchanges. In ritual kinship, for example, a man who asks another to sponsor his child in baptism believes he is indebted to the ritual sponsor, and this indebtedness influences the pattern of interaction. In the lightning-bolt stories a reciprocal exchange takes place between a human and a supernatural being. Such exchanges are familiar to the Nahuat, who carry them out during their patron saint celebrations when religious officials of the civil-religious hierarchy aim to maintain a convenant with God. The officials express their gratitude for God's gifts of nature's bounty, good health, and harmony in interpersonal relations by making ostentatious displays of wealth on behalf of all members of the community.

In a number of stories the man receives a gold ring as a reward for helping the lightning-bolt. The ring represents the creative powers in the Nahuat universe. The ring stands for a kernel of corn, the staple crop, and corn has a connection with the sun, the prime moving creative force. The connection between the ring and corn rests on several associations and implied ideas. The ring is gold, the color of corn. One storyteller (H1) described how, after the man acquired the ring, the corners of his house filled up with gleaming gold coins. This is an unmistakable reference to the way some prosperous merchants in the northern Sierra de Puebla actually fill the corners of their houses and stores with kernels of thrashed corn. It was mentioned earlier (chapter 5) that corn has a connection with the sun because a number of narrators describe a boy who plants a *milpa* (corn and bean plot) becoming the sun. One of the most interesting associations between corn and the sun occurs in the last of the eight stories (Y4). In this Orpheus-like tale, which probably has mixed Aztec and Spanish antecedents, the man flies east to recover the ring. He comes upon a tower bathed in the rays of the sun, which is a metaphor for a corn plant. The tower has two spigots of fire which actually are bells turned gold by the sun's rays. The tower refers to the corn stalk, and the golden, bell-shaped spigots probably stand for the cobs of freshly ripe corn.

Most stories describe the man being given precise instructions for keeping the wealth (item 7). The specific instructions could easily stand for the tenets of belief and religious rituals which the Nahuat contend should be taken on faith and followed with exactitude. Some of these beliefs and practices have Aztec antecedents

and serve to maintain an ethnic boundary between Indians and Hispanics. Several accounts from both communities (H1, H2, and Y3)
describe how the man is told to make or obtain square boxes or
trunks in the middle of which he must place the gold ring. The
boxes or trunks undoubtedly stand for the Nahuat view of the
universe oriented toward the four cardinal directions plus the
center. The center where the man places the ring represents the
Nahuat community in the very middle of the universe. This view
of a universe marked by four cardinal directions and a center
closely resembles that of the ancient Aztecs (Brundage 1979: 3–6).
Narrators sometimes include in their instructions ritual practices
which the Nahuat currently carry out on a regular basis. They mention, for instance, that the man must place the ring on the altar of
his home, and he must regularly adorn the altar with flowers and
spread incense (Y2). The Nahuat periodically place flowers and
spread incense around the altars of their homes and their churches
on festival occasions marked in the religious calendar.

A number of narrators describe the man losing the wealth
because foreigners come from across the sea to steal it (item 8).
The foreigners clearly refer to the Spaniards, who settled in the
northern Sierra de Puebla during the Colonial period to exploit
mines and transport ore to the smelting centers on the central
Mexican Plateau. This episode could also refer to the Hispanic
alienation of Nahuat land which occurred during the eighteenth to
twentieth centuries. Two narrators (H2 and H3) indicate that cloth
merchants stole the ring, but they obviously mean Hispanics, because the Nahuat frequently consider traveling merchants who enter their communities as Hispanics. In a number of versions, the
foreigners take the wealth from the man's wife (H1, H2, H3, Y1,
and Y2). This expresses the weakness of women and accords with
men's image of women that runs through their narrative thought.
The depiction of foreigners taking wealth from women fits with
the tendency of Hispanic men to take Nahuat women as mistresses, a common practice in all parts of the northern Sierra, but
one that is especially frequent in ethnically stratified communities
like Huitzilan.

Several stories include a final episode in which a hawk and a
mouse recover the wealth from across the sea (items 9–16). The
fact that animals recover the ring fits with Nahuat belief in an
intimate relationship between humans and animals, a belief which
has Aztec antecedents, and distinguishes Nahuat culture from that
of Hispanics (Taggart 1982a). To be sure, one can find parallel attitudes toward animals in both cultural traditions: both frequently

use animal metaphors to explore human problems, and both have the European-derived notion (Caro Baroja 1973) that some people can change into animals to punish their enemies and correct immoral behavior. But only the Nahuat depict their gods in animal form and hold the belief in human-animal companion spirits (*tonalme*). It is interesting that narrators describe how, by virtue of the intimate human-animal relationship, the man recovers wealth taken by Hispanics, who draw a sharper line between humans and animals in their culture.

The hawk and mouse stand for hierarchical relations in Nahuat society. The hawk is the stronger animal because hawks eat mice, and thus the hawk represents humans in superordinate statuses while the mouse stands for those in subordinate ones. Both Huitzilan and Yaonáhuac have hierarchy in their social structure, and these metaphors could refer to a variety of persons of higher and lower status. The hawk could refer to Hispanics, Indian men, and older members of Nahuat society, and the mouse could refer to the Nahuat, Indian women, and younger members of the Nahuat community.

The way narrators express the relations between the hawk and the mouse not only reflects hierarchy in social structure, but it also contains advice on how to deal with Hispanics. In one story (H1), for instance, the narrator describes the hawk threatening the mouse for failing to follow his orders for recovering the ring from the foreigners' house. The mouse had placed himself in danger and put the recovery of the ring in jeopardy by drinking the liquor that remained in the bottom of the foreigners' glasses after their wild celebration following their theft of the ring. This story sends the clear message that to cope with the Hispanics, the Nahuat cannot be careless or inattentive and must follow the orders of family and community leaders. The reference to drunkenness undoubtedly grows out of the Nahuat habit of piling up big bills for *aguardiente* in the stores of the Hispanic merchants, who later demand payment or the title to Nahuat land.

DIFFERENCES

The animal or human identity of the lightning-bolt or earth mother characters is the first and most obvious difference between Huitzilan and Yaonáhuac versions. All narrators connect these characters with animals by depicting them living in the forest, or by presenting them in the form of their animal companion spirits. But they also give them human identity to bridge the human and animal domains and integrate their view of the universe. The Huitzilan narrators use poetic devices with respect to these characters to separate the two domains more sharply than their counterparts from Yaonáhuac.

On the first encounter with the man, the lightning-bolts or earth mother have more animal identity in the Huitzilan stories and take on more human identity in the tales from Yaonáhuac. To be sure, overlap exists in accounts from the two communities, but table 16 describes the differences between accounts from Huitzilan and Yaonáhuac. The form these characters take in the first encounter is an indication of what comes later in the story.

Huitzilan versions 1 and 2 present the man coming upon the lightning-bolt in entirely animal form: he encounters a mute snake clearly identified as the lightning-bolt's animal companion spirit. To sharply separate the animal and human domains, the narrators insert intervals of time and space between the lightning-bolt as an animal and the same character as a human. In the first Huitzilan story, a lazy boy comes upon a mute snake cut to pieces by hunters, he patches it and goes on his way, and when he comes to the top of a hill, he finds a girl, who tells the boy she would have died if he had not helped her. In the second Huitzilan account, a man finds a mute snake whose head is chopped off, patches it, leaves it, returns some time later, and finds a boy who announces he was the snake the man had cured earlier.

Yaonáhuac versions 3 and 4, on the other hand, depict the man

Table 16. Identity of Principal Lightning-bolt Character on First Encounter, by Community and Storyteller

	Human vs. Animal Identity		
	Entirely animal	Mixed animal-human	Entirely human
Huitzilan versions			
1. A. V.	mute snake		
2. N. A. H.	mute snake		
3. M. A.		talking tiger	
4. N. A. H.		talking snake	
Yaonáhuac versions			
1. M. I.		talking snake	
2. L. V.		talking snake	
3. M. I.			girl washing
4. L. V.			girl sweeping

coming upon a lightning-bolt or earth mother in entirely human form: she appears as a beautiful girl washing and combing her hair, or as a beautiful and sensuous girl sweeping. The narrators play down the girls' animal identities by more tenuously linking them with animals, or by developing their human identities to a degree not found in the Huitzilan stories. Both describe the man, before the first encounter takes place, coming upon animals which the narrators link only indirectly with the girls. In the third version, a hunter enters the forest, his dogs chase a deer into a hollow, the man follows the dogs, and he finds a beautiful girl washing. The girl asserts her connection with the deer only by declaring that she lives in the forest. The girl temporarily changes into a spotted cow and a spotted snake later on in the story, but she plays a more prominent role in human form than any of her Huitzilan counterparts in the story. In the fourth Yaonáhuac version, a hunter shoots a bird, which falls into a lake, he goes into the water to fetch it, and he finds a girl sweeping, but the narrator does not identify the bird as her animal companion spirit. In this story, the storyteller presents the earth mother as more human than the man: she remains entirely human throughout the story, while the man assumes temporary animal identity: he temporarily changes into a hawk, an ant, a tiger, and a lion to recover the girl in an Orpheus-like version of the story. I shall refer to these differences between Huitzilan and Yaonáhuac accounts as the degree of lightning-bolt or earth mother anthropomorphization.

A number of factors connected with differences in social structure may explain this pattern. The degree of anthropomorphization probably expresses the degree to which the Nahuat of each community identify with their lightning-bolt gods. To be sure, they generally project Nahuat rather than Hispanic features on these characters in stories. One can easily see this in the way they portray Nahuat-Hispanic ethnic conflict as a struggle between lightning-bolts and Satan (see chapter 6). But the Huitzilan Nahuat would appear to express their identification with lightning-bolt gods less completely than the Yaonáhuac Nahuat by attributing to them fewer human characteristics.

Some support for this conclusion comes from other behaviors. The Nahuat in ordinary life express their identification with lightning-bolts in ways other than anthropomorphizing them in stories, and these practices by the Nahuat of the two communities correlate with the ways narrators anthropomorphize these gods in oral tradition. One way the Nahuat express identification with lightning-bolts is to declare that their animal companion spirits (*tonalme*) are snakes or lightning-bolts. Although the Nahuat assert that no one really knows who has what animal companion spirit in most cases, some claim they know because they consulted with diviners, because they are diviners themselves (lightning-bolts are believed to be clairvoyant), and because of their empirical observations. Of the two groups of Nahuat, only those of Yaonáhuac openly claimed with any regularity that they or their relatives have lightning-bolt animal companion spirits. These same Nahuat, of course, more completely anthropomorphize lightning-bolts in the stories presented in this chapter.

The degree of Nahuat identification with lightning-bolts probably hinges on several aspects of ethnic relations. The Huitzilan Nahuat probably have suppressed their lightning-bolt gods (unconsciously). For one thing, these gods have not really served them well from their point of view, because the Nahuat of this community are losing the ethnic struggle. Hispanics have achieved control over the vast bulk of the strategic resources, and they hold political power in this part of the northern Sierra de Puebla.

The heavy dependence of these Nahuat on Hispanic patronage makes them intensely ambivalent toward their patrons and the ethnic category to which they belong. To be sure, one side of this ambivalence is their deep resentment of Hispanics, expressed by attributing Hispanic characteristics to the devil, by rejecting Hispanic values, and by tenaciously holding on to their language and rituals (particularly betrothals). The other side of this ambivalence is intense coveting of Hispanic wealth and power. This promotes psychological identification with members of the dominant ethnic group and lays the foundation for subconscious receptivity to the religious personalities and ideology of Hispanics. It would appear from the Nahuat case that resisting ideational change is much more difficult for the highly subordinate Indians in a plural society than retaining overt symbols of ethnic identity like language, dress, and rituals.

One tenet of belief the Huitzilan Nahuat appear to have adopted from Hispanics that contributes to a weaker identification with lightning-bolt gods is the European Catholic idea that a human being is a divine creature separated from the world of animals or nature (Taggart 1982*a*). The Huitzilan Nahuat stress on the non-human qualities of a deified force of nature—the lightning-bolts—is consistent with this notion.

The Yaonáhuac Nahuat, on the other hand, make a more complete identification with their lightning-bolts and earth mothers because they have endured less pressure from Hispanics. Of paramount importance is their independence from Hispanic patronage, and their relatively greater degree of political autonomy. These Nahuat have less need to conclude that their gods have not served them well, because they have not lost the bulk of their land. Their relative independence from Hispanic patronage cuts down the extremes of their ambivalence toward the dominant ethnic group. They feel less compelled to hold on to their language and rituals because their resentment toward Hispanics is less intense. Likewise, they experience less psychological identification with Hispanic patrons and have consequently adopted fewer tenets of Catholicism which are inconsistent with their strong identification with their lightning-bolt gods.

A second and related difference between Huitzilan and Yaonáhuac versions is the degree of intimacy developed between the man and the lightning-bolt characters. Narrators express intimacy in these stories by the way they describe exchanges of food and sex (see table 17). The Nahuat establish their relationships of respect and friendship by means of food exchanges. They contract their most important respect relationships, which are also intimate relationships, by holding ceremonial banquets. During these banquets, the principal participants (the compadres or co-parents of ritual kinship) exchange meat from their dishes of ceremonial mole cross-sexually, to lace themselves into a sacred relationship bound by a stringent incest taboo between unmarried partners and a lifelong series of obligations. These respect relations are also intimate because partners exchange confidences and advice and render each other aid in ways uncharacteristic of other relationships. To maintain their ties, respect partners carry out periodic food exchanges during All Saints' day (October 31 and November 1), and during occasions that arise in the life of the participants (births, betrothals, marriages, and death). Narrators convey a willingness to establish intimacy between characters in stories by describing them exchanging food. They likewise describe an avoidance of intimacy by indicating the rejection of food.

Huitzilan narrators generally depict the man avoiding intimacy with lightning-bolt characters by having him reject offers of food (sometimes at the advice of a lightning-bolt himself). On the other hand, Yaonáhuac narrators describe human characters more willing to establish intimacy by accepting food from lightning-bolt characters. To be sure, one Yaonáhuac narrator depicts the man eating sparingly (Y2), but this storyteller has an interesting reason for doing so. The Nahuat generally believe that lightning-bolts have the magical ability to produce vast quantities of food from a single kernel of corn,

Table 17. Intimacy with Lightning-bolts, by Community and Storyteller

Version

H1	A. V.	girl warns man to reject food
H2	N. A. H.	boy warns man to reject food offered by his sisters
H3	M. A.	episode not developed
H4	N. A. H.	snake warns man to reject food offered by his sisters
Y1	M. I.	episode not developed
Y2	L. V.	man and woman become attracted to each other; woman tells man to eat sparingly
Y3	M. I.	man has sex with girl, then takes her to his home as his wife's servant; girl supplies food
Y4	L. V.	man marries girl

a single bean, or a small cooking pot. They hold that small quantities of their food (a single tortilla, or one spoonful of beans) are enough to satisfy an appetite. The narrator of this story depicts the lightning-bolt girl advising the man to eat sparingly because lightning-bolt food is different from human food. While this serves to emphasize the difference between humans and lightning-bolts, it also suggests the possibility of men becoming intimate with them. This is further apparent from other items of advice she passes on to the man. She tells him he must sit in a cluttered place on a battered stool and take a humble earthen bowl. She is telling him how to develop intimacy with her family by acting toward them as Nahuat should act toward each other, as equals, and avoid acting like a higher-status Hispanic. The Huitzilan narrators, by contrast, have the man rejecting food entirely, and thus they suggest that intimacy with lightning-bolts is impossible.

Another way to indicate intimacy or its avoidance is by portraying men having sex or rejecting it with lightning-bolt women. All Huitzilan narrators who develop this episode have the man reject intimacy with lightning-bolt women because they are dangerous. Yaonáhuac narrators, on the other hand, indicate how men are attracted to lightning-bolt women (Y2), have sex with them (Y3), and marry them (Y4) with no dangerous consequences. To understand the factors contributing to this difference in sexual intimacy, one must consider separately intimacy with lightning-bolts per se and men's sexual intimacy with lightning-bolt women.

Intimacy per se between men and lightning-bolt characters follows from the anthropomorphization discussed earlier. It is logi-

cal that the Yaonáhuac narrators, who more greatly anthropomorphize lightning-bolts because they more strongly identify with
them, would also depict human characters contracting more intimate relations with lightning-bolt characters. Likewise, it is reason-
able that Huitzilan narrators, who less completely anthropomorphize lightning-bolt characters, would depict less intimacy between
them and humans. The same social structural factors that promote
anthropomorphization also promote intimacy because of the logical relationship between these aspects of the stories.

Men's intimacy, or the avoidance of intimacy, with lightning-
bolt women, on the other hand, is part of Nahuat men's sexual
ideology expressed in these and other stories. It was mentioned
earlier that Huitzilan narrators describe the man avoiding intimacy
with a lightning-bolt woman lest he stay in the wild as her slave
forever (see table 17). To be sure, this episode in which the man
heeds the warning to reject food and tools offered by lightning-bolts
(men and women) may derive from Aztec antecedents. It reminds
one of the Aztecs' belief in the horrible snake woman, Cihuacoatl,
who gave men the hoe and the tumpline and forced them to work
(Sahagún 1950: 3). The Huitzilan Nahuat could have elected to emphasize other images of lightning-bolt women derived from Aztec
tradition, some of which are positive and appear in lightning-bolt
stories from other Nahuat communities. But they chose to emphasize the dangerous and threatening aspects of lightning-bolt
women because they accord with a sexual ideology that runs
through their narrative tradition.

Huitzilan men generally depict women in narratives as dangerous to the moral order because they are less socialized than
men. Stories that define more completely the essential natures of
women and men appear in subsequent chapters. It is interesting
that the image of lightning-bolt women as dangerous to men is a
special case of an androcentric sexual ideology found in a number
of cultures. Dwyer (1978a, 1978b) notes that Moroccan men view
women as threatening because they lack control over their animal-
like sexual impulses. Ardener (1977b: 23) notes with reference to
the African Bakweri: ". . . where society is defined by men, some
features of women do not fit that definition. In rural societies, the
anomaly is experienced as a feature of the 'wild,' for the 'wild' is a
metaphor for the non-social which in confusing ways is vouched
for by the senses." This kind of sexual ideology fits with the androcentric nature of Huitzilan social structure. It justifies male dominance in the family and supports patrilineal land inheritance because it explains why women cannot be trusted with land. If they

are less socialized, morally weaker, and more threatening than men, then they cannot be responsible enough to run the family estate.

The Nahuat of Yaonáhuac present a very different image of women that fits their more sexually egalitarian family structure. They attribute more human traits to the women characters who personify forces of nature. It was mentioned that in one Yaonáhuac story (Y4) the earth mother retains more consistent human identity than the man who encounters her in the forest. In some Yaonáhuac stories (Y3 and Y4) narrators assign lightning-bolt women and earth mothers a much more important place in the plot than in parallel tales from Huitzilan. There is a clear tendency for some Yaonáhuac narrators to make their lightning-bolt women supportive of, rather than threatening to, the moral order. In one version (Y3), she prevents the man from chasing away his wife, and she rejects the advances of the hired hand who schemes to seduce her. This depiction is consistent with the tendency for Yaonáhuac narrators to regard lightning-bolt women as more socialized and thus more like men.

It is interesting that the Yaonáhuac Nahuat tend to emphasize an image of women probably derived from the benevolent Aztec personality Xochiquetzal, the beautiful and sensual Goddess of Spring, who intervened on behalf of men (Brundage 1979: 159–164). It was pointed out that the Huitzilan Nahuat tend to emphasize the Aztec-derived image of the horrible Snake Woman, Cihuacoatl. Because the images that appear in the stories accord with the actual position of women in Nahuat social structure, this amounts to further evidence supporting the contention that narrative acculturation hinges in part on ideology derived from social structure.

A third difference between Huitzilan and Yaonáhuac versions is the strength of the principal lightning-bolt character relative to the man. Narrators express the strength of the lightning-bolt characters when they depict them taking the initiative, assisting, commanding, causing fear, threatening, or instructing human characters. They indicate weakness when they describe the lightning-bolts requesting help, requiring assistance without making a request, and fearing humans.

The strength or weakness of the lightning-bolt characters in different versions of the stories correlates with the position of Nahuat in the plural social structure. This is apparent from an examination of highly parallel episodes in the most closely related stories from Huitzilan and Yaonáhuac. It was mentioned earlier that the four Huitzilan versions share more common motifs with

Table 18. Incidents Showing the Relative Strength of Lightning-bolts and Men, by Community and Storyteller

| | Huitzilan | | | Yaonáhuac | |
A. V.	N. A. H.	M. A.	N. A. H.	M. I.	L. V.
Lazy boy talks to snake.	Man talks to snake.	Juan Tonto talks to tiger.	Snake calls basketmaker.	Snake calls man.	Snake calls hunter.
					Snake tells hunter to cease killing animals.
Lazy boy heals snake.	Man heals snake.	Juan Tonto offers to heal the tiger and does so.		Snake asks man to heal him in return for a reward.	Snake asks hunter to remove the rock that is crushing her.
				Man is afraid snake will bite him.	
Girl asks lazy boy to help her home.	Boy asks man to go with him because boy's father wants to thank him.	Tiger asks Juan to carry him home.	Snake asks basketmaker to take him home.	Snake asks man to carry him home.	Snake asks hunter to carry her home.
			Basketmaker fears snake will bite him.	Man fears snake will bite him.	Hunter fears snake and says she is too big and heavy for him to carry.
					Snake instructs hunter on how to carry her.
			Snake guides basketmaker.	Snake guides man.	
					Hunter fears climbing precipitous mountain on way to snake's house.

Table 18 (continued)

	Huitzilan			Yaonáhuac	
A. V.	N. A. H.	M. A.	N. A. H.	M. I.	L. V.
					Snake assists hunter to climb up to her home atop mountain.
					Hunter loses his fear of snake after she changes into a beautiful woman.
			Huge snakes rush out toward man, who fears they will eat him.		Huge dogs and man-eating tigers charge forward.
			Snake controls them.		Girl controls them.
					Hunter fears the woman's family, but she helps him overcome his fear.
Girl tells lazy boy not to eat and not to accept seeds as a reward. She tells him to ask for a gold ring.	Boy tells man not to eat any food and not to accept tools as a reward. He tells man to ask for a gold ring.	Juan Tonto asks for a gold ring as a reward.	Snake warns basketmaker not to eat food and not to accept tools as a reward. Snake tells him to ask for a gold ring.	Snake tells his brothers to bring a basket from which he removes a gold ring and gives it to the man as his reward.	Girl tells hunter to sit down on a battered stool, in a cluttered place, eat from a humble earthen bowl, eat just a few tortillas and beans, deny he helped her for a reward, re-

Table 18 (*continued*)

| | *Huitzilan* | | | *Yaonáhuac* | |
A. V.	N. A. H.	M. A.	N. A. H.	M. I.	L. V.
					fuse gifts, and ask for a gold ring.
Girl's mother tells lazy boy to obtain a box of precise dimensions.	Boy tells man to secure a box of precise dimensions.			Snake tells man to keep the ring in an empty drawer, and keep the keys without allowing his wife to have them.	Girl's parents tell hunter to place the ring in a cup on an altar adorned with flowers, to spread incense daily, to make boxes to keep the money, and to prevent his wife from touching the ring.
					Snakes help hunter leave the precipitous mountain.

Table 19. Average Ratings for Lightning-bolts, by Community

	Mean number of events
Lightning-bolt is stronger in Huitzilan tales	1.3
Lightning-bolt is equal in Huitzilan and Yaonáhuac tales	4.2
Lightning-bolt is stronger in Yaonáhuac tales	11.5
Total number of events	17

Difference of means test: $t = 13.11$ with 14.8 df, $.0005 > p$, one tailed test for comparison of mean ratings for events where the lightning-bolt is stronger either in Huitzilan tales or in Yaonáhuac tales.[3] Ratings are by ten judges.

two of the Yaonáhuac accounts (Y1 and Y2). If indeed there exist community differences in the strength of lightning-bolt characters, they should appear in comparisons of closely parallel as well as distantly parallel versions. Table 18 lists highly parallel episodes from the six most similar versions to illustrate the comparative strength of lightning-bolt characters from Huitzilan and Yaonáhuac. To ensure objectivity, ten judges compared these parallel episodes, and their average ratings appear in table 19.[2] Clearly the lightning-bolt characters in the Yaonáhuac versions have more strength than the same characters in parallel episodes of the Huitzilan versions.

The strength of lightning-bolts relative to human characters in these stories would appear to express the relative powerlessness or feeling of control over their destiny of the Nahuat in the two communities. It was noted that the Nahuat identify with lightning-bolts, and thus these characters in stories act as barometers of Nahuat images of themselves as a class relative to Hispanics. The Huitzilan Nahuat, who are powerless because they depend heavily on Hispanic patronage, depict lightning-bolts as weak. The Yaonáhuac Nahuat, who have more independence from Hispanic patronage and more political autonomy, depict their lightning-bolts as strong.

Other aspects of these stories provide further support for the interpretation that lightning-bolts are weak in stories when the Nahuat see themselves as powerless, and they are strong when the Nahuat feel they have more control over their destiny. The conditions under which the man in the stories loses the wealth (item 8) expresses perceived powerlessness vs. control. Narrators express a range of ideas about the loss of wealth. Some describe its loss as beyond human control, while others attribute the loss of wealth to human error. Huitzilan narrators generally describe human characters having little control over the loss of the gold ring. They describe foreigners or clothes merchants taking the ring, sometimes over the objections of the man's wife. This expresses the Huitzilan Nahuat view that they have little control over the course of history, and it fits with their depiction of lightning-bolts as comparatively weak.

The Yaonáhuac versions of the loss of wealth appear strikingly different when compared to the Huitzilan versions (see table 20). In three of the four accounts (Y1, Y3, and Y4), the man loses the wealth because he failed to heed a specific warning. In the fourth version (Y2), the man loses the wealth because his wife assertively searches for the ring and finds it and, therefore, goes against a warning given to her husband that he must not allow his wife to touch the ring.

Table 20. The Loss of Wealth, by Community and Storyteller

Version

H1	A. V.	foreigners take the ring from the man's wife despite her resistance
H2	N. A. H.	foreigners take the ring from the man's wife despite her resistance
H3	M. A.	clothes merchants persuade man's wife to buy their goods with the gold ring
H4	N. A. H.	episode not developed
Y1	M. I.	foreigners switch a fake ring for the real one when man's wife is left alone in the house; man had forgotten warning not to allow his wife access to keys
Y2	L. V.	man is warned not to let his wife touch the ring; one day she becomes suspicious, finds the ring, and foreigners come to steal it from her
Y3	M. I.	girl warns man not to get drunk; man ignores the warning and beats his wife and the girl, whose parents kill him
Y4	L. V.	man disobeys girl's order to empty his pockets; following his aunt's advice, he lights a match to sneak a look at the girl

Thus human characters in Yaonáhuac stories hold some responsibility for the loss of wealth, a notion that expresses the feeling of control over their destiny on the part of the Nahuat from this community. This feeling undoubtedly grows out of their independence from Hispanic patronage and their greater political autonomy.

The Nahuat stories support the hypothesis that men who lack control over important strategic resources and who occupy a weak position in the class hierarchy will develop a more male-dominant sexual ideology (Michaelson and Goldschmidt 1971: 347; Rogers 1975; Gissi Bustos 1976; Brandes 1980). The Huitzilan Nahuat rely heavily on Hispanic patronage, depict lightning-bolt characters as weak to reflect their own powerlessness, and describe women characters as less assertive, morally weaker, and more threatening relative to parallel characters in Yaonáhuac stories. The more autonomous Nahuat of Yaonáhuac express greater feelings of control over their destiny, and they depict women characters as comparatively more assertive and morally stronger.

Comparison of two highly parallel lightning-bolt stories from Huitzilan and Yaonáhuac where these characters are women illustrates the degree to which the two groups of Nahuat depict women as assertive (see table 21). The lightning-bolt woman is stronger

Table 21. Average Ratings for Lightning-bolts as Women, by Community

	Mean number of events
Lightning-bolt is stronger in Huitzilan tales	1.6
Lightning-bolt is equal in Huitzilan and Yaonáhuac tales	3.6
Lightning-bolt is stronger in Yaonáhuac tales	10.8
Total number of events	16

Difference of means test: $t = 9.52$ with 14.7 df, $.0005 > p$, one tailed test for comparison of mean ratings for events where the lightning-bolt is stronger either in Huitzilan tales or in Yaonáhuac tales. Ratings are by ten judges.

and more assertive in the Yaonáhuac version, which fits the actually stronger position of women in the social structure of this community. It has been noted that the stronger position of women in the Yaonáhuac family came about because of the application of community property law. Note how the Yaonáhuac narrator (Y2, item 16) depicts the hawk, who recovered the wealth obtained from the lightning-bolt woman, saying that it belongs to both the man and his wife.

A final difference between Huitzilan and Yaonáhuac stories appears in the way narrators construct natural metaphors for hierarchy in social structure. Some versions contain a final episode in which a hawk and a mouse recover a gold ring stolen by foreigners (items 9 through 16 in stories H1, H2, H3, Y1, and Y2). The hawk, the stronger animal, stands for humans in superordinate statuses, and the mouse, the weaker animal, stands for those in corresponding subordinate statuses. The images of the hawk and mouse in the lightning-bolt stories vary according to the relative degree of hierarchy in Huitzilan and Yaonáhuac social structure. Table 22 lists twenty similar events in five of the most parallel stories to throw into relief the different ways narrators from the two communities develop the hawk-mouse metaphor. Table 23 describes the average ratings of ten judges for nineteen of the twenty events expressing the relative strength of the two animals and illustrates the degree to which the judges believed the mouse is stronger in the Yaonáhuac tales. I excluded item number 15 in table 22 from the ratings in table 23 because judging this item required special knowledge of Nahuat culture. The item refers to the mouse eating the fish which swallowed the ring and expresses the mouse's weakness, because from the Nahuat point of view appetite control expresses strength.

Table 22. Incidents Showing the Relative Strength of the Hawk and the Mouse, by Community and Storyteller

	Huitzilan			Yaonáhuac	
A. V.	N. A. H.	M. A.	M. I.	L. V.	
Hawk offers to recover the ring.	Hawk offers to recover the ring.	Hawk offers to recover the ring.	Hawk offers to recover the ring.	Mouse offers to recover the ring.	
Hawk tells lazy boy to find a mouse to help recover the ring.	Hawk tells man to find a mouse to help recover the ring.	Hawk tells Juan Tonto to tell his brother, the mouse, that he wants him to help recover the ring.	Hawk speaks to his companion, the mouse, so that he will help recover the ring.		
Mouse fears that the hawk will eat him.					
Hawk tells mouse how to recover the ring from the foreigners' house.	Hawk tells mouse how to recover the ring from the foreigners' house.	Hawk tells mouse how to recover the ring from the merchants' house.	Hawk gives some directions to the mouse: he tells the mouse they must wait until dark before landing on the roof of the foreigners' house, and he warns the mouse about a cat. Hawk does not tell mouse how to recover the ring.	Mouse acting alone tries to recover the ring.	
Mouse does not recover the ring on first try because he fails to heed the hawk's warning to be cautious.	Mouse does not recover the ring on first try because he finds a cat in the foreigners' house.	Mouse cannot find the ring on first try.	Mouse does not recover the ring on first try because he sees the cat in the foreigners' house.	Mouse removes the ring from the foreigners' house on the first try.	
Hawk threatens to eat mouse if he does not recover the ring on the second try.					
	Hawk tells mouse how to frighten the cat and make the foreigner sneeze to release the ring.	Hawk tells mouse to cut through the paper covering the ring.	Mouse tells hawk to take him to the other side of the house, where he will make a hole		

Table 22 (*continued*)

	Huitzilan			Yaonáhuac	
A. V.	*N. A. H.*	*M. A.*	*M. I.*	*L. V.*
			and enter the house at the base of the chest containing the ring.	
Mouse removes the ring from a box, but he drops it. A foreigner picks it up.				
Mouse makes the foreigner sneeze to release the ring.				
Mouse carries the ring as the animals fly across the sea.	Mouse carries the ring as the animals fly across the sea.	Hawk tells mouse to carry the ring.	Hawk offers to carry the ring, but the mouse says he will carry it and he does.	
Mouse drops the ring into the sea because he tires from carrying it.	Mouse drops the ring into the sea because it is too heavy for him.	Mouse drops the ring into the sea because he is sleepy.	Mouse drops the ring into the sea when he tells the hawk to grab some fish.	Mouse dashes out of the foreigners' house and strikes the ring against something. The sound alerts the cat, who chases the mouse into the water, where the mouse drops the ring.
	Hawk knows that the fish which swallowed the ring will surface.	Hawk decides to wait for the fish which swallowed the ring to surface.	Hawk decides to wait for the fish which swallowed the ring to surface.	Hawk offers to fetch the mouse and the ring. He knows the fish which swallowed the ring will surface at noon.
Fisherman catches the fish which swallowed the ring.	Hawk catches the fish which swallowed the ring.	Hawk catches the fish which swallowed the ring.	Hawk catches the fish which swallowed the ring.	Hawk catches the fish which swallowed the ring.
Hawk and mouse open the fish.	Hawk tells the mouse to help open the fish.		Hawk opens the fish.	Hawk opens the fish.

Table 22 (*continued*)

| | Huitzilan | | Yaonáhuac | |
A. V.	*N. A. H.*	*M. A.*	*M. I.*	*L. V.*
	Mouse, but not hawk, eats some fish.	Mouse, but not hawk, eats the fish.		
Mouse picks up the ring.	Hawk and mouse find the ring.	Mouse finds the ring.	Hawk finds the ring.	Hawk finds the ring.
		Hawk tells mouse not to drop the ring again.	Hawk insists on carrying the ring this time.	
	Feeling the weight of the mouse, who ate the fish, the hawk asks the mouse if he ate some of the fish. The mouse denies it.		When the animals reach land, hawk scolds the mouse for not giving him the ring in the first place. The two animals quarrel.	
Lazy boy first asks the hawk what he wants for a reward.	First the hawk and then the mouse ask for something to eat.	Juan Tonto first asks hawk what he wants for a reward.	Man first asks hawk what he wants for a reward.	Hunter first asks mouse what he wants for a reward.
Hawk says he does not want a reward.		Hawk says he does not want a reward. Both animals say they do not want money.	Hawk says he does not want a reward.	Mouse and hawk say they do not want a reward.

Table 23. Average Ratings for Mouse, by Community

	Mean number of events
Mouse is stronger in Huitzilan tales	5.6
Mouse is equal in Huitzilan and Yaonáhuac tales	3.8
Mouse is stronger in Yaonáhuac tales	9.6
Total number of events	19

Difference of means test: $t = 4.57$ with 16.9 df, $.0005 > p$, one tailed test for comparison of mean ratings for events where mouse is stronger either in Huitzilan tales or in Yaonáhuac tales. Ratings are by ten judges.

Yaonáhuac narrators generally depict the mouse taking more initiative, being more assertive with the hawk, and more competently carrying out tasks on his own than the mouse in the Huitzilan stories. In one Yaonáhuac version (Y2) the narrator completely reverses the positions of the two animals by describing the mouse rather than the hawk meeting the man first and offering to recover the ring, and by depicting the mouse receiving his reward before the hawk. This is a strong expression of a more egalitarian social structure, because the Nahuat place a great deal of emphasis on order as an indication of relative status. On ceremonial occasions, for example, food and drinks are served to invited guests in order of their rank.

SUMMARY

The remainder of this book provides a fuller picture of the differences between Huitzilan and Yaonáhuac oral tradition established in this and the preceding chapters. It will be useful to summarize the major differences discussed so far. The stories from Huitzilan have undergone more Hispanic acculturation: they have fewer Aztec religious personalities and express a sharper dichotomy between humans and animals consistent with the culture of the dominant ethnic group. Parallel stories from Yaonáhuac have retained more Aztec-derived religious personalities and express a more intimate relationship between humans and animals. These differences have a direct connection to the degree of Nahuat identification with Aztec-derived personified and deified forces of nature and men's images of women.

The following chapter expands upon the Nahuat identification with their Aztec gods. It compares parallel stories to illustrate that those Nahuat who closely identify with lightning-bolts also depict these religious personalities assertively supporting the human moral order by punishing those who sin. It also provides a more complete picture of Nahuat sexual ideology by discussing the image of lightning-bolt women, who punish men, and the position of women in the family.

The support lightning-bolt women give to the moral order in stories rests on Nahuat men's general ideas of the moral nature of women and men. Chapter 10 compares biblically derived stories that define the essential natures of the sexes. The ideas about men and women contained in these stories illustrate why some Nahuat see women supporting the moral order, while others believe women threaten it.

Men's general ideas of the moral nature of women and men pivot on the ways the Nahuat from each community place women in metaphorical space. It has been noted that both groups conceive of the earth as a landmass with stylized spatial domains. The center is the domain of humans, which the Nahuat juxtapose against the periphery, which is a wild and asocial place. The tales compared in chapter 11 illustrate that some Nahuat—those who have a more symmetrical view of the sexes—generally regard men and women as nearly equally human and thus belonging toward the center of the Nahuat universe. But other Nahuat—those whose view of the sexes is more asymmetrical—place women toward the wild and stress their less socialized nature relative to men. Comparison of biblically derived stories reveals that the Nahuat with the asymmetrical sexual ideology have developed a woman-as-animal metaphor further to explain and elucidate the contrasting natures of men and women.

9. Lightning-bolts Who Punish Sin

Thou hast made thyself into a rabbit

A number of storytellers remarked that they consider it the main function of their oral tradition to uphold the Nahuat moral order. They tell numerous tales describing the horrible fates of those who refuse to conform to Nahuat standards of ethical and moral conduct. Their term for *story—neiškwitil* or *neiškwiltil*—means *lesson with moral significance,* and those who listen to stories direct most of their comments to the moral message.

Storytellers from both communities express the moral messages of their tales in similar fashion. They generally juxtapose the forest (the domain of animals) with the town (Nahuat civilization). They metaphorically describe how deviant persons find their destinies in the forest because they act like animals with uncontrolled impulses rather than socialized human beings with impulse control. They depict in gruesome detail how deviance can bring severe retaliation from the community: patricide is punished by burning alive; a woman's adultery brings her husband's brutal revenge; an adulterous man loses his penis in the beak of the diviner bird.

Hispanics altered Nahuat ethical and moral thought by introducing the concept of sin—the idea that breaking moral rules earns the wrath of the gods. Aside from blasphemy, few crimes were believed to bring direct punishment by the gods in pre-Hispanic Aztec thought (Vaillant 1966: 132). Those who broke moral rules did not await punishment in life after death because post-mortem destiny hinged more on how one died than on how one lived. Even sexual sin, such a concern to the Spanish, did not appear in Aztec belief before the Conquest. Sahagún's informants regarded sexual pleasure as a gift from the gods (Garibay 1970: 117). To be sure, the Aztec warned their daughters against sexual promiscuity and adultery, but they did not believe such behavior brought supernatural punishment. They sought to control sexual conduct with a deep concern for family honor, a sense of shame, and men's fear of dissipating their finite supply of sexual energy and thereby losing their ability to satisfy their wives' sexual voracity in old age (Garibay 1970: 117–128).

But the friars and the Hispanic settlers firmly established the concept of sin, particularly sexual sin, in Nahuat thought. The Nahuat have adopted the Hispanic idea that one's destiny after death depends on moral conduct in life. Sinners end up as slaves of the devil, who lives in a cave in the forest. The less tarnished go to paradise (*Talocan*), where *milpas* grow tall, animals graze on rich pastures, and one can buy things in stores much as one does in life on earth. Narrators from both communities tell numerous moralistic tales describing supernatural beings who punish the wayward and the evil. The gods who punish sin are the major ones in Nahuat belief—the sun (Jesus or God), the saints, and the lightning-bolts.

DIFFERENCES IN MORALITY TALES

The two Nahuat groups have developed different ways of telling the same morality tales because they have different images of the supernatural agents who punish sin. The Nahuat of both communities describe the sun (or Christ) and the saints punishing the immoral, but the Yaonáhuac Nahuat tell far more stories of lightning-bolts who uphold the moral order by dealing directly with sinners. This difference in narrative ethical thought derives partly from their more positive self-image as Indians, which they metaphorically express as powerful lightning-bolt deities. They accept, rather than reject, their Indianness, which they express in folktales by describing human characters developing more intimacy with lightning-bolt characters, and by depicting lightning-bolts upholding the Nahuat moral order. They tell more stories of semidivine characters transforming themselves into their lightning-bolt animal companion spirits to punish sin. These stories rest on the prevalent Nahuat belief of nagualism, a belief widespread in Mesoamerica (Villa Rojas 1947) that individuals can change into animals to correct immoral behavior as well as punish their enemies.

But lightning-bolts change into women as well as men, and thus their images in folktales also pivot on the position of women in Nahuat social structure. Women in Yaonáhuac folktales are generally more competent and supportive of the moral order than their counterparts in Huitzilan folktales because of their higher status. The more positive Yaonáhuac image of women translates into women as lightning-bolts who assertively correct the immoral behavior of men.

LIGHTNING-BOLTS IN COGNATE FOLKTALES

Narrators from both communities tell of lightning-bolts who punish humans for blasphemy: they tell of the great drought caused by
humans swearing at the lightning-bolts when they brought rain.[1]
But Yaonáhuac storytellers relate far more accounts of lightning-
bolts who uphold the moral order by punishing humans for other
sins. The comparable characters in the Huitzilan cognates of these
stories do not have lightning-bolt identities. Comparison of two
cognate stories—The Tiger in the Forest and The Adulterer—illustrates the difference between Huitzilan and Yaonáhuac morality
tales.

THE TIGER IN THE FOREST

The versions of this morality tale of attempted murder from the
two communities express the contrasting Nahuat self-images. The
hero is a man who personifies the Nahuat in the plural society. He
meets an evil man in the guise of a tiger who tries to eat him in
the forest. Narrators from Huitzilan and Yaonáhuac place the
aborted crime in the forest because they regard it as a place filled
with animal-like unbridled forces that can bring the destruction of
the Nahuat moral order. The forest is where the devil makes his
home, and it is the place of destiny for those who refuse to conform to the rules of Nahuat society. One Huitzilan narrator (Huitzilan version 1) turns the central conflict between the hero and the
tiger into an ethnic struggle between Hispanics and Indians by
giving the hero clear Nahuat identity and making the tiger his
Hispanic patron. But only in the Yaonáhuac tale does the hero kill
the tiger by turning into a lightning-bolt. His counterpart in the
Huitzilan story must use an Hispanic tool—a rifle—to do the same
job.

HUITZILAN VERSION 1

*1. One day a man went to work in the highlands, where he found
a patron, for whom he worked many days. Then he decided to ask
for his pay: "I want my wages." "Why not?" replied his patron,
who added, "But wouldn't you like to go hunting first, and get
some meat from the forest?" "With pleasure," said the man. His
patron gave him a fine gun, and the man knew a lot about arms.*

*2. They went into the forest, where the patron said, "Now you
wait here. I'm going to walk around for a bit." He departed and*

circled around, taking the dogs with him. That patron was evil. He decided to become a man-eating beast [tekwani] and said to himself, "I'm going to eat that worker so I won't have to pay him."

3. *Meanwhile, the worker waited. He thought he heard the dogs barking, but they didn't come near him. Then he heard a beast screaming, and he thought, "It's going to eat me." He listened as the screaming came closer. "If God wants it to eat me, it'll eat me," he thought. Then he saw it. A huge beast burst out of the forest.*

4. *The man fired a shot, but the beast didn't fall. It didn't fall until the fifth bullet. The man went back to his patron's house and spoke to the patron's wife, saying, "Has the patron returned?" "No," she said. Then the man told her, "Well, he just left me in the forest and he didn't come back for me. A man-eating beast was about to eat me, but I shot it." Then that lady [šinola] became angry because she knew what her husband was doing to the workers. He worked them but he didn't pay them. He took them to the forest and there he ate them. "Pay me," demanded the man. "No, I won't," said the woman. So then he told the other workers, and they forced her to pay him.*

5. *Then they went to skin the beast. They split open the hide and found the patron's clothes inside. The workers told the man it was a good thing he killed their patron because he was always doing this to his workers.* STORYTELLER N. A. H.

HUITZILAN VERSION 2

1. *A man was in the plaza of this hacienda. The hacienda was like a town with a plaza, someone in authority, and a judge. He met another man, who asked him, "You also go on the hunt, don't you? Don't you go after badger and whatever other animals?" The first man replied, "I do." The second man said, "Well, I know that there is a tiger in that forest. The hacienda owner is bringing his calves [and the tiger might eat them]." "Really?" said the first man. "Really!" replied the second, who added, "Well, we really looked for it, but we couldn't find it, but I know where it is. If you want to, let's go." The first man said, "I'll go. Just let me make some purchases in the plaza and we'll go." He made his purchases, and they went to his house. The first man said to the second, "Wait for me here. I'm going to get my gun." He went to his house and found his gun. He removed one of the hairs from his head and put it into the barrel, along with some tobacco and some garlic. He rejoined the second man, who was waiting for him in*

the road. The second man asked, "Is this the gun? Let me see it."
He looked it all over. "Fine," said the second man, who added,
"Let's go."

2. The second man, who invited the first man to go with him
into the forest, had a serape, a knife, and a pouch [morral]. They
went into the mouth of the forest, and the second man said, "You
go that way and I'll go this way. If you find it, you call me, and if I
find it, I'll call you."

3. So they went off, and the one who had the gun found it first.
But it wasn't really a tiger. The first man stooped under a big tree
and watched. When he saw the tiger coming, he thought, "That
tiger comes from where my companion went. But how shall I call
him without that animal coming to eat me?"

4. So he didn't call his companion and quickly aimed his rifle
and fired a shot. God had decided the tiger wouldn't eat him, and
so it was to be that he shot the tiger in the forehead. So there that
animal fell.

5. He thought, "Well, what shall I do with this animal? It's
big. Now where did my companion go? It'd be better for me to
skin it while he is returning." He quickly opened up the animal to
skin it. He opened it up across its belly and there he saw the hat,
the serape, the knife, and the sandals of his companion. That man
had turned into a tiger.

6. He reflected, "Now I'm not going to skin it. I'm going to tell
the authorities." He went back to the hacienda, and he immediately
spoke to the judge. He told the judge exactly what happened. How
he came to the plaza. How that man had taken him, saying he knew
where the tiger was in the forest. How he found the man's things
inside the animal. They went to see the tiger. Many went, and they
made a wooden stretcher and brought the animal [to the haci-
enda]. They gave a lot of things to the man who shot it. They gave
him a house. They gave him cattle. He was sitting pretty. The end.

STORYTELLER D. A.

YAONÁHUAC VERSION

1. Once there were some of our brothers from the highlands—a
man and his son. The man, who was a diviner, knew there was
work in the coffee harvest in Cuetzalan after All Saints' day [No-
vember 1]. So he went to Cuetzalan, where he found some humble
people [masewalme] who owned a coffee orchard, and he asked
them for work. They gave work to the diviner, who was like a
lightning-bolt. His patron had a tiger as an animal companion

spirit [tonal]. After about eight days, the highlander asked for his wages to buy some clothes. But his patron said, "No. I won't have money until I sell the coffee. I'll sell it in about a month and a half." So the highlander continued working for another month and a half. He asked for his money again, but his patron said, "I still don't have it." But his patron did not want to pay him, because he was evil. He just wanted to work his men without giving them their wages. The highlander was angry, and he quarreled with his patron, saying, "Either give me the money or don't give me the money!" His patron replied, "Do you want to take the money from me by force?!" They got angry with each other and exchanged more angry words.

2. Then the highlander picked up his satchel and his clothes and returned home. He went on foot because there were no cars then. His patron warned, "It'd be better if you go home, or I'll cut you up with my machete." Then he added, "But we'll see each other on the road." There was a big forest near the home of the man from Cuetzalan.

3. A big tiger appeared in the road the highlander was taking, and the highlander declared to his son, "O son, there [is our patron, who] is going to pay us our wages. You stay here for a moment. Wait for me. That animal is sleeping. Don't make a sound. I'm going on an errand and I'll come back to you in a moment."

4. Then the boy saw a cloud and saw his father rise up into it. His father rode inside that cloud on the wind, and he killed that tiger with a bolt of lightning. It wasn't long, perhaps a quarter of an hour, and the highlander returned. "Grab your satchel and let's go, because that animal is dead," he told his son, adding, "That's the man from Cuetzalan—our patron. He didn't pay us. Let it be enough that his animal companion spirit died. The moment this animal died our patron died." STORYTELLER F. V.

Narrators express the ethnic hierarchy or egalitarianism of their communities by the way they identify the characters and the way they develop the central conflict beween the tiger and the man. Both Huitzilan narrators express the ethnic hierarchy of their social structure by including both Indian and Hispanic characters. The narrator of the first version makes the Indian identity of the protagonist certain by describing him as a migrant worker, nearly all of whom are Nahuat rather than Hispanics in the northern Sierra (item 1). He assigns Hispanic identity to the evil patron by describing his wife as a lady, using the term *šinola*, which means *Hispanic woman* (item 4). The narrator of the second Huitzilan version stages some of the action in a prerevolutionary hacienda, a clear symbol of an Hispanically dominated society (item 1).

But the Nahuat, like other Indian groups in Mexico (Colby 1966), both resent and identify with the dominant ethnic group, and the two Huitzilan narrators, who probably feel this more deeply than their Yaonáhuac counterparts, express both sides of their ambivalence. The first Huitzilan narrator expresses the negative side by having the Indian worker kill the Hispanic patron (item 4). The second narrator expresses the positive side by turning the conflict into a contest between two lower-status persons and adding the rags-to-riches ending to his story. He has the protagonist given many valuable things—a house and cattle—by the owner of the hacienda for saving his livestock (item 6). The narrator probably includes cattle because they are an obvious symbol for Hispanic wealth and power. Spaniards brought cattle to Mexico after the Conquest, and many Hispanics who settled in Huitzilan converted into pastures large tracts of highly visible land on the slopes of the mountains. These tracts remind the Nahuat of the vast quantities of land they lost to the Hispanics in the last 100 years.

The Yaonáhuac narrator expresses the more egalitarian social structure of his community by including no Hispanic characters either in the main plot or in the background of his story. His tale is about humble people (*masewalme*), meaning the Nahuat (item 1). The action takes place between Yaonáhuac and Cuetzalan, a large *municipio* consisting of many Nahuat to the northwest in the lowland coffee zone (item 1). A number of people from Yaonáhuac actually used to travel to the Sunday market and work in the coffee orchards of Cuetzalan before the paved highway made Tezuitlán more accessible.

It is interesting that the hero of this tale acts more assertively with his evil patron than his counterpart in the Huitzilan tale (see version 2). He argues, he gets angry, he and his patron exchange angry words, and they threaten each other (item 1), and the hero finally kills his patron, who became a tiger (item 4). Characters standing for the Nahuat in Huitzilan tales are much less assertive with characters representing Hispanics, mirroring their actual subdued behavior with the dominant group. The protagonist in the first Huitzilan version kills his Hispanic patron, an assertive act to be sure, but unlike his counterpart in the Yaonáhuac version, he does so without knowing the tiger's true human identity (item 4).

THE ADULTERER

The second set of cognate tales consists of two versions of a story about a married man who commits adultery while working as a migrant on a plantation in the hot country. The story focuses on a common moral dilemma created by the long absence of migrant laborers who travel to the coastal plain and stay away from their homes for months at a time. The Huitzilan and Yaonáhuac versions of this story express both the contrasting self-images of the Nahuat as a class and men's images of women for the two groups.

The stronger Yaonáhuac self-image comes through in the way the storyteller from this community describes punishment for the migrant worker's adultery. He describes a lightning-bolt taking the form of a snake and wrapping around the adulterer's neck, giving him a severe case of magical fright. This is another case of the stronger Yaonáhuac self-image expressed as a lightning-bolt god, who upholds the moral order by directly inflicting punishment on sinners.

The two versions capture the contrasting images of women in the way the storytellers from Huitzilan and Yaonáhuac describe the sexual identity of the character who inflicts punishment. The stronger image of women in Yaonáhuac thought is evident in the way the Yaonáhuc narrator has the adulterer's semidivine wife change into her lightning-bolt animal companion spirit to punish her wayward husband directly and assertively. The Huitzilan narrator expresses a more passive image of women by describing the father of a girl deceived by the adulterer taking revenge for the wrong done to his daughter.

HUITZILAN VERSION

1. *One time two men from Tachco [a small hamlet near Huitzilan known for the manufacture of wooden spoons] went to the lowlands to work. Their patron had a daughter, and one of the men found her pleasing. He told her he would serve [marry] her, and so it was that he stayed there for a long time. After a while, he decided to go home to see his father and mother. He went home and did not return, and those in the girl's house grew impatient. The girl was all alone waiting for him to come back.*

2. *One day another man from Tachco went to the lowlands to sell spoons. He passed by the house where the girl's family lived and asked if they would buy some of his wares. They said, "Yes, we'll buy some, but where are you from?" The spoon-seller replied,*

"I'm from Tachco." The girl's parents asked, "Well, there was a man who came here who said he too was from Tachco. Do you know him?" The spoon-seller said, "Yes, I know him." The girl's father [probably] said, "Well, he hasn't returned. He lied, saying he was going away for a short time to visit his father and mother, and he said he would come right back. He has a wife here. We gave him this girl. He said he didn't have a woman there." But to that the spoon-seller said, "No, he does have a woman there. He has children too."

3. The girl's parents said, "Well, we really loved that man so much, here is a loin cloth [that we've made for him]. We want to send it to him so that he can wrap himself with it. Take it to him, if you'll do us this favor." They gave it to him wrapped in a handkerchief, and they said, "Don't go to his house to deliver it. Call to him from far away in the road so that he'll come to meet you. Just show him a little of [the loin cloth], and then give it to him and get out of there quickly." And that is just what he did. He left it with the first man from Tachco, who felt it grow heavy. The loincloth had turned into a snake, and when he opened the handkerchief, the snake bit him. He died, and the handkerchief turned into an owl [kwošašaka]. When they held the wake, the owl perched above the house and screeched and screeched until the man was buried. After they buried him, the owl went to the lowlands and announced, "Yes, now it's done. They've buried him."

STORYTELLER D. A.

YAONÁHUAC VERSION

1. Once there was a member of the work gang [cuadrilla] whose wife had very strong blood. His wife adored him. She never did a bad thing to her husband because he never hit her, he never scolded her, he never swore at her, and he never criticized her work. And then one time, the man went to work in the work gang. He stayed there for a long time, not just for a day or a few months, but for a year. He didn't like working [in the highlands] because wages were low. The time came when that man found a sweetheart.

2. There was gossip as always, and one of the companions of the cook—the cook was his sweetheart—told the man's wife about his infidelity. But the wife said, "Well, he wouldn't do it because I know the man. We have children, and the man never gets angry and is never drunk." However she was really angry, although she acted as if nothing had happened.

3. *Then one day her husband announced, "I'm going to the work gang again." The little woman said, "Fine." That little man was a little proud of what he knew. Even though he didn't know something, he would thrust himself forward as if he did. Then the work gang came across some snakes—some horrible, vile ones. The man boasted, "I grab them when they're alive." But his companions warned, "Well, we don't grab them, because we're people from earth. We'll die if they bite us because they have poison." Well, that man grabbed one of the snakes anyway, and he wrapped it around himself as if it were a necktie. The snake which he wrapped around his neck was really his wife. Because she was kind of a diviner, she turned herself into a snake in the pasture when her husband slept with his sweetheart. The others just stared at him in fear. He stood apart from his companions, who surrounded him and watched to see what would happen. He tried to remove the snake from his neck, but he couldn't do it. The snake tightened its grip, and the man's eyes popped out as he felt the snake coil more tightly.*

4. *His companions declared, "We must remove the snake because if the labor recruiter, or the authorities, or his wife see it, they'll think we did this to him out of nastiness." One of the companions warned, "If we hit it with a machete, we'll cut the man's throat. If we poke it with a machete, it'll be the same. If we hit it with clubs, we'll also kill the man." There was a guasima tree nearby, and its branches were like hooks. They cut two hooks, each two meters in length, because the companions were afraid of the snake—it was big. One hook was put on one side of the man, and the other hook was put on the other. Some pulled from the left side, and others pulled from the right side. There they were like buzzards grabbing a piece of dead horse flesh. They removed the snake. The man was almost white. He was frightened by that snake because it was cold. The snake slithered off after they threw it onto the ground. A marksman shot at it, but the bullets didn't strike it.*

5. *Fever grabbed the man, and he said, "I'd better go home because I can't work. Fever has grabbed hold of me because of the scare from that snake." He lived around Zacapoaxtla [the* cabecera *of the former district which lies between Tetela de Ocampo and Tlatlauqui], and so he came home by bus. He came home, but he couldn't find his wife. He returned to the lowlands looking for her, but his companions told him to return home. The man went back home for the second time and found his wife. "Why did you come home?" she asked. "I came because fever grabbed me. I didn't feel*

right in that place because it was so hot. I came looking for you, but you weren't here," the man said. "Let me feel if you are really ill," said his wife. The man wasn't ill anymore. The wife said, "Look, why didn't that woman you have in the work gang cure you? She's the reason I gave you the lesson [neiškwitil]. I was the snake you wrapped around your neck. I wasn't here when you came home so that you would realize what happened; so that you'd obey me. If you're thinking of looking for your sweetheart, then the fever won't leave you. But if you stay here, you won't have the fever." That man didn't go back to the work gang even though he could earn more money working there than here.

STORYTELLER F. V.

The Yaonáhuac narrator develops the semidivine lightning-bolt identity of the adulterer's wife in a variety of ways. He says she has strong blood (item 1), he indicates she is clairvoyant (item 3), and he tells how bullets cannot kill her snake animal companion spirit (item 4). It is interesting that snake symbolism is just the opposite in the two versions of this story. The snake is a comparatively positive symbol in the Yaonáhuac tale: it is the animal companion spirit (*tonal*) of a virtuous lightning-bolt woman who draws her wayward husband back into the moral order. But the snake has an entirely negative connotation in the Huitzilan version of this story: it is an instrument of witchcraft carried out with diabolical intervention. The Huitzilan narrator makes it clear that the girl's father invoked the devil by mentioning the owl (*kwošašaka*) (item 3), whom the Nahuat regard as the devil's helper.

The snake was an ambivalent symbol for the ancient Aztecs, a fact apparent from examining their anthropomorphized snake gods. On the one hand is the very ominous Snake Woman, Cihuacoatl, who gave men the hoe and the tumpline and made them work (Sahagún 1950: 3). On the other is the Feathered Serpent, Quetzalcoatl, a figure with a benevolent side who created the race of humans and helped obtain their sustenance in the last creation (Paso y Troncoso 1903: 28–30; Brundage 1979: 102–128). I suspect the friars and Hispanics attached negative value to snakes, once regarded as ambivalent in pre-Hispanic Nahuat thought. Since the Huitzilan Nahuat have experienced greater pressure to change their thought to conform to that of the dominant group, they have more completely suppressed the positive side of their ambivalent attitude toward snakes in oral tradition.

The two narrators depict very different images of women concordant with the position of women in the social structure. The Huitzilan narrator reflects the comparatively weak position of women in his community by making women characters peripheral to the plot. He depicts the major conflict taking place between the adulterer and the girl's parents, and he uses the male spoon-seller as an intermediary who delivers the instrument of death (the loin cloth turned poisonous snake).

The Yaonáhuac narrator, on the other hand, reflects the stronger position of women in his community by making the wronged woman a powerful character (a lightning-bolt) and by giving her a more central place in the story. He describes how the wife directly corrects her husband's deviant behavior, and he uses an interesting metaphor linking the husband's moral conduct with the state of his physical health. He describes the wife telling her husband that if he returns to the work gang and takes up again with the cook, he will fall ill with fever, but if he stays with her, he will enjoy good health (item 5).

This narrator also makes the principal female character a woman of virtue by telling how she adored her husband and never did a bad thing to him (item 1), and by describing her showing restraint when told of his infidelity (item 2). He contraposes the virtuous wife to the wayward husband with an interesting synecdoche in which the husband's sexual promiscuity stands for other kinds of deviant behavior. He tells how the adulterer is also arrogant of his knowledge and thus acts in ways uncharacteristic of ordinary people. The narrator develops his distinctiveness by telling how he grabs the snake, something ordinary people (taltikpakwani) would not do (item 3). He tells how, after the snake wrapped herself around his neck, he stood apart from his companions much as an arrogant person would alienate himself from Nahuat society (item 3). The following chapter describes how Huitzilan narrators tend to depict women as the less virtuous sex.

ASSERTIVE WOMEN IN OTHER STORIES

Comparison of cognate versions of The Adulterer shows that women have a stronger image in the Yaonáhuac story, and this probably stems from the stronger actual position of women in the family of this community. The adulterer's wife is assertive—she directly punishes her husband for his infidelity—and assertive women characters appear more often in other narratives from Yaonáhuac. Women characters in the folktales from this community more frequently take the initiative, play a stronger role in decision making, affect to a greater degree the outcome of action, and win contests with and apply punishments to men. To be sure, women are generally less assertive than men in the bulk of the cognate narratives from both Huit-

Table 24. The Assertiveness of Women in Cognate Tales, by Community

Name of narrative in appendix 1	Story no.	Episode no.	Summary of episode	
			Huitzilan version	Yaonáhuac version
Women characters openly assertive with their husbands				
The Lazy Husband	3–4	4	The wife applies no punishment to her lazy husband turned sparrow-hawk.	The wife punishes her lazy husband turned buzzard by chasing him away and refusing to let her buzzard turned husband feed him.
Women characters openly assertive with their fathers				
The Man Who Won the Hacienda	19–20	3	A boy who never bathes and wears a tunic enters a princess's bedroom by pulling on a rope that she dropped for her suitor. Her father catches the boy in the girl's bedroom and declares she must marry him, like it or not.	A charcoal-seller enters a princess's bedroom by pulling on a rope that she dropped for her suitor. The girl receives him and has him bathe and put on new clothes, and she presents him to her father as the man she wants to marry. Her father accepts him as his son-in-law.
The Fisherman	21–23	4	A gentleman offers his daughter to a man who is searching for his brother locked in a mountain (story 21). A man is given the daughter of a general because he kills a twelve-headed serpent (story 22).	When the first of three brothers passes by a large house with a girl standing in the upper window, the girl tells her father that she wants to marry him. Her father sends soldiers to bring the man to her.

zilan and Yaonáhuac. This is consistent with the male-dominant family that prevails in both communities. But Yaonáhuac storytellers describe women as more assertive than comparable characters in cognate narratives from Huitzilan. Table 24 presents tale segments from a variety of storytellers from both communities and indicates a consistent difference between Huitzilan and Yaonáhuac cognates for the variable of women's assertiveness.

10. Adam and Eve

The harlot

The Nahuat tell more stories about sexual sin than any other kind. Their term for sin (*tahtakol*) primarily connotes sexual relations between unmarried partners. They have little tolerance for sexual promiscuity on the part of either men or women. They apply their term for a sexually promiscuous person (*kalayon*) to both sexes, and they express their disapproval of promiscuity by asserting that the sexually loose among them have dogs for animal companion spirits, because they believe dogs mate indiscriminately. Their concern with sexual sin derives from the disruptive effects of adultery accusations on their social order. Men readily believe their wives will be unfaithful if given the chance, and they are quick to defend their honor by grabbing their machetes. Women, who have equal intolerance for men's dalliance, are quick to take their complaints to the *municipio* authorities to punish their promiscuous husbands.

The Nahuat attempt to control the moral conduct of husbands and wives by surrounding themselves with a network of ritual kin for whom they hold an exceedingly rigid incest prohibition. The Nahuat believe their ritual kin will uphold the moral order by exerting pressure on their spouses to conform to the Nahuat standards of sexual conduct and by reporting cases of sexual deviance.

Nevertheless, despite their vigilance and that of their compadres, opportunities for sexual promiscuity frequently arise. Men spend many weeks and even months working as migrants in the lowlands. They pick up with loose women in the hot country, and their wives sometimes find lovers in the home community. Sexual infidelity, a major concern in real life, is excellent stuff for myths.

SEXUAL SIN BY MEN VS. WOMEN

Nahuat men, like their counterparts elsewhere (see Blaffer 1972; Collier 1974; Turner 1974; Dwyer 1978*a*, 1978*b*), regard women as the more sexually threatening sex. They believe women are more sexually voracious, morally weaker, and a greater danger to the moral order than men. They express their view of women in myths about the origin of the sun and the moon in which they assert a man became the sun and a woman became the moon. This metaphor expresses the strength of men because it links men with the heat and light from the sun, the prime moving forces that bring moral order out of chaos. It expresses the weakness of women by connecting them with the forces of darkness and cold which work to undermine the Nahuat moral order.

A number of factors contribute to the image of women as morally weak and sexually threatening. Chapter 8 illustrated that this androcentric sexual ideology develops in part from men's weak position in the plural social structure. The Nahuat who have a generally weak position relative to Hispanics develop an androcentric sexual ideology to compensate for their comparatively low status. Such an ideology supports androcentric patterns of family life and enhances the position of men relative to women by justifying why men should control the family estate.

It has also been pointed out that this sexual ideology is isomorphic with androcentric patterns of family life that stem from factors over which Nahuat men have little control. One such factor is the general scarcity of land, which promotes patrilineal land inheritance throughout the northern Sierra de Puebla. Because men control the bulk of the strategic resources, because there is more agnatic male solidarity with virilocality, and because men are older than their wives, the balance between the sexes tilts toward male dominance. When women are subordinate, they cannot easily contradict male authority openly and so they must exert their influence on family decision making more indirectly than men. To be sure, some women are assertive with their husbands, and it is also true that the status of women changes with age. It is lowest when a woman marries into her husband's parental family household. It improves when the couple establishes their own independent domicile, and it increases further when a woman becomes the mother-in-law to her sons' wives. It reaches its highest point when a woman becomes the custodian for the patrimonial land after her husband's death. But at all stages in the cycle, the position of the Nahuat woman is weaker than that of the man at comparable stages. To be sure, men have a more positive image of the women who are their mothers, because women who have attained a high rank in the social structure are believed to represent less of a threat to the moral order (Taggart 1977: 299–300). But I contend that when women have a generally weaker structural position, they must be indirect and secretive with the dominant sex, and this contributes to their image as sexually voracious and threatening. One spectacular form of indirect and secretive deviance is sexual promiscuity, and Nahuat men both hold this as a real worry and also turn it into a dramatic metaphor in their tales to connote a variety of other forms of disobedience on the part of their women.

Women appear to help maintain this androcentric sexual ideology because the social structure places some women in conflict with others. The prevailing practice of virilocality places a mother in conflict with her sons' wives. A young bride normally spends the first years of her marriage with her husband's parental family. Nahuat mothers, like their counterparts elsewhere (see Foster 1948; Lewis 1951; Nutini 1968; Vogt 1969; Chang 1970; Collier 1974), are very jealous of their daughters-in-law. By offering sex, young brides have alienated their sons' affections, and mothers frequently retaliate by criticizing the work of their daughters-in-law and attacking their moral character. Quarrels between the two can tear the patrilocal extended family apart here, just as it can elsewhere (Collier 1974: 93). The Nahuat try to ameliorate tension in this relationship by dividing the kitchens and splitting the work routines of women, without dividing the granary and splitting the extended family household (Taggart 1972: 137–138). Nevertheless, the mother-in-law and daughter-in-law conflict, which has a sexual basis, remains a major reason the Nahuat regard women as sexually threatening.

The Yaonáhuac Nahuat appear to have less need to develop as pronounced a male-dominant sexual ideology for several reasons. They have less need to compensate for their status in the class hierarchy because they depend less heavily on Hispanic patronage and have more control over their community government. A shift toward bilaterality and other exogenous changes have promoted more egalitarian sexual relations in the family. Because Yaonáhuac women acquire more land through inheritance, they can play a more direct role in family decision making. They have less need to resort to covert tactics that men find threatening to exert their influence in family affairs. Thus men have less need to describe women as less socialized and more animal-like than men. To be sure, women do not acquire as much land through inheritance as men, and patrilocal residence creates tensions between a mother and her daughter-in-law that disrupt and threaten family unity. For this reason, Yaonáhuac men probably attribute some animal traits to their women. But as women assumed a more direct role in family decision making by virtue of their greater control over strategic resources, men appear to have responded by developing a more symmetrical sexual ideology.

ADAM AND EVE

A number of cognate stories in the oral tradition of Huitzilan and Yaonáhuac express the contrasting images of women for the two Nahuat groups. The most important of these is the biblical myth of Adam and Eve, which the friars introduced to the Nahuat in the seventeenth century. For most Nahuat, this myth describes the creation of the first man and woman at the beginning of the First Era of Creation and establishes the essential moral character of the sexes. Four versions of this story—two from each community—follow.

HUITZILAN VERSION 1

1. Adam was the sole survivor after the flood. When he made a fire to heat his tortillas, smoke rose to the heavens and reached Jesus. First, Jesus sent the sparrow-hawk to discover who made the fire, but the sparrow-hawk could not find who it was. Then Jesus sent the buzzard, but when it reached the earth, it ate the flesh of the dead animals and people and became soiled. So it could not return to heaven. 2. Then Jesus sent the hummingbird, who found Adam alone, without a wife to make his tortillas. Jesus visited Adam, who asked for a wife. Jesus felt sorry for him, and so he told Adam to sleep, and 4. he made Eve out of Adam's rib. When Jesus presented Eve to Adam, he said to Adam, "Have only one woman. And you, Eve, have only one man." 3. Jesus told Adam, "I didn't really want to give you a wife because that will mean many will be planted, causing me to bear a lot of sin, and I won't be able to endure it." Adam replied, "I don't want to sin. I just want to eat, to have clean clothes, and to have someone to keep me clean." So it was, and Jesus returned to the heavens. 13. But one day Eve decided to do the laundry [in the river], and a muleteer spoke to her, saying, "Run away with me." Eve refused, telling him that he was a drunk and Adam didn't drink and he supported her well. She told the muleteer that Jesus told her not to have two men and that if she did, she would be punished. But she deceived Adam and had the muleteer's child. 14. Within a year, Jesus came to tell Eve that she behaved badly and that now he was bearing her sin. To punish them both, he gave them skins to wear. And so they were. 20. Jesus returned to the heavens, and after that, Eve had a child every two years until she couldn't plant anymore. She had ten children. Each woman had ten children until there were many. Afterwards, Adam decided to marry her, and when they had their marriage celebration, the muleteer died from too much aguardiente.   STORYTELLER J. H.

HUITZILAN VERSION 2

Long ago, there was a great God in heaven but there was no earth, only an abyss. But God decided to make the earth for his children. 1. After he made the earth, he made Adam. 2. But God saw that Adam was tired of living alone, and so he had Adam sit down and sleep. 4. He removed a rib and made a companion, a woman. When Adam awoke, she was there. They were nude. They lived together for a long time and grew accustomed to each other. God told them that there were many things in the big orchard, and that there were good things and bad things. He told them to eat only certain things, and then he returned to heaven. Then the devil came along and tricked them. He told them not to believe God, and he told them that there was this apple which was good to eat. He told them that if they ate it, they would remember more [they would be wiser]. He told them to abandon God and not to believe God because he was tricking them. The devil said to watch as he ate it and see if he would die. 6. The devil began eating the apple, and it is said that Eve also ate it. 5. After they ate it, the devil changed form and sat in tree with an apple in his mouth. 9. Eve decided that she liked it [eating the apple]. 7. Then the apple was given to Adam to eat. It was put in his mouth. But Adam said that his father told him not to eat it. 12. After he ate it, the apple stuck in his throat, and then the devil went away. 9. And they liked it now. Eve liked it. They went to where they saw the apple and pulled it down rapidly and cut it. But the tree left them and went to heaven and reached God, who came right away and found Eve eating the apple. 10. Adam quickly hid, and so God only found Eve. Afterwards, Adam and Eve were ashamed. 11. God told Eve that since she received the devil and gave him her hand when he greeted her, she would serve him. He told them that she sinned. 14. He said that Eve would bear all her children with great pain. She would bear her children inside her. 19. She would show all of the animals how to seed themselves. 15. He told Adam that he would work to eat. He told Eve that she would have sons and daughters, but with much punishment. Eve was sad, but what could she do?
                                    STORYTELLER J. P.

YAONÁHUAC VERSION 1

One time God our father had a fruit orchard. But in that orchard
he had a tree of pears. He left Adam there to care for it. 1. God
formed Adam from mud. 2. He left him in the orchard so that no
one would enter it. Adam was alone and had no one to talk to. So
he just slept all day long. That animal came, walking around to
see if the caretaker was taking care of things. So the devil told
God that Adam wasn't a caretaker because he just slept. The devil
said that was because he needed a woman companion to talk to.
The devil told God to go see Adam, who would be sleeping at two
in the afternoon. So God came to the orchard and found Adam
fast asleep. 4. He removed a rib and formed mother Eve and laid
her to one side of Adam. When they awoke, Adam didn't know
whence she came. Before, Adam's ribs were complete, but now
our rib is cut in half because mother Eve came from there. Adam
and Eve lived together, they talked to each other, and they looked
after the orchard. Then the animal went to the orchard and told
them to eat the fruit, telling them that it was very good. But
[Adam] said no because God our father told him not to eat it.
They could eat other fruit as much as they wanted. The devil said
that God didn't want them to eat it because if they did, then they
would win over him by a degree. And he cut it for them to eat. 6.
and 8. Mother Eve ate it, but secretly. They both ate it. She was in
the middle of eating it when God found her. So mother Eve swallowed it. And father Adam swallowed it. 12. He tried to put a big
one in his mouth, but he couldn't and it stuck in his throat, where
it remains as our Adam's apple. God shouted at them. The fruit
stuck in Adam's throat, and Adam couldn't answer him. As for
mother Eve, the fruit she ate passed through her throat and now
forms her breasts. She didn't have them when she was born, but
when she began to grow up, her breasts grew. 15. God said that
now they had eaten it, they had to work. 16. Then the animal
returned and decided, the story says, to make them have sex. He
lay mother Eve down and told Adam to place himself over her.
But they didn't know how to do it. They just grabbed each other
without touching. So the animal showed them. 17. Adam got
down and he liked it. Father Adam liked it. And then God our
father caught them and asked what they were doing. No one answered. God caught them giving sin to the world. Before, the
world was clean. Adam said to Eve that they should ask their
father for forgiveness. 18. But Sr. Santiago hit Adam with his
sword and made him swollen. He told him that he was not going

*to help them anymore because they had given sin [to the world].
20. He said that they were now going to fill up the world with
people. For that reason, there are people everywhere.*

STORYTELLER F. J.

YAONÁHUAC VERSION 2

*Long ago there was no earth. When God our father existed before
us, no one lived on earth. This earth was dark. When God our
father decided to make the earth, the heaven was not blue as it
is now [it was dark]. 1. God decided to make a man first, so he
formed him out of a ball of mud. He moistened the earth and
made a ball of mud and formed an image. Then he stood it up and
he put life into it, but the man couldn't talk. So God our father
told the Holy Ghost to make the man talk, and so the Holy Ghost
went into the man's mouth, and the man spoke. 2. The man was
alone on earth. It was dark. At that time, there was also the devil,
and the devil wanted to marry the man. The devil tricked him,
telling the man to marry him. God didn't want the man to obey
the devil, so he decided it was not good that Adam was alone. So
God decided to make a woman, a companion whom we call "our
wife." But long ago she was known as a companion. 4. When
Adam fell asleep, God removed a bone from Adam's left side and
made a woman for Adam out of the bone. He removed the bone
from under his arm. So Adam and the woman awoke together. But
God punished them, because he didn't give them permission to be
in a garden where there was fruit which they were not to eat. But
that animal, the demon, tried to win him over, even though Adam
was now with a woman. The devil told Adam that they ought to
get married. Adam told the devil that if he wanted to get married,
someone must bring water for the celebration. The devil offered to
bring the water, and Adam gave him a basket with which to bring
it to fill the cauldron. But when the devil returned with the basket, nothing fell into the cauldron because all the water had run
out. So by the time the chicken crowed, the cauldron wasn't full.
So the devil went away. But as always, the devil worked to win
over Adam, and so he offered him fruit from the garden. 7. But
Adam refused because God didn't give him permission. The devil
told him to eat it anyway, because no one would know. He said
that God wouldn't see him. 5. and 6. The devil climbed into the
tree and cut it and gave it to the woman from above. The man ate
it too. The woman swallowed the fruit, and just as the man cut it
and ate it, God caught them. God asked them what they were*

doing, and why they were in the garden. 12. God startled Adam as he swallowed the fruit, and so it stuck in his throat. As for the woman, who had already swallowed it, the fruit remained as her breasts. God abandoned them because they sinned. 15. He told them to go away forever from the garden and find something to eat for themselves. That is the reason we work in order to eat. We are in another place that is not the same place as where we were, where our ancestors named father Adam and mother Eve were.

STORYTELLER L. V.

SIMILARITIES

The images of Adam and Eve in the four tales fit closely with the male-dominant family system that prevails in both communities, but they also vary with the differences in the position of women. Table 25 contains key items abstracted from the tales that illustrate the similarities and the differences between versions from Huitzilan and Yaonáhuac.

The four storytellers express the male-dominant family common to both communities in a variety of ways. All place Adam on the earth before Eve, and they depict how a divine agent made Eve from Adam's rib. All describe Eve as morally weaker than Adam, although they do it in different ways. Storyteller F. J., for instance, links Eve with the devil and immorality by depicting God making Eve at the devil's suggestion. J. H. does it by depicting Eve, but not Adam, breaking the rule of monogamy. J. P., F. J., and L. V. all have Eve eating the forbidden fruit before Adam. Both J. P. (Huitzilan) and L. V. (Yaonáhuac) depict Adam, but not Eve, resisting temptation by initially refusing the apple, pear, or forbidden fruit. J. P. describes God telling Eve that she will serve the devil for accepting the fruit from him.

The three storytellers who depict Eve accepting the forbidden fruit before Adam not only imply that she is the morally weaker of the two, but they also mean that she has a greater inclination toward sexual deviance, because eating the fruit is a metaphor for sexual intercourse for the Nahuat for a number of reasons. When the devil climbs the tree to offer Eve the fruit (see versions of J. P. and L. V.), he places himself above her as a man places himself above a woman in the Nahuat position for sexual intercourse. Eating has a link to sex because eating and conception have a connection in Nahuat belief: if a woman eats a twin fruit or vegetable, for example, she may have twins. When Adam and Eve eat the apple, L. V. describes them as sinning (*tahtakoke* = they sinned), a Na-

Table 25. Summaries of Adam and Eve Tales, by Community and Storyteller

| | Huitzilan | | Yaonáhuac | |
	Storyteller J. H.	Storyteller J. P.	Storyteller F. J.	Storyteller L. V.
1.	Adam survives the flood.	God makes Adam first.	God forms Adam from mud.	God makes Adam from a ball of mud.
2.	Jesus decides to make Eve because Adam has no one to make his tortillas.	God decides to make Eve because he sees that Adam is tired of living alone.	At the devil's suggestion, God decides to make Eve to keep Adam awake and make him a better caretaker of the orchard.	God decides to make Eve to prevent Adam from marrying the devil.
3.	Jesus is reluctant to give Adam a wife because that would mean many would be planted, and then he would have to bear a heavy burden of sin.			
4.	Jesus makes Eve from Adam's rib.	God makes Eve from Adam's rib.	God makes Eve from Adam's rib.	God makes Eve from Adam's rib.
5.		The devil changes form and sits in a tree with an apple in his mouth.		The devil climbs a tree and offers the forbidden fruit to Eve from above.
6.		Eve eats the apple before Adam.	Eve eats the pear before Adam.	Eve eats the forbidden fruit before Adam.
7.		Adam resists when the devil offers him the apple.		Adam resists when the devil offers him the forbidden fruit.
8.			Eve eats the pear secretly.	
9.		Eve likes the apple, then they both like it.		
10.		Adam hides when God comes.		
11.		God tells Eve that since she received the devil, she will serve him.		

Table 25 (*continued*)

	Huitzilan		Yaonáhuac	
Storyteller J. H.	*Storyteller J. P.*		*Storyteller F. J.*	*Storyteller L. V.*
12.	The apple forms Adam's apple.		The pears form Eve's breasts and Adam's apple.	The forbidden fruit forms Eve's breasts and Adam's apple.
13. Eve deceptively has the muleteer's child.				
14. Jesus punishes Adam and Eve by giving them skins to wear.	God punishes Eve by making her bear children inside her body, causing childbirth to be painful.			
15.	God punishes Adam by making him work to eat.		God punishes Adam and Eve by making them work to eat.	God punishes Adam and Eve by making them work to eat.
16.			The devil teaches Adam and Eve how to have sex.	
17.			Adam likes sex.	
18.			Sr. Santiago strikes Adam with his sword and makes him swollen and tells Adam to work to eat.	
19.	Eve shows animals how to seed themselves.			
20. Eve gives birth to a child every two years until she has ten. Each woman has ten children until there are many.			The world is filled up with people.	

huat word which, when used in ordinary conversation, means illicit sexual relations. The punishments and consequences for eating the fruit have an explicit sexual connotation: painful childbirth (J. P.), showing the animals how to seed themselves (J. P.), acquiring breasts and the Adam's apple (J. P., F. J., and L. V.), and filling up the world with people (J. H. and F. J.).

DIFFERENCES

Eve in these tales is more sexually voracious in versions from the community where the position of women is weaker in the family. J. P. (Huitzilan), for example, stresses how Eve, when tempted by the devil to eat the apple, not only accepts it from him, but also likes it, meaning that she likes sexual intercourse (item 9). F. J. (Yaonáhuac), on the other hand, stresses Adam's pleasure and ignores Eve's response when the devil teaches them how to have sex (item 17).

Because Eve is more sexually voracious in the versions from the community where the position of women is weaker, it follows that storytellers from the same community would also depict her as more inclined toward sexual deviance. J. H. depicts Eve committing adultery despite Jesus's admonition against sexual promiscuity (item 13), while his Yaonáhuac counterparts are less explicit about this aspect of Eve's behavior. Because storytellers from Huitzilan tend to stress Eve's sexual voracity, and her inclination toward sexual deviance, they also focus punishment on her rather than on Adam. J. H. (Huitzilan) has God making Adam and Eve wear skins for Eve's adultery with the muleteer (a sexually related punishment applied to both, but specifically linked to Eve's sexual deviance) (item 14). J. P. (Huitzilan) has God telling Eve that she will serve the devil for receiving him (item 11), and describes God punishing her by making her bear children inside her body, causing childbirth to be a painful experience (item 14). By contrast, storytellers from the community where women have a stronger position direct more punishment toward Adam. It is true that storytellers from both communities describe God expelling Adam and Eve from the garden and making them work to produce their food, a punishment directed toward Adam, because Nahuat men do the bulk of the agricultural labor (item 15). But F. J. (Yaonáhuac) adds an episode in which Sr. Santiago (the patron saint of both communities) strikes Adam with his sword for introducing sin to the world (item 18).

It also follows that storytellers from the community where the position of women is weaker would also regard her as a greater threat to the social order because of her sexual voracity. It is of interest to mention that sexual jealousy is a major cause of fatal or near fatal machete fights in Nahuat society, and thus sexual deviance is actually a cause of social disruption. Storyteller J. H. (Huitzilan) describes Jesus reluctantly giving Eve to Adam because he fears that "many will be planted," making him bear a heavy burden of sin (as one carries a burden with a tumpline) (item 3). "Many will be planted" connotes sexual promiscuity as well as the idea that many will be born into the world. Planting is a metaphor for sexual intercourse that has rich connotations for the Nahuat if one considers their experience and beliefs. The Nahuat plant their fields with digging sticks, sharply pointed instruments that they drive into the ground to make holes for corn and bean seeds. Men plant the earth, which they represent as a beautiful young woman or a benevolent old woman in their oral tradition, by plunging their digging sticks rhythmically into her surface.

By contrast, storytellers from the community where the position of women is stronger tend to depict Eve as introduced for positive reasons. F. J. has God make Eve to keep Adam from falling asleep and to make him a better caretaker of the orchard (although God acts at the devil's suggestion). L. V. portrays God introducing Eve to prevent Adam from marrying the devil and falling under his, rather than God's, influence (item 2).

In sum, storytellers from the two communities use different synecdoches (selecting parts to represent the whole, or anatomical particularizing [Sapir 1977a: 15]) to depict Adam and Eve. Those from Huitzilan select sexual voracity, sexual deviance, and a threat to the social order to represent Eve and apply the contrasting traits of sexual restraint, sexual morality and moral strength, and support of the social order to Adam. Narrators from Yaonáhuac change parts of this pattern by switching sexual voracity from Eve to Adam, deemphasizing Eve's sexual deviance, and dropping a threat to the social order from the list of traits connected with Eve.

This pattern of contrast in the sexuality of women characters runs consistently through other cognate narratives told by other storytellers. Table 26 contains the summaries of parallel segments from other cognate tales told by seven different narrators (four from Huitzilan and three from Yaonáhuac). It illustrates that the sexuality of women characters varies inversely with the status of women in other narratives of Nahuat oral tradition: female characters are more sexually voracious, deviant, and dangerous when women have low status in the social structure. Together with the Adam and Eve tales, this supports the conclusion that the image of women's sexuality varies with the position of men and women in Sierra Nahuat society.

The Huitzilan narrators of the tales that appear in table 26 single out for emphasis the frankly sexual from among the many complex facets of the man-woman relationship. They depict women craving and asking for sex from their men and portray sexually deviant women endangering the food supply and committing horrible crimes (matricide). Yaonáhuac narrators, on the other hand,

Table 26. The Sexuality of Women in Cognate Tales, by Community

Name of narrative in appendix 1	Story no.	Episode no.	Summary of episode Huitzilan version	Yaonáhuac version
Women characters as sexually aggressive				
The Jealous Man's Daughters	25–26	4	Daughters are confined to their house by their father. They pray to God for a way to satisfy their sexual desires. A boy disguised as a maid gives them sexual pleasure.	Closely watched daughters try to resist the sexual advances of three boys disguised as women who try to seduce them in the steam bath (*temascal*).
The Fisherman	21, 23–24	5	A man who looks like his older brother sleeps with a princess, who is the older brother's wife. He places his sword between himself and the princess. The princess asks him to remove it so they can have sex.	A man who looks like his older brother comes to the house of the princess, who is the older brother's wife. She gives him supper and he goes to sleep.
Sexually aggressive women characters as dangerous				
The Fisherman	21, 23–24	1	By committing adultery and feeding fish to her lover, the fisherman's wife causes the fish to be ill.	The fisherman's wife does not commit adultery or cause the fish to be ill.
The Girl Who Killed Her Mother	27–28	2	The daughter who kills her mother is depicted as having a huge sexual appetite.	The daughter who kills her mother is not depicted as having a huge sexual appetite.

play down women's sexuality and emphasize other aspects of the relationship between men and women. They have women showing sexual restraint and describe women loving their husbands in ways other than the purely sexual. Yaonáhuac narrator L. V. describes a wife loving her husband by using the word for love (*kitahsota* = she loves him) that connotes respect rather than carnal love.[1] Because they play down women's sexual appetite, they also depict them as less threatening and do not generally connect heinous acts of deviance to sexual voracity.

11. Men : Women : : Culture : Nature

Mother with child

Nahuat men's general ideas of the moral nature of men and women pivot on the ways men place women in metaphorical space. It has been mentioned that a key spatial metaphor runs through Nahuat narrative thought. The Nahuat juxtapose the center against the periphery of their universe. The center is the human community where human social life is governed by rules that make up Nahuat morality. It contrasts with the periphery, where unbridled, primordial forces exist that are both creative and destructive. These forces are locked in a tense contest whose outcome determines the fate of Nahuat civilization.

The Nahuat generally regard humans as socialized beings with control over their animal-like impulses. They regard these impulses as dangerous to orderly social life and emphasize the need for control and restraint. They consequently disapprove of behaviors that imply a lack of impulse control and explain deviant social behavior by making an analogy between the deviant among them and the animals who inhabit the forest in the periphery. They emphasize impulse control in a variety of ways in ordinary life. It is considered improper, for example, to show submission to hunger and wolf down food. In narratives, characters who are out of control find their destinies in the wild and dangerous periphery.

The Nahuat generally recognize that the deviant among them who act like animals can be both men and women. Their stories describe deviant members of both sexes perishing or undergoing perpetual and infinite punishment in the periphery of the universe. Examples include a boy lacking appetite control who perishes when his patron sends him on an errand from which he does not return. The Nahuat also tell of an unfaithful wife who is carried off by the devil to a dangerous and ugly place in the periphery where she repeatedly experiences a bizarre and painful sexual rite.

This chapter compares biblically derived stories to illustrate that some Nahuat place women in metaphorical space more toward the periphery than men, while others place both sexes generally closer to the center of the universe. The stories express how the Huitzilan Nahuat, but not their counterparts from Yaonáhuac, have changed biblical stories by adding a woman-as-animal analogy sharply to delineate the essential differences between the sexes.

The woman-as-animal metaphor of Huitzilan men is a special case of a general tendency in sexual ideology noted by Ortner (1974), Ardener (1977*a*, 1977*b*), and others. It was mentioned that Ardener (1977*b*: 23) contends many rural societies place women toward the wild in a universe defined by men. Ortner (1974), applying the language of Lévi-Strauss (1969), suggests that women are generally regarded as closer to nature while men are closer to culture. This tendency in sexual ideology is said to derive from the generally held perception of women's physiology. Women menstruate but men do not, the role of women in procreation is more obvious than the role of men (see Barnes 1973), and women, but not men, produce breast milk to feed infants. Sexual ideologies resting on these facts of human physiology emphasize the natural creative functions of women and the artificial or culturally creative functions of men.[1]

This argument rests on an assumption that does not apply equally well to the Nahuat of Huitzilan and Yaonáhuac. It assumes a sharp dichotomy between culture and nature (or humans and animals), but such a pronounced dichotomy exists more among the Huitzilan Nahuat, who adopted a view of the universe more consistent with Judeo-Christian thought (see chapter 8).

Moreover, this argument, which rests heavily on the role of the sexes in reproduction, might help account for some of the general features of Nahuat sexual ideology that cross-cut all communities in the northern Sierra de Puebla. But it cannot explain the variations between the Huitzilan and Yaonáhuac stylized images of women which men express in oral tradition. The Nahuat of both communities describe procreation in the same way. They assert that it is the result of sexual intercourse between a man and a woman when a substance ejaculated by the man mixes with another substance secreted by the woman to create an infant in the mother's womb. They are aware that pregnancy will not occur if a couple practices abstinence, and some recognize that women can be impregnated by artificial insemination in hospitals. Likewise, the role of women in childrearing and the Nahuat preception of that role are identical and cannot contribute to differences in sexual ideology for Huitzilan and Yaonáhuac men. Because the two communities share such close historical, linguistic, and cultural antecedents, one can control background variables that could conceivably contribute to differences in men's images of the sexes.

This book has presented the thesis that social images in oral tradition differ for the Huitzilan and Yaonáhuac Nahuat because of notable differences in social structure. This argument can be extended to explain why some Nahuat place women closer to nature and other Nahuat do not. Let us turn to a comparison of biblical stories illustrating how some Nahuat re-work their versions to incorporate a woman-as-animal metaphor. They are the same Nahuat who depict women as morally weaker, more sexually voracious, and a greater threat to the moral order than men.

THE FLOOD

The tales which most clearly define the essential qualities of men and women are stories that describe their origins. The Nahuat believe there were two eras of creation—the Era of Darkness and the Era of Light—and they describe how, at the beginning of each, humans populated the world. For most narrators the story of Adam and Eve, discussed in the previous chapter, describes how God created the first man and the first woman at the beginning of the Era of Darkness. This story expresses how the Nahuat from the two communities define the sexuality of men and women. This chapter considers the story of The Flood, which describes how the Era of Darkness came to an end and tells how humans repopulated the earth at the beginning of the Era of Light. It has been mentioned that humans and animals were alike during the Era of Darkness and became distinguished during the Era of Light. The cognate versions of The Flood illustrate how some, but not all, Nahuat have elected to connect the distinction between humans and animals to their asymmetrical sexual ideology.

Storytellers from both communities tell a story of the flood clearly derived from Genesis, but they weave in different ideas derived from a variety of sources, including pre-Hispanic Aztec thought. These additional elements incorporated into the common cognate core express the contrasting views of women. On the one hand, the Yaonáhuac version, which appears first, expresses a symmetrical view of the sexes by giving both Noah and his wife human, rather than animal, origins. For these Nahuat, neither women nor men are necessarily closer to nature, a view that complements their notion that women are not necessarily more sexually voracious and threatening to the moral order than men. On the other hand, the Huitzilan version, which appears second, expresses a close relationship between women and nature with a metaphor that describes how Noah's female dog evolved into a woman with whom he propagated a new human race.

The Yaonáhuac and Huitzilan cognate versions of The Flood consist of four episodes which are identified with the letters A, B, C, and D in the following texts. The tales from the two communities share the following themes. A man, whom I shall call Noah, is told to build an ark because the world is going to come to an end (episode A). He does so, and a great flood destroys the world, and all the animals and humans who did not board the ark perish (episode B). After the water recedes, God sends angels to earth to find out what happened. But the first of these eat the flesh of the dead animals and become the buzzards we know today (episode C). Noah survives the flood to repopulate the world (episode D).

The dog-woman metamorphosis appears in the final episode (D) of the Huitzilan version. This metaphor has two clear meanings: it depicts Nahuat-Totonac ethnic relations and expresses the Huitzilan image of women as closer to nature than men. The Huitzilan narrator describes how Noah speaks Nahuat and his dog-turned-woman speaks Totonac. Totonac is a language of the Maco-Mayan family that is completely unintelligible to the Nahuat, whose language belongs to the Aztecan family. Huitzilan is an entirely Nahuat-speaking *municipio* that is adjacent to two Totonac-speaking ones (Zongozotla and Zapotitlán de Méndez). This metaphor clearly explains the Nahuat conception of the genetic relationship between the groups and explains the unintelligibility of the Totonac language by asserting that it derived from the barking of a dog. The Nahuat express their moral superiority over the Totonacs with the analogy men : women : : Nahuat : Totonac. But this is only one meaning, because the metaphor also clearly expresses the Huitzilan men's view of their women. This will become evident from an examination of the facets of the metaphor which are identified with the numbers 1 through 9 in the Huitzilan version of the story.

YAONÁHUAC VERSION

A. It was dark at that time. It was always dark. There lived people called Gentiles during that time when it was dark. It was an ancient time. They were very tall. They grew up to be terribly tall because they never endured heat. They lived when it was dark. There were just a few stars giving light. There were seven stars for those people who lived then. So then God changed the world because the time had come. God put a man on earth so that he might build an ark. He was to build an ark so that God could put in all of the seeds. He put in a pair of Christians—a man and a woman, corn seeds, sheep—a she-sheep and a he-sheep, a he-

donkey and a she-donkey, and a cow and a bull. It was the same
for everything in the world. He put in a pair of everything. God put
a man there so that he would build an ark. God told him to call
his companions to help with the ark because a time was going to
come when all were going to perish. The Jews [his companions]
said, "It's not true! You're lying to us! Where did you see that
people would perish? We won't make the ark. You make it yourself. No one is going to help you." Well, the man extended a great
effort to make the ark. It took 100 years to make it. We now say a
century. God told him to put just one window on the north side.
B. So then when things came to an end, when it was Judgment Day
for them to die, a storm appeared from the north. It turned black.
The clouds rose. It became very dark—so much so that no one
could see. And the wind started to blow very hard. And then those
Jews, those Gentiles ran when they saw the wind and the rain coming with great force. When [the storm] began they started pounding
on the ark with their hands. Hands were huge then. They struck at
the ark trying to open it up. Their headman told the man inside to
open it up. But the man inside replied he wouldn't let them in because they hadn't helped him. If they had helped him he would
have let them in. But it was God who, from the beginning, had them
disobey so that just the seeds would enter the ark. So when the
great rain came—the Book now calls it the Universal Flood—it
rained for forty days and forty nights. It rained extremely hard.
The water rose halfway up to heaven. Nothing could be seen. The
entire world was filled with water. All the people perished. Everyone drowned except those who were inside the ark. It took a long
time for the waters to calm.
C. Now there were what we now call buzzards. They say they
used to be angels in heaven next to God. He sent the angels to
earth, telling them, "Go walk about and see if the ark is resting."
They came. Nothing had calmed. The water was still high. God
sent them another time, saying, "Go walk about again. Find out if
it has calmed or not." He sent them and they returned. "Water is
everywhere—it is over the entire world. Only one very tall tree
appears. The tip is showing," they said. "Well now, let the water
drop some now," God said. He sent them again, telling them, "Circle around to see if the water has calmed." When those angels
landed on the earth, there was land. They found the dead in some
parts and they decided to eat them. God saw them. They didn't
know he watched them. They went back to heaven, and God
asked, "Why did you stay?" "We stayed a long time because we
walked all over," they replied. "Did you eat anything?" God asked.

"We didn't eat anything," they replied. "Let's see. Open up," God demanded. They opened their mouths. The meat they had eaten was stuck in their teeth. So God told them, "Just as you went to eat dead meat, so it will be that you will eat it wherever you find it. Now go away from me here!" Well, they were angels before but, because they sinned on earth by eating dead meat, our God destined them to eat as they do now. Where they see a dead animal, they eat it.
D. So to change the world again, father Noah came to be. He had children. His children came to be, and there were a lot of them. Those children were a large family. A new world was made.

STORYTELLER L. V.

HUITZILAN VERSION

A. Well, yesterday or the day before there was this man who was preparing the forest for planting. He worked day in and day out. He cut down a lot of trees. But when he came to the forest one day he exclaimed, "The trees are all standing again. Why are they standing? Who did this?" He went back to preparing the milpa for planting again. He came the next day, and again it was the same. The trees were standing where he had cut them down the day before. The man wondered, "Well, who is doing this? I work. I do my work and now when I return I find no sign of where I worked. It is forest." Well, again that man went to work to prepare the field for planting. And again he came back, and the trees he felled were all standing again. He asked, "Who is doing this? Well now, I'm going to see." He watched during the night. He waited around where he worked. He saw the trees getting back up, and he saw who was doing the work. He saw a rabbit lifting up the timber. He raised them all up again. The man declared, "Well, it's you who is doing it! I've cut them and I'm tired because I've been working for several days now cutting down the trees. I come back and it's back to the way it was before. Why do you do this?" "Well, let me tell you," the rabbit responded. "The day will come when the world will be lost, and if you work, you'll work in vain. It would be better that, instead of working your milpa, you find a big box and go into it, because the world is going to be lost. Get hold of a chicken that will crow right at midnight. And get hold of a parrot to put on top of that box. 1. And you'll have to take along that dog. Don't leave it behind," added the rabbit. "But if it isn't true?" the man asked. "What do you mean 'If it isn't true?'!" replied the rabbit. "Well, I've warned you." Well, that man who was working in the forest got hold of a big box. He got hold of a chicken. He got hold of a parrot. And he always did have a dog. So then he shut them up tightly into that box. He closed that box well.

B. *When the water came it floated, and he was closed inside that box along with the dog, but not with the parrot. He took along the chicken. It too was inside the box, but not the parrot. He left it on top of one of the corners of the box to tell him when the water began, how high they climbed, if they had reached the summit or if they hadn't. The water rose and rose and rose. Four days passed, and the parrrot said, "Well, it has climbed half way from the earth to heaven. It has climbed half way, for the water is still rising." Well, they went on. It rose and it rose. The parrot said, "You'll feel it hit when we arrive at heaven. You'll feel it, and I'll tell you, 'Now we've arrived.'" When the water reached heaven the box hit and made a sound like striking glass. The parrot said, "Now we've reached heaven. Now we're going back down." "For how many days will we go down?" the man asked. "Since we were eight days climbing," the parrot said, "it'll be another eight days before we reach the earth." When the water began to recede they descended. They say the man felt it descend for eight days. When the eight days had passed he was on the ground.*

C. *From there, yes, Jesus knew the world had come to an end. There wasn't a thing left. The world was clean. After a while Jesus sensed smoke rising. He thought, "Well, why is something smoking again? The world doesn't have any more Christians. I made them all perish." Then Jesus told the buzzard, "Now then, you go see what is happening on earth. I'm going to die of this smoke again." The buzzard came to earth. He began eating meat. "Well now," God said, "he went off and hasn't come to tell me how it is. He hasn't come back up here. Now you, angel, go find out how the earth is. What is it that's smoking? I made our brothers all perish." The eagle came. The same thing happened. The intestines of animals, of beasts of burden, were strewn all over. The angel came and began picking up and eating the intestines. God grew impatient and sent the hummingbird. "Now you go. The angel went. The buzzard went and no one has informed me. Go see them but watch that you don't stay there. Watch out that you come back," God warned. "No," said the hummingbird, "I'll go but I'll make only a single turn." And the hummingbird came. And those who were eating the meat didn't even notice that the hummingbird passed. He went by quickly, whistling through the air as he went,*

and he returned to his patrón *[God]. "I've come,* patrón," *he said.
"Well, fine. What's there?" God asked. "Well, the buzzard and the
angel are both eating," the hummingbird told him. "But who has
survived? Who is making smoke?" asked God. "A man survived.
A man and a dog survived along with a chicken," replied the
hummingbird.
D. "The man was eating the meat. You had all the animals perish.
Now that man is stripping away all the meat. But the intestines
are strewn about. The angel is picking them all up," added the
hummingbird. God asked, "And the buzzard?" "He's picking up all
that's left," replied the hummingbird. "And did you eat anything?"
God inquired. "Me? No. I didn't want to land on the earth. I didn't
even pause in the air," replied the hummingbird. "Ah good," said
God, and then he asked, "But you saw how things are?" "Well,
they're working beautifully," the hummingbird answered. "The
man who survived is with just a chicken and a dog. They're cleaning up all the meat that is strewn about there. He's picking it up,
cleaning it, and frying it." "Ah good. Well, that's a fine thing," God
said. 2. The man cleaned up the world and then began working in
the* milpa. *He was working in the* milpa, *and he took the dog with
him. He went with her to the* milpa. *Around nine or ten o'clock
the dog would come home. Now that man didn't have anyone to
grind his tortillas. But when he came to eat there were tortillas.
The dog was female. She took care of him. She made the tortillas.
She went off again to see her master. 3. When the man came
home, there were the tortillas. "But who makes my tortillas?" the
man wondered. "I don't have anyone to take care of me. And I
always take the dog, that female dog," the man thought to himself. 4. And so he watched. He went to work, taking the dog. And
he saw that from ten or eleven o'clock the dog wasn't there. "Perhaps she also went to work," he thought. "Who makes the tortillas?" he pondered, and then he resolved, "I'm going to see." He
glanced around for the dog. The dog didn't appear. The man went
to see. He approached silently and carefully. 5. He found a woman
grinding tortilla dough. A hide was lying there. The dog was grinding tortilla dough, but she was a girl. 6. He quickly grabbed ashes
and threw them on the hide. 7. The girl stood up and nearly cried.
"Why did you do that? Aren't I taking good care of you?" she said.
8. "It's fine the way you're taking care of me," he said. "But you
shouldn't have done that to my clothes," she protested again. "But
wouldn't it be better now for me to serve [marry] you?" the man
said. The woman who used to be a female dog left her skin, her*

hide, and became a Christian. 9. The woman now speaks Totonac and the man now speaks Mexicano [Nahuat].   STORYTELLER A. V.

Huitzilan narrators may have adopted rather than developed the metaphor of the dog-woman metamorphosis they incorporated into the biblical story of Noah, because it has a wide distribution in Latin America (see Drummond 1977: 847–848; Adams, personal communication, 1980).[2] But I contend Huitzilan storytellers chose to modify the biblical story with a metaphor (whatever its source) that expresses an asymmetrical view of the sexes by asserting the primordial animal (dog) nature of women but not men because women have a weak position in the social structure. An examination of the metaphor makes this clear.

The dog-as-woman metaphor expresses several facets of sexual relations as Huitzilan Nahuat men perceive them—the indirect and secretive nature of women, men's moral superiority, the suspicions men have of women, men's underlying fear of women's sexual promiscuity, and the ideals of male sexual initiative and female coyness. This metaphor, which makes an analogy in which Noah's dog : Noah :: wives : husbands, is absent in the cognate version of Noah's Ark from Yaonáhuac. Thus it is likely that the men living in the more male-dominant community of Huitzilan incorporated it to explain the nature of women.

The metaphor the Huitzilan Nahuat have woven into the biblical story has nine elements: 1. Noah boards the ark with his female dog; thus the dog is a companion to Noah just as a wife is a companion to her husband; 2. After the flood, Noah works his *milpa* and the dog makes his tortillas, just like the sexual division of labor between husband and wife; 3. Noah is unaware that the dog makes his tortillas because she does it secretly, just as husbands are unaware of the conduct of their wives, who are secretive with their husbands; 4. Noah becomes suspicious and spies on the dog, just as husbands are suspicious and vigilant of their wives; 5. Noah discovers a woman grinding tortilla dough and finds a dog skin (by describing a woman evolving from a dog, while keeping Noah entirely human, the storyteller expresses how women are more animal-like than men: I contend that the Huitzilan narrator implies that because women descended from dogs, they are more sexually voracious and promiscuous on the grounds that in ordinary discourse, the Nahuat give sexual promiscuity as a salient characteristic of dogs); 6. Noah prevents the woman from wearing the dog skin, just as men, who are morally stronger, prevent women from returning to their primordial animal-like state: this clearly expresses the moral superiority of men over women; 7. the dog-turned-woman protests, just as women ideally should be coy with men; 8. Noah proposes that he and the dog-turned-woman live together as man and wife, just as men ideally should take the sexual initiative with women, despite the underlying nature of women implied by the woman-like-animal analogy; 9. Noah speaks Nahuat and the woman speaks Totonac, just as husbands have difficulty understanding their wives because of their secrecy.

In the Yaonáhuac cognate, on the other hand, the storyteller has not reworked the biblical story of Noah by describing animal origin either for Noah or his wife. Moreover, I did not find the motif of a female dog who sheds her skin and marries her master either as an episode or as a separate tale in any of the 175 narratives that I collected in this community. I contend the Yaonáhuac version of Noah's Ark expresses a more symmetrical view of the sexes because it fits with the more egalitarian relations between men and women in this part of the Sierra Nahuat area.

SUMMARY

Several factors combine to explain why some Nahuat but not others place women toward the wild by asserting their animal origins. The Nahuat who express the woman-as-animal metaphor are the same ones who have experienced more narrative acculturation. One aspect of this process is the more complete incorporation of the Catholic doctrine that humans are divine and distinguished from animals. The absorption of this doctrine into their oral tradition stems from their greater dependence on Hispanic patronage and their weakened identification with their Aztec-derived gods, who are deified forces of nature. A comparison of lightning-bolt stories earlier in this book illustrated that these Nahuat anthropomorphize their lightning-bolt gods less than their counterparts in other communities, where the Nahuat are more independent of Hispanics. By more completely incorporating the Christian doctrine setting up a sharp separation of humans and animals, they have set the stage for a woman-as-animal metaphor to delineate sharply the contrasting nature of the sexes.

To be sure, both groups of Nahuat exhibit some tendency to distinguish humans from animals, while at the same time holding the belief that humans and animals have a close relationship. The Nahuat from both communities, like their ancient Aztec ancestors, emphasize that humans and animals differ because only the former are socialized. Both groups of Nahuat hold the belief that humans have animal companion spirits (*tonalme*), and they assert that some among them (*nagualme*) can change into animals to punish their enemies or correct immoral behavior. I only contend that Huitzilan narratives expressed by men reflect a shift in emphasis toward this Christian doctrine.

The Nahuat from Huitzilan have a greater need to employ a metaphorical device to distinguish the sexes because they have a much more androcentric social structure. Sexual hierarchy promotes social distance and antagonism between the sexes, leading to a sexual ideology that sharply distinguishes the moral character of men from women.[3]

12. Conclusions

The well-taught daughter

A debate over the relationship between symbols and social relations has focused on the existence of dual organizations in human society (see Lévi-Strauss 1960, 1963: 132–163; Maybury-Lewis 1960).[1] Out of this debate came the suggestion that members of every human society may organize their thoughts according to antithetical categories, although polar thinking may have more importance for some than for others. There was a call for further research on the social as well as formal link between dyadic and triadic symbolic structures (Maybury-Lewis 1960: 40–43). This study has attempted to identify the social structural correlates for different degrees of polarization in Nahuat narrative thought.

Comparison of parallel stories has illustrated a number of consistent differences between the narratives from the two communities. Narratives from Huitzilan and Yaonáhuac have developed two variants of a common cultural model in accord with changes Hispanics have brought to their social structure. It will be useful to recapitulate what they have in common before turning to how they differ.

The common cultural model described in part II consists of a series of homologous juxtapositions of spatial and temporal categories, forces of creation and destruction, and social images. This model has a tripartite structure because a number of concepts mediate between the homologous juxtaposed categories (see the figure). The Huitzilan and Yaonáhuac variants of this model differ most markedly with respect to the mediators.

The most important mediating concept linking the contraposed categories in the common model is the belief that humans have animal companion spirits (*tonalme*). The most conspicuous characters in stories personifying this belief are the lightning-bolts, the synthetic characters that combine elements from both Aztec and peninsular Spanish tradition. The modern-day Nahuat describe them with animal and human identities, and thus they have them bridge the center and the periphery of their universe. They also use them to connect other important polar concepts including the masculine sun and the feminine earth to help tie the other parts of the Nahuat view of the universe into a whole.

YAONÁHUAC TRIPARTITE MODEL

The Yaonáhuac variant of this model retains its tripartite structure because narrators emphasize the mediating role of lightning-bolts in two ways. First, they depict them with a balance of human identity as well as animal identity: they present them as beautiful and sensuous women and have them live in the forest and sometimes appear as snakes, tigers, and deer. Second, they describe them directly interfering in human affairs by punishing those who sin and upholding the human moral order. The images of these characters in Yaonáhuac stories reflect an integrated view of the universe in which the human domain in the center and the animal domain in the periphery have a tightly woven relationship.

HUITZILAN DUALISTIC MODEL

Narrators from Huitzilan collapse this tripartite model into a dualistic one by doing the following. They stress the animal rather than the human qualities of lightning-bolt characters in stories, and they consequently place them more toward the wild periphery

meditators	
lightning-bolts as wisemen	lightning-bolts as snakes and tigers

center	periphery
north	south
right	left
day (noon)	night (midnight)
summer solstice	winter solstice
present	past
heat	cold
light	darkness
Christ	devil
Christians	Gentiles/Jews
humans	animals
Nahuat	Hispanics

Nahuat cultural model

of their universe. They seldom depict lightning-bolt characters upholding the moral order of humans by punishing those who sin. They place lightning-bolt and other women further toward the periphery with a woman-as-animal metaphor to contrast sharply the moral nature of the sexes. The image of lightning-bolt characters in Huitzilan Nahuat stories reflects a more dichotomized view of the universe, particularly with respect to the relationship between the human domain in the center and the animal domain in the periphery. The differences between the Yaonáhuac and Huitzilan models are not absolute, but reflect a shift in central tendencies apparent from a comparison of parallel stories.

CULTURAL MODELS AND SOCIAL STRUCTURE

The tripartite model from Yaonáhuac and the more dualistic one from Huitzilan probably evolved from a common but unknown prototype. These models undoubtedly developed in accord with changes Hispanics brought to Nahuat social structure. It would appear that the tripartite model in the Yaonáhuac stories changed less from the pre-Hispanic original. To be sure, the lightning-bolt characters in both sets of Nahuat stories have close parallels with a number of ancient Aztec religious personalities, particularly the serpent gods (Quetzalcoatl, Coatlicue, and Cihuacoatl) and other related deities (Nanahuatl and Xochiquetzal). But they appear in greater numbers, they are more completely developed, and they perform more of their ancient functions in the stories from Yaonáhuac. Perhaps most important, these religious personalities have balanced animal and human identities, consistent with a more integrated view of the human and animal domains, in Yaonáhuac as well as ancient Aztec tradition. This contrasts sharply with the Huitzilan Nahuat, who place these characters out of the center and in the periphery, and who replace them more completely with religious personalities taken from peninsular Spanish tradition. They have absorbed to a greater degree the Judeo-Christian separation of humans and animals into their view of things.

The Yaonáhuac Nahuat have retained the tripartite model for several reasons. First, their political and economic autonomy relative to the Hispanics has permitted them to resist pressure to change their beliefs to conform to those of the dominant ethnic group. Second, their tripartite model fits a social structure where there is comparatively little polarization in ethnic and sexual relations.

The more dualistic cultural model in Huitzilan narratives appears to have developed with the pronounced ethnic and sexual hierarchy in the social structure. To be sure, both groups of Nahuat have antagonistic relations with Hispanics, and men stand in social opposition to women in both communities. The Nahuat from Huitzilan as well as Yaonáhuac make a clear distinction between their domain in the center and that of Hispanics in the periphery of their universe. Men in the two communities clearly delineate themselves from women by describing women as the morally weaker sex. But the ethnic and sexual hierarchy in Huitzilan social structure leads to a more dualistic model for two reasons.[2] First, the Nahuat feeling of powerlessness reduces their identification with Aztec-derived religious personalities, and thus they do not anthropomorphize lightning-bolts as much as other groups of Nahuat. Their strong psychological identification with Hispanic wealth and power has caused them to adopt tenets of Hispanic Christianity, including a dichotomized view of the universe in which humans are sharply distinguished from animals. Second, ethnic hierarchy promotes sexual antagonism because Nahuat men develop an androcentric sexual ideology to compensate for their weak position relative to Hispanics. A strong androcentric sexual ideology develops with actual sexual antagonism between men and women, one manifestation of which is comparatively high rates of divorce in Huitzilan relative to Yaonáhuac (see table 27). A direct connection exists between sexual antagonism in social life and a dualistic cultural model which plays down the role of lightning-bolt mediators. In Nahuat stories, lightning-bolts who mediate frequently appear as women, probably because mediators generally have anomalous qualities and women appear to men as the anomalous sex. Mediators have anomalous qualities because they bridge gaps between contraposed domains. Women probably strike men as the anomalous sex because of their obvious human qualities, coupled with

Table 27. Rates of Divorce, by Community

Status	Huitzilan		Yaonáhuac	
	Number	Percent	Number	Percent
Married but never divorced	882	80.2	661	93.1
Divorced one or more times	218	19.8	49	6.9
Totals	1100	100.0	710	100.0

$x^2 = 56.2$ with 1 df, $p < .001$ (two tailed test)

their procreative functions, which could cause men to attribute to women animal-like functions. MacCormack (1980: 9) suggests that women can function in systems of belief as the mediators between culture and nature because they socialize children and cook, and thus transform natural entities into cultural ones, and this could easily apply to the Nahuat. Whatever may be the case on a more general level, Huitzilan men have an unusual degree of sexual antagonism in their social structure because of the pronounced androcentrism in their families. They express this antagonism when they strip women of their human qualities and reduce their mediating functions.

The Aztecs are an important case because they developed a culture entirely different from those related to Judeo-Christian tradition. Their view of the universe in general and their notion of the relationship between humans and animals in particular differ in many ways from the views brought by the Spanish colonists to the New World. This book describes how contemporary Aztec-speaking groups developed different synthetic cultural models based to different degrees on Aztec and European prototypes. These models grew out of everyday experience as the Nahuat competed with Hispanics for land, as they learned to adapt to varying degrees of Hispanic domination, and as men and women altered their relationship. The Nahuat express the more invariant aspects of these models in narratives, whose rigidity they preserve by re-telling them as they heard them. Their narratives perform the important function of guiding them through a very complex and hard world.

The very rigidity of narratives makes them particularly useful tools for detecting different patterns of thought between two or more groups.[3] The models described here by no means exhaust all of the cultural variation created by the uneven pattern of Spanish settlement in the Hispanic world, let alone in the northern Sierra de Puebla. Further research using the method of controlled folktale comparison can provide a fuller picture of historically related cultural models and their transformation.

Appendix 1. Story Summaries

This appendix contains the full text of stories mentioned in the preceding chapters. Conclusions about the common and different features of Huitzilan and Yaonáhuac folkloric world view, as expressed in narratives, rest on these texts as well as on those which appeared in the body of this book. Each text in this appendix contains numbers to facilitate the identification of important episodes referred to earlier. There are ten sets of cognate stories, and the reader is invited to make comparisons to identify differences and similarities between Huitzilan and Yaonáhuac narrative tradition not already mentioned.

The 30 stories in the body and 28 stories in the appendix of this book represent the most popular and important of the 280 narratives I collected and transcribed in the two Nahuat communities. The reader may write me for more information on the entire corpus of material collected in the Nahuat area.

NARRATIVES CONTAINED IN APPENDIX I

1. THE SUN AND THE MOON, by M. I. of Yaonáhuac

1. A man with a donkey passed by a lake and found two children, a boy with his head in the water and a girl with her feet in the water. They were naked. The man took them home. His wife put diapers on them, and the man and his wife raised them.

2. After they were grown up, the boy asked his adoptive father for his inheritance and that of his sister so that they could work on their own to help their father. It was agreed, and the next day their father took them to a very large lake and told the boy how he had found them, and how he brought them from there so that they wouldn't be injured by the water. The lake, he declared, was their inheritance.

3. The girl started working first. She carried sand into the water. The boy carried rocks into the water. They were making a dam [filling in the lake]. The man, the adoptive father, came home, and the boy and the girl worked hard. But they couldn't do much. The boy decided that they would make a rope, one for each of them, and climb two mountains. Each would crack a rope in the

valley between them. It worked. The mountains crumbled and filled up the lake and extended the plain. Once done, the [boy probably] said, "Now we're going to make it grow. We're going to put a town here for our brothers."

4. Meanwhile, their father worried because they didn't come home to eat. Their mother told him to go see them and take them something to eat. She fretted about where they were sleeping, and she grew concerned because they hadn't taken their clothes. Their father went to find them and came across a big town. He found them working, and he was astounded at what they had done in just three days. He walked through the town for three more days and still hadn't seen it all. The boy said, "We still have some more to do. I've just begun." Their father marveled at the huge streets and big houses. He told them that he brought their lunch. The father asked who fed them. "We go out there," the boy and girl replied. Then they invited their father to stay there. "You pick the room you'd like and you two live here. We've adorned it for you." The father agreed. [The boy probably] said, "Good. Let my mother see it."

5. The father went back home and brought his wife. When he returned, he called to the girl, "María." She answered. He asked, "Your brother?" The girl replied, "He's working way over there." Then he came. The father agreed to stay because he was getting old and couldn't work much anymore. The boy told him, "We're going to finish and we're going to do another job that we still have to do. We won't be coming back." The father and mother went to bring their things. When they returned, their children told them they had finished. They took them for a spin in their very fast car, but even though they ran around all day, they couldn't circle around all the streets.

6. The boy and the girl told their father and mother, "You two stay here. It's for our brothers who'll come too. Let them live here." Their father asked, "Where are you going, children?" They replied, "Into the heavens. Tomorrow we'll pass by to see you." María said she would see them at night. The boy said he would see them during the day, but he said they wouldn't speak. The boy became the sun and the girl became the moon.

2. TWO MEN, by M. A. of Huitzilan

1. Once there were two men working alone. They were brothers, and they decided that one should make the tortillas and prepare the meals while the other worked in the fields.

2. One day the brother who made the meals decided to go over a hill and watch his brother work in the valley below. He saw that his brother had cleared a large area of about six hectares. Again he returned to watch his brother, and he saw him clear a very large field. He climbed up the hill a third time, and this time he saw two men working with plows and oxen. But when he went to where he saw them working he found only his brother. He asked his brother about what he saw, and the brother replied, "I'm here alone." The one who prepared the meals said, "That's not true. I saw two men working here." The other said, "Let's not talk about it." He climbed the hill a fourth time, and again he saw two men working in the valley below. But no one else was living in the forest at that time. There were no other human beings.

3. When the two brothers awoke, much corn had grown overnight. The two men lived on that corn, and when they had consumed it, they resumed working. The brother who worked in the *milpa* made only one trip to his plot, and he waited for the crop to mature. They harvested another huge crop which filled two granaries. The brother who prepared the meals asked again, "Who is helping you?" "No one," replied the other. "I just shout to God. He is the one who helps me. That is why we have such a good harvest."

4. They continued to have good harvests from then on. More and more corn grew, and human beings began to appear and fill up the area, making a community in the forest. First there were a hundred human beings or so, and then there came more and more. So it was that people were planted.

3. THE LAZY HUSBAND, by N. A. H. of Huitzilan

1. A man had a wife who asked him to work. She gave him his tortillas every day so that he'd go to work, but every day he just sat down at the edge of the forest and ate his tortillas without doing anything. One day the woman asked him, "Did you work much?" He replied, "Yes." Then he asked her to buy some corn for him to plant. The woman found some corn and gave it to him, but instead of planting it, he dug a hole and threw the corn into it.

2. One day the woman again became impatient, and she asked her husband, "I wonder what it's like where you planted?" He said there was fresh corn, and she asked him to take her to see it. The man took his wife to a field of fresh corn that didn't belong to him, and then he left her there to cut it. They returned and ate the corn.

3. The next day, the man went off again to the edge of the forest. A sparrow-hawk was above him [in a tree], and he had been there

every day. The man spoke to him, saying, "What are you doing there? You're just screeching. If I were you, I'd be grabbing some turkeys and eating them." The man told the sparrow-hawk to come down to the ground and change clothes with him. The sparrow-hawk was reluctant at first, but he finally did it, and they changed all of their clothes, including their faces.

4. The man went off to sit in a tree, and the sparrow-hawk went to the man's house, where he found his wife. Since it was late, the sparrow-hawk–turned–man and the woman ate supper, and then the woman decided to go to sleep. But the man, who was still thinking like a sparrow-hawk, couldn't lie down to sleep. The woman insisted that he lie down, but he was afraid to do it. The woman grabbed him to make him lie down, and then he explained he was accustomed to sleeping sitting up because he was a sparrow-hawk and was not her husband. He explained that he changed clothes with her husband at his request. He told her he did it reluctantly. He said that her husband didn't do any work at his *milpa*. He told how he just sat down at the edge of the forest and ate the tortillas she had given him. He told her that her husband didn't plant the corn she had picked, and he offered to take her to where he really had planted the corn she had given him. The sparrow-hawk–turned–man said that he would really work if she wanted him to take her husband's place. The woman agreed, and he told her that he wouldn't change clothes with her husband. The day came when he took her to where the lazy husband had planted, and he explained how the husband had dug a big hole and threw the corn into it.

5. Meanwhile the man–turned–sparrow-hawk was screaming above, and he decided to try and grab some turkeys. But he was unable to do so because they ran into the bushes. He became weaker and weaker, and he finally fell to the ground on the spot where he had sat before. The sparrow-hawk–turned–man and the woman worked hard together. The woman expressed dismay that her husband had done no work while she gave him his tortillas every day. The sparrow-hawk–turned–man and the woman grew accustomed to each other, but the man–turned–sparrow-hawk died.

4. THE LAZY HUSBAND, by L. V. of Yaonáhuac

1. One time they chased a lazy man to work so that he would support his wife. But he sat down underneath a tree in the shade, and there he lay face up day after day. He did that every day.

2. One day his wife said, "You must have worked a lot." He replied, "Uh huh. I worked a lot. You just give me my tortillas."

3. But one time when he was lying there a buzzard approached him. The bird circled about and turned on an angle as he made his circle. He flew beautifully. The man pondered about how beautiful the buzzard looked. "If only I were he. That buzzard doesn't work to eat as I have to work to eat. It'd be better if I were a buzzard," he said to himself. The buzzard perched nearby, and the man jumped up and said, "Wouldn't you like to lend me your clothes for a while so that I might know how you live?" "Of course. I'll lend them to you," was the buzzard's reply. The buzzard lent the man his feathers, and that lazy man flew around and liked it.

4. He returned and asked the buzzard, "Let me borrow your clothes for a long time." "Sure, go ahead," replied the buzzard. The man added, "You stay here and do my work. I was clearing the weeds and rubbish from that field. I have some seeds at home for planting. My wife will come to feed me. I'm going to fly around and then I'll try to come back in time to change my clothes and eat. But if you're eating when I return, then you can give me some tortillas." The buzzard agreed to all this and put on the man's clothes. He put on his machete, his huaraches [sandals], his trousers, and his shirt. He grabbed the file and sharpened his machete and started to work. He worked and worked and worked and worked and liked it. The little woman came and found him there. "Now you've worked a lot! You hadn't worked the time I came before, but now you've done a lot." The little woman had brought eggs, tortillas, and atole. She respected him now and invited him to eat. The buzzard-turned-man lit into the meal and liked it. The woman did not know he was not her husband, but she noticed that he smelled terribly. "You smell awful," she said. "Perhaps you smell that buzzard which landed over there nearby," explained the buzzard-turned-man. The buzzard which landed was really her husband, and he approached them. The man who turned buzzard could no longer speak. The little woman said, "Get up and throw a rock at that filthy animal." But the buzzard-turned-man replied, "No. Let it be." So the little woman got up herself and threw a stick of wood at the man-turned-buzzard. "Horrible, filthy animal," she said. The buzzard-turned-man said, "I'm going to toss him a tortilla." But the little woman protested, "What! I didn't make these tortillas for it to eat!" She chased the man-turned-buzzard away. After she left, the husband complained, "You didn't give me a tortilla!" But the buzzard-turned-man explained that the little woman wouldn't let him. "Well now, we'll change our clothes," said the

man-turned-buzzard. He tried to remove his clothes, but the feathers dug into him. When he pulled they hurt. He tore at them, and they bled.

5. He knew that he would have to stay that way. He asked, "What'll I do to eat?" The buzzard-turned-man said, "Well, I always went to where I saw smoke rising and there I would land to eat." So the man-turned-buzzard flew off. He saw smoke rising where a forest was on fire and flew into it. That is why part of the buzzard is bare and why it is dark. He returned and told what happened. "Look for a thin column of smoke rising. There you'll find a dead animal or some filthy thing. And if you don't find a dead animal, you'll find something filthy like excrement. That's how you'll eat. I like how your wife fed me."

5. THE LIGHTNING-BOLTS TAKE NAWEWET FROM COSOLIN, by J. H. of Huitzilan

1. Nawewet[1] used to live on the Cosolin.[2] The lightning-bolts [kiuteome = rain gods] feared that the town [Huitzilan] would be lost in a flood, and so they decided to go see the Nawewet. They baptized him Juanito, and they invited him to a dance. "It's really nice where you live. There is a lot of water," they remarked. "Yes, but the water is mine," replied Juanito. The lightning-bolts urged, "Let's go. You're going to visit us. We'll feed you. You'll eat and you'll dance and then you can come back here." Juanito agreed, saying, "I'll go, but wait for me. I must see which package to take. I'm ashamed to go empty-handed." The lightning-bolts replied, "Don't be ashamed."

2. At about eleven o'clock at night they took him to the celebration. They went through the water [by way of the river], and Juanito grew tired while they journeyed because he carried such a heavy burden. His burden was a big piece of mountain like that church tower over there [gesturing]. He left his burden right there in the middle of the river below Tuxtla.[3] There is a big hill in the middle of the [Zempoala] river with ocote trees on it. Juanito goes there to eat the wood.

3. When they arrived, they saw arches of flowers decorating the cave, only they were not flowers, but rainbows. The water of the river whistled loudly like a guitar. The lightning-bolts said, "We've arrived. Now the musicians will play. Now that you don't have your burden anymore, you can dance." They gave Juanito a lot of aguardiente, and he got drunk. They told him it was his saint's day, but he didn't know for sure because he didn't know how to

read. The lightning-bolts told him he would stay there. "I've got my home," Juanito protested. But the lightning-bolts explained, "You could have killed us off with a flood.[4] It would have ended the world. It would be better if the world isn't lost by water again. You'll always have meat. The water will bring fish, or drowned animals, or even human beings. You won't have to eat tortillas." And a gentleman spoke to him, saying, "Listen, isn't it great what these people are saying? You won't have to buy clothes either because the water will bring them to you."

4. It was really raining when he arrived there. The lightning-bolts said, "It's your saint's day [June 24]. It'll always rain when it's your saint's day." Well, Juanito stayed there. He got drunk, and the lightning-bolts left him there sleeping. When he awoke there was nobody around. He is still there now. Sometimes, about in July, one can hear him whistling when he plays in the water. He more or less knows his saint's day, but he doesn't know it exactly. The lightning-bolts will not let him know. Because if he knew, he would throw a big celebration and bring a huge rainstorm and we would perish another time.[5]

6. THE MAN WHO SAID WHEN IT WOULD RAIN, by A. V. of Huitzilan

1. Once there was a man who had a lot of workers who prepared a field for planting. One day when it was very hot, he decided to gather his workers together and ask them if anyone knew when it would rain. He wanted rain to make the crops grow. "We don't know," said the workers. "Just God knows that." And standing in the rear was a little man who looked sick and stupid. He said that rain was not far off and that, although it looked sunny now, clouds would come and it would rain in two or three days. The co-workers presented him to their patron. The man had white hair. "Is it true you know when it'll rain?" asked his patron. "Well, I don't know. But it is said that clouds will come tomorrow or the next day and then it'll rain," said the man. His patron replied, "If it doesn't rain in four days, I'll go to your house and shoot you with five bullets. If it does rain, then I'll give you half of everything I have—my houses, my animals, and my land. My workers who heard me are the witnesses."

2. The man went home, and when he rose on the third day, he told his wife, "Get up. Pack me some tortillas, and I'm going away." The man went into the forest, where he came across a hummingbird, then a redbird, and finally a buzzard. He ignored the

first two birds when they called him. The buzzard succeeded in engaging the man in conversation. The man told the buzzard what happened, and the buzzard said, "But he won't shoot you. You'll arrive at a place where you'll find a big stone. Tilt it and follow the road you'll see behind it. You'll see a big house far away, and there you'll find the water."

3. The man followed the directions and reached the house. He came upon a woman grinding dough for tortillas. "Ah, son, why did you come here? None of my children from earth comes here. I'm glad you came, my son," she exclaimed. The man explained what happened. "Sit down and wait for my children. They went visiting, but they'll come back," said the woman. The man waited, and after a short while those boys [telpočkame] came. They were nude, and they were wet with perspiration, and they were tired. "How glad we are that you came. We don't see Christians from earth here," they said. The man explained to them what happened. The boys told him why it hadn't rained. "When [your patron] sees that it's going to rain, he gets angry because no one can work. He wants the sun to shine so that his men can work. He gets angry and swears at the rain. Go now quickly. Take this rain cape. Go and climb on top of your house. We'll just take a bath and we'll go right over there," they said.

4. The man took the rain cape and returned, although he didn't know how. It started to rain a little, and wind shook his house and a lot of rain fell. On the fourth day much rain fell. On the fifth day his patron, the owner of the hacienda, held a huge celebration. He adorned his house and the roadway with flowers. He treated the man and his wife like gods by putting them on an altar. He held a dance and divided his holdings.

7. THE MAN WHO SAID WHEN IT WOULD RAIN,
by M. I. of Yaonáhuac

1. There once was a drunk who got drunk and went to the front of the government palace and shouted. A policeman came out and grabbed him, asking what he was doing. The policeman reminded him that there was a drought. The drunk replied, "But how am I to blame? You're the stupid ones. I wish it to rain in three days." The policeman ran him off. The next day another policeman went to call on him to tell him to see the town president, who wanted him to explain why they were the stupid ones. The president confronted the drunk and told him that if it didn't rain in three days, they would kill him and burn him for lying. The drunk asked how he could

bring rain, and the president replied that would be his problem.

2. The man went to his wife and told her prepare his meal. The drunk fled and went into a forest [*kwoyo*]. In the afternoon of the next day he reached a pasture in the middle of the forest.

3. There he found Tonana [Our Mother] inside a hut. She was sweeping. The drunk asked for lodging, and she obliged. Tonantzin [Our Little Mother] is the mother of the lightning-bolts. She finished sweeping and hid the drunk inside the house, putting his head in the corner and covering him with a straw mat. She hid him from her children so that they would not strike him. Her children came home. They were small and had very curly hair. "There is a boy who came from far away," their mother told them. She explained what had happened to him. The boys uncovered the man, who explained that it had been some time since it rained in his town. "I got drunk and shouted, and they threw me in jail," he said. "I told them that I wanted it to rain in three days. I told them they were stupid. The town president told me that if it didn't rain in three days, then he would kill me," the drunk added. The boys explained, "But we haven't gone there for this reason. We used to go there all the time, but they swore at us. So we decided that it would be better not to go." They added, "Now we go somewhere else, farther away, where they don't say anything. We work for the plants so that they'll have water and grow better. We don't go places to do damage." The drunk told them he had no money. The boys said to him, "That's not important. We'll go to your house. You buy a candle and you decorate a table and you light that candle. Put chairs around the table as if it were for your compadres so that we can rest there. And you tell the president to tell the rest not to swear at us for working there again."

4. The drunk came home and did as the lightning-bolts told him. He lit the candles, and the clouds came and the lightning-bolts emerged. It thundered loudly and a rain shower began. It was a very heavy one. The lightning-bolts came to rest at the table. The lightning-bolts warned the people of the town to leave quickly because a wall of water would come. It continued to rain steadily.

8. THE ORIGIN OF CORN PLANTING KNOWLEDGE,
by M. F. of Huitzilan

1. The first lightning-bolt awoke after breaking open Sustenance Mountain and found no Christians anywhere. The corn was dirty and had been stepped on. He resolved to gather up the corn despite its condition.

2. He planted the corn so that he would have fresh ears before anyone else. He planted his *milpa,* and it produced quickly. The others came and asked what he had done with his *milpa* to make it grow. So he told them how to plant. He said, "Roast the corn first and then plant it." They took his advice and roasted a lot of corn and planted it. But it didn't sprout even after a month. They came again to ask the first lightning-bolt why it didn't sprout. He said, "Perhaps the earth is bad. Perhaps it is too cold. Prepare a lot of *nixtamal* [corn boiled in lime water] and plant that." They followed his instructions, and two months passed. There was no crop. They saw that the first lightning-bolt's corn was ready to harvest.

3. Out of envy they knocked down his *milpa* with wind. Then they went to see him, and he asked why they had done this. He said, "I'll tell you how to plant, but first you must attach the stalks of my *milpa* so that it will be just as it was before and nothing will be lost." He stressed that his *milpa* was about to be harvested.

4. They attached all the pieces of the stalks so that the *milpa* was as before. They attached the pieces with mucus from their noses. For this reason, at the foot of the stalk now it looks as if there are drops of mucus. They told the first lightning-bolt that they repaired his *milpa.* He told them how to plant corn. "Put the corn in water for a day and then plant it," he said.

9. THE ORIGIN OF CORN PLANTING KNOWLEDGE, by F. J. of Yaonáhuac

1. Nanawatzin awoke after cracking open Sustenance Mountain and releasing the corn. He found no one else around. The other lightning-bolts left the corn residue strewn all over. Nanawatzin gathered up the remainder of the corn and loaded it on his mules. He knew that the other lightning-bolts would want another favor.

2. He planted his *milpa,* and the other lightning-bolts decided to see how Nanawatzin had done it. They asked him how he had planted his corn. He replied, "Prepare a lot of *nixtamal* and grind it into dough. Throw the dough into a hole." They did as told. When the lightning-bolts checked their *milpa,* they found that it had not sprouted, even though Nanawatzin's *milpa* had fresh ears of corn by this time. Their *milpa* filled up with weeds. They decided that Nanawatzin had not told them the truth.

3. They resolved to knock down Nanawatzin's *milpa* with wind and rain. This made Nanwatzin very angry, and so he went to see the other lightning-bolts. He told them, "Restore my *milpa* and

I'll tell you the truth." They replied, "If you really tell us the truth this time, then we'll repair it."

4. Nanawatzin told them to attach the broken pieces of the stalk with the mucus from their noses and with their saliva. The lightning-bolts made the wind blow in the opposite direction to re-erect Nanawatzin's corn crop.

10. THE ORIGIN OF CORN PLANTING KNOWLEDGE, by J. M. of Yaonáhuac

2. The lightning-bolt children asked their father what he did to make his crops grow. Their father said, "Roast the corn and then plant it." They did as told, but the corn didn't sprout. They came to their father again and told him that their corn had not sprouted. The father then said, "Prepare some *nixtamal* and plant that." They followed his instructions. But nothing happened, and they told their father that their *milpa* didn't sprout. "You don't know how to plant corn," he said. "You're not telling us the truth," they replied.

3. The three brothers exchanged opinions among themselves. They decided to knock down their father's *milpa*, and they did it with wind. "Why did you destroy my *milpa*?" their father asked. "Because you didn't tell us the truth," they said. "I'll tell you the truth, but first you must repair my *milpa*," demanded the father.

4. Again the three brothers exchanged opinions. They decided to attach the pieces of the stalks with their nose mucus. For that reason, it looks as if the roots of the stalk drip spittle.

11. THE COMPADRE AND THE CHILE THIEF, by F. J. of Yaonáhuac

Once there was a compadre who had a chile patch far away. One day there came a heavy rain. The compadre was a wiseman [lightning-bolt with clairvoyant powers], and he divined that someone was stealing his green chiles. The thief could not get away from the chile patch because of the heavy rain. The compadre decided to let the thief cut the chiles and fill up his sack. He saw the thief fill the sack and tie up the mouth. He saw him prepare to load the sack with his tumpline. So the compadre decided to act. "I'll make him leave it there, and tomorrow I'll fetch it," he said to himself. He removed a burning stick from the hearth and threw it to the corner of the chile patch where the thief was squatting to load the sack with his tumpline. A *nauwiyak* [fer-de-lance] came toward him quickly and chased him off. It wanted to bite him, and it came very close to doing it. The snake didn't let him take the sack, and the next day when the rain had stopped, the compadre brought the sack of chiles.

12. THE TIME THE DEVIL LOST THE WAGER, *by J. P. of Huitzilan*

1. God decided to live in heaven, and the devil wanted to take command of the Christians on earth, God's children. But God didn't want it that way because when he left the devil in command, the devil would eat one of God's children when the sun came out. The Christians were becoming fewer. God asked Sr. Santiago if he realized how many of their children there were. Sr. Santiago also realized that there were not enough. They both decided to see the devil when the sun came out because that was when he ate one of their children. They wanted to remove him from his work. They found him at the precise moment that he was eating a Christian and one of them [God or Sr. Santiago] hit the devil to remove him from his work.

2. Then the devil decided to go his own way. One day God won over him completely. The devil said, "I'll bet you can't tell me who my parents were." God didn't know because he hadn't met them. God asked Sr. Santiago, but he didn't know either. "When I awoke, that man—the devil—was already there. He is ageless," said Sr. Santiago. Then God spoke to sleep, who didn't know either.

3. Sleep told God, "Talk to thirst. I'll grab him when he goes to eat. We'll both get him to tell us who his parents were." When the devil went to eat he became very sleepy. He went to sleep and thirst came along and asked him. The devil said that his father was black dysentery [*tiltikalawak*] and his mother was white dysentery [*ištakatiltik*]. He said that when he was born, he was turned upside down [possibly referring to a breech birth], and his mother was the very old woman [*simi lamatzin*]. He said that when he was a child she passed him four times between her legs, she breast-fed him, and then tossed him away. He grew up to be thin because he was reared on smoke. Thirst went immediately to tell God. Thirst asked, "Did you hear what the devil has said?" God replied, "Yes. Now tell sleep to let go of him."

4. The devil awoke and ate. He remembered God was waiting for him in the road. He wanted to beat God and command the Christians. He went quickly to find where God waited for him. But

God told the devil who his father and mother were. He told him that he had been turned around and passed four times between his mother's legs and abandoned. He knew that he was nurtured on smoke. So God won the contest, and he continued to command his children on earth.

5. The devil decided to go to his headquarters, and he told God to wait for him to return and they'd go hunting. "I'll bring my carbine," he said. He made twelve small dogs to take with them into the forest. He lined them up and blew in their faces as he whipped them so they would bark. They all fell over, and he asked God, "Why didn't they come to life?" God made some big dogs. The devil went back to his headquarters. He opened up his house and found that all of his guns were melted together. There was just one Remington, but when he tried it out, it exploded. So he decided to go hunting without any gun. He told God, "Whip the dogs." But God blessed them instead. God looked right at the devil, face to face. God had made the dogs go without food, and so they really chased the devil. They chased him and chased him into a mountain. There the devil went to stay forever. He went into that mountain.

6. God held a celebration. He went to bless the devil's abode and spread a lot of incense around. The guests drank wine. They were God's apostles. They began to play the trumpet. The devil sneaked back and spoke to God. God asked, "What do you want?" The devil replied, "I've come because the dogs are sleeping. They injured me. They bit me. I won't threaten this house anymore. Please may I have just one of your children." God denied him. The devil wanted permission to go in, but God refused. The devil asked for a little sauce in which the meat of the banquet was boiled. God didn't have time to tell the devil where he was born because the dogs chased him away.

13. THE TIME THE DEVIL LOST THE WAGER, by L. V. of Yaonáhuac

2. Once God our father met the animal [the devil]. The devil demanded, "Tell me who your parents were and who my parents were." God didn't know who his own parents were, let alone who were the parents of the devil. If God couldn't solve the riddle, then the world would belong to the devil. God had to meet the devil in eight days at noon and tell him the answer to the puzzle. He was to meet the devil at the crossroads.

3. God wondered what to do. He decided that San Pedro

should put a cantina on a hill where the devil climbs up out of a canyon. San Pedro put water—*aguardiente*—in his cantina. When the devil arrived he asked for a cup of water. He drank some and asked for more. He got drunk and rolled around in the dirt in front of the cantina and started talking. "I'm going to meet God," he said. "I asked him who his parents were and who my parents were and I know that God doesn't know. God's father was the wax candle [*cerita*] and his mother was copal [for incense]. My parents were the ash in the middle of the fire and the thorny heart of the century plant [maguey]. My grandfather was the forked tree and my grandmother was the whirlwind. My cousins were the noises one hears the wind make in the hollows. My aunt is the crying woman [*la llorona*]."

4. The devil awoke and went off, but San Pedro reached God first and told him what the drunk man had said. San Pedro had written it all down. The devil came and God told him the answer to the riddle. That animal lost the wager.

14. THE CRUCIFIXION OF CHRIST, by J. H. of Huitzilan

6. When the Jews killed Jesus, they struck him. They attacked him. They chased him. They grabbed him and hit him with sticks of wood. They stabbed him with a knife, they struck him with a machete, and they shot him. When they hit him, Jesus said, "Oh God, oh God, why do you hit me? I don't have sin." The Jews replied, "Yes, you do have sin because you have become like a god." They cut him to pieces, and they whipped him.

8. They dug a grave and threw in the pieces of his body and covered him up. After they covered him up, the Jews were happy. They went to fetch a chicken and put it on top of the grave. They told the chicken, "Now we've buried Jesus here, but now you stay here. If you see the ground moving because Jesus is trying to escape, shout loudly so that we'll come so that we can hit him again."

10. Well, within four days he rose. The chicken saw the ground move. Jesus appeared a little bit and spoke to the chicken, saying, "Don't shout so that I can flee." The chicken replied, "Well, that's fine, but only if I go where you're going." Jesus answered, "If you go there you'll have eternal life with me. You'll have eternal life when they kill you. When you see that I'm in the middle of heaven, then you shout. When the Jews come, you flee, but continue shouting as you flee. You'll accompany me and I'll know how to feed you."

11. When the chicken shouted, the Jews came quickly. They brought clubs, machetes, knives, daggers, and stones. They wanted to hit him, but they couldn't. He went up to heaven to be in charge. Now Jesus is in charge. No one else is in charge.

14. When Jesus went, he punished the blackbird [*papa*]. When it feels it is going to lay eggs, it doesn't lay them. It lays them one week later. When Jesus arrived in heaven, he told the redbird [*čičil-totot*] that it had a very fine heart. "Well now, you'll sing when I ask," said Jesus to the redbird. As for the *primavera* bird [*kwita-totok*], Jesus said, "Let's see, you'll sing as you can." But when Jesus arrived in heaven, the redbird couldn't sing. He couldn't find the redbird in heaven, but he did find the *primavera*, and it is he who has the fine heart. It sings well and it won. [See episode 5 in story 15.]

15. THE CRUCIFIXION OF CHRIST, by F. J. of Yaonáhuac

1. The Jews lived and God our father lived with them. But God our father could perform miracles. And as much as the Jews tried, they could not equal them. Wherever God our father went, he didn't take any tortillas. Nevertheless, when the time came to eat, he fed his apostles their lunch or their coffee. The Jews tried to do the same thing, but they could not. The Jews had a king, but their king was not the equal of Jesus.

2. So they decided to capture him and kill him because they feared that he would reign. They tried to figure out who he was because all of the apostles had the same face and were the same size. The Jews decided to ask one of the apostles. They offered to pay him to show them who he was. They said they'd give him seven coins. They decided that the apostle would identify Jesus by kissing his feet. The apostle identified Jesus the next morning, but Jesus knew what was happening. The Jews gave the apostle the seven coins. He brought a sack, and they threw the seven coins into it. The apostle didn't even see where they fell.

3. Then things went on as if nothing had happened. That evening everyone gathered around God our father, and he gave them supper. After they finished eating, he told them that one had turned him in to the Jews so that they would kill him. The apostles all lined up and each said to him, "And was it I who turned you in?" He said no to each one until he came to the one who did turn him in to the Jews. The apostle didn't have his crown. When this apostle saw that the others had their crowns but he didn't have his anymore, he asked for forgiveness and for pardon, and he said, "It

would be better to return the seven coins so that you'd give me my crown again." But God our father said, "You turned me in and I'm happy." The apostle pleaded, but he didn't give it to him. God our father fled. The Jews chased him. Jesus went into the forest.

4. He came upon some men who were working and asked them, "Children, what are you doing?" They replied, "We're cutting here to plant corn." God told them that tomorrow they should bring their baskets to harvest their crop. He added, "Some persons will come asking when I passed by here, and you should tell them that I came by here when you were cutting down the forest to plant. You had then plowed the land, put the earth over the roots of the corn stalks, doubled over the ears of corn to dry, and now you're about to harvest the crop." Then God our father went on ahead. The Jews saw signs of where Jesus had passed through. Jesus came upon some others, whom he asked, "What are you doing here?" They replied, "We're planting some stone." They didn't tell Jesus the truth. "Good, then when some persons come and ask about me, you tell them that I passed by here when this hill was being born," said Jesus. He went on further and saw the Jews coming closer. He couldn't flee from them. The mountains grew larger, and the men who said they were planting stone said to the Jews that the mountain was beginning to grow when Jesus passed them. Jesus found some others, whom he asked, "What are you doing here?" "We're planting some trees," was their reply. A big forest appeared with rotting wood, fungus, and debris [*pastle*].

5. The Jews chased him further. Jesus saw that they were about to catch him, so he went into another forest. There were blackbirds [*papame*]. The Jews said, "Jesus must be here because the blackbird says that he sees his father." The Jews also went into the forest. God our father saw that he couldn't flee anymore, and he realized the blackbirds were turning him in. So he threw himself down on the ground and covered himself with debris from the forest floor. The partridge saw where he was exposed, and it covered God our father so that the Jews wouldn't see him. The Jews arrived and spread themselves out, but they couldn't find him. So they left. Since the blackbirds were turning Jesus in to the Jews, God our father made them defecate blood every day from Good Friday.

6. When they caught Jesus, they took him to a town and made the people gather together to see that they had captured the divine prisoner. They tied him on a cross, but he didn't stay there. They grabbed him. They attacked him, and they really hit Jesus Christ. They killed him.

7. The Virgin of the Soledad [*Tonantzin*] and San Juan were helping him. But the Jews struck them just as they had struck Jesus. After the Jews hit him they say that the Virgin la Veronica cleaned him with her apron. They grabbed her and struck her too just as they struck him. They even crucified San Juan. It was Good Friday when the blackbird turned Jesus in and the Jews caught him.

8. They lowered him from the cross and told a carpenter to make a coffin. They took him to the cemetery in a procession led by a torch. They blew cornets. They buried him. They told a stonemason to build a tomb so that he wouldn't escape. But the Jews were not sure. So they put a chicken on the tomb and told it to shout if he tried to leave so that they could catch him again.

9. The mole [*topo = tusa*] decided to go into the grave to see if he were alive or dead. God our father was alive. The mole felt that he was alive. God our father said to the mole, "Now that you've come, now you'll stay here forever." So the mole stayed there and didn't return to tell the Jews.

10. Jesus spoke to the chicken, asking, "Do me a favor and don't shout when I leave. They [the Jews] will take many pieces out of you. Each piece will be a chicken, and you'll reign in the world. Every house will have a chicken." The chicken was nude then; it didn't have any feathers. Jesus said he would give it clothing. Jesus told the chicken, "Don't shout until you see that I've gone far, until I've gone way up." The chicken was happy. It did not turn Jesus in to the Jews.

11. Jesus went. The chicken did not turn him in. When the chicken finally shouted, the Jews rushed out to chase him. But they never could have caught him. He rose up into the heavens. All of the apostles were sad. "Well now, how shall we speak to him?" they asked. Well, he came to see them. "When will you come again?" they asked him. "I'm going to live in heaven, but Sr. Santiago will go with you," he said.

12. Jesus went to see Sr. Santiago and sent him to earth, saying, "Right now go see what the Jews are doing." Sr. Santiago came with his horse, and the Jews grabbed his horse and killed it. Sr. Santiago told God about this, and God told him to gather together the legs of his horse and shout three times, and he would see that his horse got up again. Then Jesus told him, "Then you hit the Jews. Take a sword, one that has been used." Sr. Santiago came and killed all the Jews.

13. Because the carpenter made the coffin for God our father,

he didn't bless his work. That's why carpenters earn so little. The same is true for the stonemasons and the Jews.

16. THE HUNTER, by L. V. of Yaonáhuac

1. Once a hunter went for a walk in the forest to look for animals—wild boars, doves, badgers, or armadillos. This time the lightning-bolts took away his permission to hunt. They bewildered him, and instead of leaving the way he came in, the hunter went farther into the forest and got lost. He came across some lumbermen who were sawing up some trees.

2. "What are you doing?" he asked them. "Making a living," they replied. "Would you tell me where I can find the road to get out of here?" asked the hunter. "We've seen you. You've passed by us but you've never spoken to us," they replied. "We'll give you directions for getting out of here, but do us a favor first. We have to deliver this wood, but our cook hasn't come to feed us. Would you go to our house and help us by making our meal?" they added. "Since that's how it is, then I must go," said the hunter. "Leave your carbine," said the lumbermen. "We'll feed you. You'll find our house way down there [*tanipa* = north] where you got lost in the forest. Go inside but go cautiously. You'll find our cook there. Don't speak to her. She doesn't understand. We'll tell you what to do. Look for the pot of corn and put it on to boil. Put the dinner pot on the fire also. Get the beans and put them into the dinner pot so that we can eat when we get there."

3. The hunter left his carbine with them and went off. He came to the house and went inside. He saw a frog sitting on the metate. He snatched a piece of wood and hit the frog. She tried to run under the metate, but she couldn't save herself. The hunter almost killed her. He thought she was just an animal, but she was the cook for the lumbermen. But they weren't really lumbermen. They were lightning-bolts.

4. Well, the hunter put the pot of corn on to boil and put wood on the hearth to make a really big fire. He put a lot of corn into the pot just as we do here. But the lightning-bolts put just one kernel of corn into the pot to boil. The hunter did the same with the beans. He put a lot of beans into the dinner pot. The pots overflowed, and a lot of the meal was lost.

5. Well, afterwards he started to open things up in the house. He found a beautiful horsewhip and he found a belt which he strapped around his waist. He saw some beautiful clothes and put

them on. He came across a beautiful instrument—a trumpet—hanging on the wall. He pulled it down and put it to his mouth. He ran over to some pots inside the house. Some held the wind, others held hail, and still others held rain. There were many other things which he did not understand. He removed the lids from the pots. He looked in and tried to put the lids back on. But as he tried to put the lids back on, the wind escaped with force. It was the same for the hail and the rain. The wind rose with clouds and rain.

6. The lumbermen looked over to their house. They saw it get very dark. The rain and hail came from there. "Who knows what our helper is doing inside the house. Let's see. People will perish in the rain. Let's go calm the storm," they said. When they arrived they couldn't find the hunter. He had traveled up with the wind. He put the trumpet to his lips, and there was a loud clap of thunder. The lumbermen dressed themselves. They carried their own whips. They cracked their whips and surrounded the wind, rain, and hail. They calmed the tempest and brought it back into their house. "Why did you do it? You nearly destroyed us. It'd be better if you went home," they told the hunter. "Take your pay. We aren't bad people," they added. They gave him gifts. They gave him a gourd jug. They gave him a ring. They gave him some stones which were like crystals. He would eat forever with their gifts, but he had to stop hunting.

17. JUAN BARAJERO, by N. A. H. of Huitzilan

1. Once there was a man called Juan Barajero. That man didn't like to do just any kind of work. He only liked to support himself by playing cards. There came a day when he didn't have enough money to feed his children. He decided to leave his house and set out on the road. He told his mother, "If I run into God, I'll talk to him. But if I run into the devil, I'll talk to him too." He ran into a man and asked him if he would like to play cards. "No," said the man, "but someone else is coming along who would like to play with you." Then the man added, "If you hadn't invoked me first, then you would have run into the devil first, and you would not have beaten him. Since you invoked me first, you'll beat the devil in the card game."

2. Juan did indeed beat the devil five times. Juan took the devil's clothes and his horse. But afterwards he told the devil not to feel badly because he beat him. He asked the devil to tell him where he lived and what was his name so that he would work for

him to repay him. "I'm Deodan de Oro and I live in the bowels of the earth," replied the devil.

3. One day Juan went to look for the devil to make good on his promise. He passed through four communities looking for Deodan de Oro, but no one knew where he lived. Finally he ran into an old woman who lived where there was no one. She told him how to find the devil and return safely. She said, "You must cross four bodies of water. A wild beast [tekwani] will carry you across the first one. A water dog [aitzkwinti, which could possibly be a manatee] will take you across the second one. An animal [okwili] will take you across the third. And an eagle [tenitz] will take you across the fourth. You'll find the devil's daughter washing [in the river], and she'll have a necklace, some earrings, a ring, and ribbons lying about nearby. Pick them up. When she looks for them, give them to her. Talk to her, because she'll bring you back safely to earth."

4. Juan did exactly as told. The devil's daughter, Blanca Flor, agreed to help Juan if he really would go off with her. She warned Juan about her father. "He really just wants to eat you, but he won't do anything if you take me away," she said. Juan arrived at the house of the devil. Deodan de Oro gave Juan four huge tasks. "Clear a field stretching across half of the earth and plant it with chiles," he said. Juan went to Blanca Flor and she helped him by getting ants to do the work. "Build a bridge from here to the other side of the sea so troops can meet in the middle and fight," demanded the devil. Blanca Flor helped Juan again by making a bridge with a rainbow. Two kinds of ants met in the middle and fought. Blanca Flor made it rain, thunder, and lightning to make it sound like war. "Recover a gold ring that I dropped in the middle of the sea when I went to market," said the devil. This time Blanca Flor helped Juan by cutting around the diameter of her finger with a knife. The blood dried, and she took off a ring of dried blood that turned into gold. "Grab an untamed horse that no one has been able to grab hold of and tame it," insisted the devil. This horse could run seven thousand leagues. Blanca Flor helped Juan again. "Let's fetch a mare who runs a thousand leagues and with her you can rope the wild horse," she told Juan. "Hit the wild horse and barricade it to tire it out and then it'll be tamed," she said.

5. After Juan finished the last task, Blanca Flor said, "My father just wants to eat you. Let's flee on the mare that runs one thousand leagues." To escape her father, Blanca Flor foiled him in many ways. She put a cup filled with her saliva on the floor of her room. When her father called to her the next morning, the saliva

answered him. But her father discovered what happened, and he
went out after them on the horse that ran seven thousand leagues.
When Blanca Flor saw her father approaching, she spit on the
ground and made a very thick mud, and her father couldn't pass
through it. When her father came after them again, she threw
down her mirror, which made a big lake. When she saw him come
after them again, she threw down her comb, and it turned into a
corral. When she saw her father coming again, she threw down
some of her hair, which turned into a forest. When he came still
another time, she told Juan, "Sit down in the road and I'll become a
bunch of bananas. Offer to sell them to my father, saying, 'two for
five.'" Juan did as told. He refused to answer the devil, who asked
about the couple. He just said, "Two for five," as he offered the
devil some bananas. When the devil came again, Blanca Flor turned
herself into a village, and she made the mare into a church, changing its tail into a church tower. "Ring the church bells," she told
Juan. When the devil came and asked about the couple, Juan announced that the priest was coming to give a mass. Deodan de Oro
swore, and the couple escaped.

6. Juan and Blanca Flor arrived safely on earth. Blanca Flor
warned Juan that he would forget about her because they would
throw incense on him, erasing his memory. That was what happened. Juan returned to his mother. He found he had been gone
four years while thinking it was only four days. Juan's mother
decided to arrange for her son's marriage. The day of the ceremony
arrived, and Juan suggested that his mother ask Blanca Flor to help
prepare the food. He had heard that she knew how to prepare a
meal very quickly. His mother told him to bring her, and so he
went to visit Blanca Flor. She agreed to help prepare the food. Juan
asked her to make some dolls to dance with, and she agreed to this
as well. Blanca Flor made one doll to look like Juan and made
another one like herself. When the music of the marriage celebration started, the dolls started to dance. The doll looking like Blanca
Flor struck the one looking like Juan on his behind. She reminded
him of the time when he took her ribbon, her necklace, her earrings, and her rings worth thousands of pesos. She told him about
helping him clear and plant the field, about making the bridge,
about making the ring, and about breaking the horse. Then Juan
remembered who she was, and he told his mother that Blanca Flor
had saved him. He abandoned the girl he was supposed to marry,
and took Blanca Flor as his wife.

18. *JUAN BARAJERO, by L. V. of Yaonáhuac*

1. One day Juan Barajero told his wife, "Fix me my lunch. If I can find someone to play cards with, let him be the devil."

2. Juan left his house and took to the road, where he came upon the devil. The two started playing cards. The devil let Juan win first. But then the devil won everything from Juan, including his life.

3. Juan went back home and told his wife, "I'm going to pay this debt to the devil." Juan left his house again and went on and on. He came across some animals in the forest—the buzzard, the tiger, and the rabbit. The buzzard spoke to him. "Since I fly about the earth, I see where people go to get lost," said the buzzard. That was the home of the devil. The buzzard took Juan, and along the way he gave him instructions. "I'll leave you at the entrance to the devil's home. But don't go to his home. Instead go to the edge of the water and stand where a girl [Blanca Flor] brings water. She'll want to marry you in return for her help. You should agree so that you can win out over the devil. But don't you tell the devil that the girl is your wife," instructed the buzzard.

4. Juan followed the buzzard's instructions exactly. He met Blanca Flor and agreed to take her away in return for her help. The two of them went off to see the devil so that Juan could pay his debt. "Build a mountain in my farm three leagues high and have it ready for me by noon tomorrow," demanded the devil. Juan went to Blanca Flor and told her what the devil requested. "Get some earth and moisten it to make a ball of mud. Then fan it with your hat to make the ball roll. It'll get larger and become a mountain," she told him. It worked, and Juan returned to the devil for more instructions. "Plant seeds of papayas, bananas, melons, watermelons, and a lot of other fruit and bring me the ripe fruits at noon tomorrow," said the devil. Again, Juan went to Blanca Flor. "Take these seeds and plant the fruit, sapling by sapling. Water the plants and you'll see them grow right before your eyes. The fruit will be ready by noon tomorrow," said Blanca Flor. Juan completed the task and returned to the devil for even more instructions. "Put a floor of crystal over the earth and sea and encircle it with a fence," commanded the devil. This time Blanca Flor said, "Take this mirror and put half into the water and half on the ground. It'll expand across the sea. Stick this knife into the ground over and over again and a fence will grow around the crystal on the earth. I'll go into the water to plant the rest of the fence in the sea. You'll have to chop me up with this knife and throw me into the water. Be careful

and don't spill any of my blood," she said. Again Juan did as told and it worked. Blanca Flor re-emerged as if nothing had happened. But she noticed that a piece of her finger had fallen to the ground when Juan chopped her up. Now it was missing. "It will serve as a sign," she said. "My father will say, 'Now you've paid me what you owed me, I'll pay you.' He'll say, 'What do you want?' Tell him you want a girl. But there are a lot of us. We'll make a circle in front of my father. We'll look exactly alike. You won't know me except for my finger. When you find me, say, 'I want this one,'" Blanca Flor explained. Juan did exactly as told.

5. The devil left them alone. Blanca Flor told Juan, "We must flee to your home." So they ran off on a horse called Devours Leagues. They took off, but the devil mounted a faster horse called Runs with the Wind. To get off to a good start, Blanca Flor filled a cup of saliva that answered when her father called them. She put pots in their bed so that her father thought he stabbed Juan when he went into their room at night. But the devil finally realized that the couple had fled. Blanca Flor saw her father approaching, and so she told Juan, "You change into a dead horse. I'll change the horse into a dog, and I'll change myself into a bird." But afterwards she saw her father approaching again. She changed Juan into a man carrying a basket of bananas and she turned into his wife. Their horse became their dog. The devil finally ran out of time and couldn't pursue them any more. The chicken crowed after three in the morning, and the devil wasn't free to chase after them anymore.

6. The moment the chicken crowed, Blanca Flor became a woman from the earth [*taltikpak siwat*]. The couple arrived at Juan's house. "Take me to your mother. If we're not careful, your mother will kiss you and then you'll fall asleep and when you wake up, you'll have forgotten about me," she said. But Juan refused her request, and when his mother kissed him, he forgot about Blanca Flor. Juan decided to look for a wife [the narrator makes no mention of the wife who appeared in episode 1]. Blanca Flor was living with Juan's aunt. She was a diviner and knew of the wedding, and so she persuaded the aunt to go with her to the celebration. She found a new suit of clothes for the aunt. Blanca Flor also made a doll to look like Juan. During the wedding celebration she danced with the doll, speaking to it and hitting it with a whip. She reminded the doll how she had helped Juan, and then she delivered Juan to the devil.

19. THE MAN WHO WON THE HACIENDA,
by N. A. H. of Huitzilan

1. Once there was a man who had a son. That son grew up without ever taking a bath. He wore a tunic and never changed his clothes. He and his clothes were very, very black. But he wasn't lazy. He worked hard in the *milpa*. One day his parents decided he should look for a wife. His father said, "Go look for your eye." He meant go look for a girl. "Perhaps it'll be in the church," he added. But the boy didn't know what his father meant. He went to church and saw the eye of a dog and then told his father. This time his father told him, "Go to the cafe." He returned and said, "I saw the eye of a chicken." So then his parents sent him to the butcher shop, and when he returned he told his parents that he saw the eye of a bull. So this time they sent him to the town square.

2. They say he sat down at the edge of the square because he was ashamed. Then he decided to look around. There were a lot of people. They say there was a man who had three daughters. Some of these princesses were in the second story of his big house. The boy heard them talking. He saw a well-dressed person come by. The girls dropped a piece of paper down to him. The paper told him to meet them that evening when it got dark. It told him to climb up to them at eight o'clock that night. The note said, "We'll drop a rope down for you between eight and ten o'clock."

3. That boy decided he would come before the well-dressed gentleman arrived. He went to the place where he found the rope and jiggled it so that the girls would pull it. He climbed up into their room and stayed there. He slept with them. The next morning the girls' parents awoke. Their father asked their mother, "What are our daughters doing? Why don't they get up? Go call them." She did just that, but the girls didn't get up. So their father went to see them and found them with the dirt-stained boy. "Right now," he said, "even though you don't want to, just as you slept with him, one of you will marry him. You'll marry him because you slept with him." So the dirty boy married one of those girls.

4. He began working with the girls' father, who was very rich. He worked with the plowboys. The workers asked him where he lived. "I'm in the house of that king," he replied. "When would you be with a princess?" they said. They refused to believe him. Word got around to another hacienda owner, who said to the boy, "If it's true, then you'll make a wager with me. If she comes to feed you, then you'll take all that I have. My house and hacienda will be yours. If she doesn't come to feed you, I'll give you five bullets.

Each one of my workers will shoot you once and you'll die."
    5. The boy returned to his wife and said, "I'm not well."
"Why?" she asked. He explained what happened. He told the girl's
father, "He said she's to come to feed me tomorrow noon. If she
comes I'll take all that king has." The girl's father asked, "What'll
he give you if she doesn't come?" "Five bullets," he replied. So the
father-in-law said, "We'll feed you tomorrow." At noon the next
day the other hacienda owner saw them coming to feed the boy.
"What I have is yours," he said. The dirt-stained boy became
very rich.

20. THE MAN WHO WON THE HACIENDA, by F. J. of Yaonáhuac

    2. One time a charcoal-seller went into town. There was this
girl who was up above in a building. She was looking down. There
was a boy below, and he was talking to her. "Well, it's about time
we get married," he said. "Yes. You come at nine or ten tonight. I'll
wait for you," she said. "How will you see me? How shall I call to
you so that you'll come out?" he asked. "I'll let a rope fall. You pull
on it. I'll be sleeping and it'll wake me up," she replied. The charcoal-
seller heard everything, but he played dumb.
    3. The charcoal-seller came ahead of the boy. He tied himself
with the rope and tugged on it so the girl would pull it. He went up
into her room. He wasn't the one she expected. "Well, you've
climbed up here. Another one was going to come. Well, it'll be you
then," she said. The charcoal-seller was so sooty. He was stained
with grime. "How shall I present him to my father?" she asked.
That girl was ashamed. She took him into the bathroom. She took
him to wash. He changed. He put on all new clothes so that he'd be
like the girl. He put on new trousers, a new shirt, and new shoes.
When the sun came up, she took him to her father. She presented
him as if he were the son-in-law. "Well, I'm going to marry him,"
she said. "You're going to marry this boy, eh?" said the father. "We
were engaged yesterday, and I told him to come. Since he came, I'm
presenting him to you now," said the girl. "Well, that's how it'll
be," replied the father.
    4. So there they were. The charcoal-seller was accustomed to
work. He saw others going to work and wanted to go with them.
"Don't go. Stay here," said the father-in-law. His daughter was a
princess, and she didn't speak to just anyone. But the charcoal-
seller was bound to go. He said, "I'm going to go to work with the
oxen." The girl and her father told him not to go, but he was very
stubborn. "Well, go," they finally said. So he went. He put on his

stained and grimy clothes and went off. He started plowing the edge of the field. Along came a rich man, who asked him, "Are you working here?" The charcoal-seller replied, "The rich man sent me here to work. I want to prepare the field for planting." "Who is going to feed you?" asked the man. "The princess," was the charcoal-seller's answer. "That's not true," said the man. "I've married her," declared the charcoal-seller. "When will she come?" the man inquired, "Perhaps at two-thirty," said the charcoal-seller. The man didn't believe him. "We'll make it a bet. If she comes, then all my hacienda will be yours. And if it isn't true, then I'll give you five bullets," said the man.

5. Now the father-in-law was watching. He went to his son-in-law and asked what had happened. The charcoal-seller told him, and added, "He also wanted to marry her. He said he had money. He told me you didn't want the marriage." The father-in-law said, "Don't be afraid." He returned to his house and told his daughter what happened. She quickly prepared dinner and took it to him in the car. They sat down to eat. "Son of a whore. I've lost," said the rival suitor. The charcoal-seller took his hacienda and became a rich man like his father-in-law.

21. THE FISHERMAN, by R. M. of Huitzilan

1. Once there was a man who lived mostly from fishing. He caught fish and sold some to buy corn. He went along for a long time, but then his wife did a bad thing. He brought fish to her, and she would invite another friend [her lover] to eat the fish meat. This made San Miguel angry because when the woman's lover ate the fish meat, it made San Miguel's children, who were the fish, ill.

2. One day the fisherman went to catch fish, and he found San Miguel standing there. San Miguel said, "You can take some fish but don't take many. Take just three. You can eat one and sell two. As for the fish you eat, plant the bones in three corners of your garden. When the sun comes up, you'll see what'll appear." San Miguel gave him the fish. Before he had given him many. The fisherman did as told, and when the sun came up he found three boys. They all had the same faces. San Miguel told him, "You take those children into your home." The fisherman went again, and San Miguel gave him another three fish with the same instructions. This time he found three dogs. San Miguel gave him yet another three fish, and the fisherman found three horses. San Miguel gave him three more, and this time three saddles appeared.

Finally, he gave the fisherman three more fish, and three swords
appeared. "Now don't take anymore," said San Miguel. "Tomorrow
when the sun comes up, you saddle the horses for your boys and let
them take to the road that passes by your house. They'll know where
they'll end up," he added.

3. The fisherman did as told, and the boys went away. They
came to three roads. Each one went off on one of the roads. The
oldest said, "If someone dreams of me tomorrow, you must go
down the road I take and follow it. The same goes for the next one.
I'll cut the bark of this tree. If you come looking for me and you see
this tree bleeding, then you'll know I'm not all right."

4. He went on and came to the house of a gentleman. That
gentleman had a daughter, and he asked the boy, "Where are you
going?" The boy replied, "Over there." The gentleman said, "You
stay here and take my daughter." With that the boy stayed. They
slept and it dawned. They ate. The boy was happy there. There was
a window. He asked the girl, "Tell me about that house. What is it
called?" She said, "The place where You'll Go But You Won't Return." The boy replied, "I'll return. Now I must saddle my horse,
and you'll see if I don't." Well, he came to an old woman who was
sewing in front of a fine house. She grabbed him, and he went
inside that house. It was well sealed.

5. The next day the next brother came. He also slept with the
princess. But he put his sword between them. "Leave your sword
over there," she said. "No. I won't. It's mine," he replied. The sun
rose again, and they washed their hands. The boy stood by the
window. "Where is that house? What do you call it?" he asked.
"Well, I've been telling you it's called You'll Go But You Won't
Return." She watched him go away.

6. The next day the third one came. He also slept with the
girl. It dawned and he ate. Again he stood by the window. "Where
does that road go?" he asked. "I've been telling you!" she replied.
"You haven't told me," he said. "Sure I have. Three times now
you've asked me. Don't you listen?" said the girl. "But I want to
know," said the boy. She told him.

7. He grabbed his horse and saddled it. He mounted and took
off with his dog and his sword at his side. He came upon the old
woman sewing in front of the house. "Where are my brothers?" he
asked. "They're here," she replied. "Why did you lock them up?"
he wanted to know. "I locked them up because they came here but
they won't come back," she replied. The boy said, "Oh yes, they'll
return." He drew his sword and cut her to pieces. He killed her and

opened up that house. The people! Those who didn't return! It was a big house and it was filled. He took them out. Son of a whore, he took many out of that house.

8. Well, the three brothers returned. They were all alike. "Well, this one is the gayest. You went to get them. Now you'll run things here," someone said to the youngest brother. They sent the older brothers to be in charge of separate towns. They all came to be *hacendados* [owners of haciendas].

22. THE FISHERMAN, by N. C. of Huitzilan

1. Once there was a fisherman. He really liked children, but he didn't have a single one.

2. One time he went fishing and threw his hook in the water. It got stuck, and he went into the water to release it. Someone spoke to him and said, "Do you like fish?" The fisherman replied, "Yes. But I don't do it just for fun. I'm poor. I sell them to support myself." The man said, "Now we won't be able to give you many. We'll give you just three." From then they always gave him just three fish. "You have a garden. Plant the skulls in three corners," said the man. Three boys appeared, and they all had the same faces. The fisherman went again to the edge of the water and was given three more fish. He planted the skulls and three identical swords appeared. He did the same with three more fish, and this time there were three equal horses. Again he planted three fish, and this time three saddles appeared. He planted yet another three, and three identical dogs appeared. "Now let those brothers take to the road. Each one should go his separate way," the man told the fisherman.

3. So those children went off and came to a fork in the road where three roads went off in different directions. They let one take the left fork, they let another take the right fork, and they let the oldest take the middle fork. The oldest said, "We're going to cut this tree. If something happens to us, you'll see this tree bleed." Each one cut the tree with his sword.

4. The oldest brother went down the middle road and reached a store. "Where are you going?" someone asked. "Don't go there, because there is a big animal. It has twelve heads," he added. But the boy replied, "Good. I'll strike it down. I have my good dog. I have my good sword. I have my good horse." He came to where the animal was. It was in the water and wore the face of a fish. He killed it and cut out its twelve tongues with his sword and put

them into his pocket. He went on and came to a store. "Where have you been?" someone asked. "Over there," said the boy. "No one goes there," said the person. The boy showed him the twelve tongues. "If you killed it, they'll give you the girl," the person said. "She's the general's daughter," the person added. "While they were talking, along came a charcoal-seller. He reached the general first and delivered the remains of the dead animal. So the general gave him the girl. She put her arms around his neck and kissed him, and he really enjoyed it. But then the boy arrived. "Why are you passing through here?" asked the general. "I killed the animal back there," replied the boy. "I brought its tongues," he added. "But the charcoal-seller killed it," said the general. The boy replied, "Let him open its mouths and count the tongues." They believed the boy and sent the other one away. "Leave him with five bullets," said the general. They shot the charcoal-seller, and the boy rested with the girl. There was a house far away. It could be seen only by straining the eyes. The sun came up, and the boy asked the girl, "That house. What is it called?" "You'll Go But You Won't Return," she replied. "But I shall," said the boy. "I have my good horse and my good dog." He went. There was an old woman there. She quickly grabbed the boy by his waist when he dismounted and put him in jail. There he stayed.

5. This made the other brother dream of him. When he reached the tree he found it bleeding, so he came. He found the girl. "You've come, son," she said. "Yes. I've come," replied the boy. It got dark. He also slept with the girl. But he didn't want to sleep [have sex] with her, because he put his sword between them. And the sun came up, and he said, "Where is that house?" "Oh God, son, have you forgotten what I told you? You'll Go But You Won't Return," she replied. He went off, and the old woman grabbed him too.

6. So the third brother went off. He reached the house of that girl. He climbed up [to the second story], and when the sun came up, he asked, "And what is it?" "Oh son," said the girl. "I've told you many times. You'll Go But You Won't Return." "I'll return," said the boy.

7. He left rapidly on his horse. When he arrived, he dismounted and drew his sword. He quickly struck the old woman while she was sitting down. He struck her with the blunt end until she couldn't get up anymore. He opened up the house, and there were a lot of troups inside. They all came out. There were many! They started blowing cornets, and along came the three brothers.

8. One of the brothers took the girl. As for the other two, the

general said, "Now you'll work here. You take all these soldiers. You'll know where you'll want to put them to work."

23. THE FISHERMAN, by L. V. of Yaonáhuac

1. One time there was a fisherman who caught fish. He brought them home. He ate them. His wife ate them. He also gave his female dog fish to eat. He gave his mare the water from washing the fish.

2. Well, the little woman had triplets. The dog had three little dogs. The mare had three baby horses. The fisherman planted the wings of the fish in his flower garden. The wings sprouted into three big swords. The children were big when they were born. The baby dogs were also big from the time of their birth. Well, they all grew up to be just alike.

3. The time came when the oldest boy said, "Papa, it would be a good thing if you'd give me a horse and I rode off to where I'd like to." "Take it," said the fisherman. "And what'll you give me as inheritance?" asked the son. "Just take a dog and a sword. There is a sword in the garden. One is for you," replied the father. The boy took to the road.

4. He passed through a town. He went through a big plaza where a girl was standing [on a balcony] of a big house. That house had big windows. The girl was looking around. She said to her father, "Papa, that boy who is coming with the fine horse and the fine dog, I like him. Perhaps I'll marry him." "Well, if you like him let's talk to him," replied the father. He was a rich man who had a lot of soldiers, and he sent them to bring the boy. "Come. Our patron calls you," the soldiers told the boy after they overtook him. They brought him. The girl loved him. She started to talk with him. She really wanted him. "Where are you going?" she asked. "I'm just taking a walk. Who knows what I'll find," he replied. "Well, don't go anywhere. You're going to stay here with me because I love you. I've told my father already, and you stay with us here," she said. Well, that boy looked out from the second floor and saw a revolving mountain. It looked like a merry-go-round. It was big and it smoked. "Well, that mountain?" he asked. "It's called You'll Go and You Won't Return," said the girl. That boy was courageous and grabbed his horse and dog and went off. He went into that mountain and was lost.

5. They grew impatient at his home. "Papa, my brother doesn't come. I'm going to look for him," said the next oldest. His father gave him a horse and dog and sword identical to the ones he

gave the oldest son. He went off asking about his brother. He passed by the same town, and the girl spotted him. "Papa, my sweetheart is coming over there. Go talk to him, because he's passing by the house and he isn't coming up. He doesn't recognize anything. Why does he behave like that? Has he forgotten us?" said the girl. The soldiers quickly brought him. "Why didn't you pay any attention to us?" asked the girl's father. The boy quickly realized that his brother had passed by here. "I'm just passing by now because I'm going on an errand. I'm coming from my house," replied the boy. "You stay here. This is your home too!" they said. He went up to a higher floor and saw the mountain through the window. "What is that mountain that's smoking and revolving?" he asked the girl. "That is You'll Go and You Won't Return," she said. "Well, let's see," he said. That boy also went into that mountain to stay, along with his horse, his dog, and everything else that he took with him.

6. Now the youngest brother said, "I'm going to look for my brothers." He left with his sword, his dog, and his horse, which were just like the others. He came to a big square in the same town. The girl saw him pass right by. She exclaimed, "There goes the boy, my sweetheart! He doesn't want to come in. He's ignoring me. Let's see if they can overtake him." The patron chased after him, and the soldiers overtook him. "Why did you ignore us? You passed by and you didn't come in. Have you forgotten us?" they asked. "No," said the boy, who realized his brothers had passed by. There was that girl who loved him. It was as if he were her husband. Her husband made her happy. He was like her husband, but he wasn't really. He climbed up onto the floor above and saw that mountain through the window. "What's that mountain that's revolving and smoking?" he asked. "Oh, that one far away is You'll Go and You Won't Return," she said. "Well, I'll be sure to return," he said.

7. Since he was the youngest, he was more intelligent and braver. "My brothers have gone there. I'll go right into it with my machete in hand," he thought to himself. He reached that mountain swinging his machete. He hit those who were in that cave. Who knows what kind of cave it was. It was probably the cave of the devil. That place was the underworld [miktan]. That house was burning. He cut up what he came across. He found a cauldron. A fire was heating it. He dumped it over and put out the fire. He removed his brothers with the flat of his sword. He circled around and struck those who were in that place. He saved everyone and brought them back.

8. He came to his sweetheart. She saw the three identical brothers with their identical horses, dogs, swords, and clothes. The brothers had identical faces. She didn't know who was her first husband.

24. THE FISHERMAN, by M. I. of Yaonáhuac

1. Once there was a fisherman who lived on nothing but fish.

2. It came to pass that his wife had three sons who were exactly alike. All of them were tall and blond. It also happened that the fish in the river came to an end. The last fish caught by the fisherman was the mother of the fish. She said, "Now you've caught me. My children are gone. You've finished them all. But you have three sons, and they are all the same. Now you take me and eat me. But you chop me all up, and as for the dirty water, you give it to your mare. And you give some of that dirty water to your dog. As for all my bones, don't throw out a single piece. Put them where there is a big ant hill. You bury them there. And when your mare gives birth and your dog gives birth, on that day you take out my bones. Those bones of mine will be your children's inheritance." That little mare had three horses. That dog had three little dogs, and they were all the same color.

3. Well, the children grew up. They said, "Father, we're going to look for work." "Good. Take your inheritance," said the fisherman. He gave them each a sword, a horse, and a dog. They took off and came to a crossing. They found a tree, and the oldest said, "You go put a slash in that tree. We're all going to cut it. When the cut bleeds it'll be because something has happened to us. You'll know who is in trouble by remembering who made which slash. We'll make a custom of visiting this tree once a month. We won't look for each other unless something happens to one of us." Each one took a different road.

4. The oldest brother went to stay.

5. A new month came, and the second brother found the slash bleeding where the oldest brother had cut the tree with his sword. So he followed his brother and came upon a princess standing on a balcony. She told him, "Turn around. Tie up your horse over there and climb up onto the balcony. I'll go meet you." He was a fine boy with his dog and his horse and his sword. She thought he was her husband [she married the oldest brother]. It came about that he looked out into the distance and saw a mountain. "What's the name of that mountain?" he asked. "Haven't you gone there already?" the girl wondered. "Me? But I don't remember," he said. So

then he realized in his heart that his brother was in that mountain. She said, "Its name is, You'll Go and You Won't Return." She gave him supper, and he went to sleep. He thought to himself, "I'm going over there." "Don't go, because you won't return," pleaded the girl. "I'll return," he said. He went and reached a big door. That mountain was revolving. A buzzard came and closed the gate. He was locked inside. The *cayime*[6] were dancing. They were going round and round in circles.

6. That one went to stay, and another one arrived. "What's the name of that mountain?" he asked the girl. "But don't you know?" said the girl. "It's called the mountain where You'll Go and You Won't Return!" He was fed supper and went to sleep.

7. The next day it dawned, and he saddled his horse and went off. "Well now, I'm not going to stay," he said. "I'm going there to fight with metal." He came to a big open entrance and found his brothers there in the middle of the patio. They were having fun. He went in quickly and drew his sword. The buzzard came, and he rapidly cut it to pieces. "Come on! Outside!" he shouted to his brothers. He went over to look at the seven revolving cauldrons. They were revolving, and he ran in and cut across each cauldron with his sword. They say a flock of white doves rose up. They were human souls. "Hurry up! Let's go!" he shouted. They left there in a hurry.

8. They went back to where the princess was. She didn't know to whom she should speak. They all greeted her. She didn't know who was her husband. They were all the same. There were three identical dogs, three identical horses, and three identical people. She set a table for them and gave them supper. She didn't know what to do about them. But one stayed and the others left. She recognized the one who stayed.

25. THE JEALOUS MAN'S DAUGHTERS, by J. S. of Huitzilan

1. Once there was a well-dressed gentleman who had three daughters. They were grown girls, but he didn't let them go out of the house. Because he was a well-dressed gentleman, he had a big house. Since he had a big house, he kept the girls on the second floor. Even if they just asked their father for permission to take a walk, he would say no. This went on until they were big—sixteen and seventeen years old.

2. There was a boy who wondered, "Why won't that well-dressed gentleman let his daughters go out?" He decided to teach himself how to do kitchen work. He taught himself how to make

tortillas, how to make meals, and how to wash things. He let his hair grow to be like that of a woman. He combed it to look like a woman's hair. He resolved, "Now I can do the work in the kitchen. Well now, I'm going to speak to that well-dressed gentleman so he'll hire me."

3. He went to speak to him and asked for work. The gentleman liked what he saw and said, "Well, why not? Sure! My daughters are over there. You'll help them in the kitchen." He wanted to hire him right away, and so he told him, "You come in a little while. Come tomorrow." The boy said he would come in a little while. He started working with the daughters. He began preparing meals and making tortilla dough. The girls thought he was a woman. The gentleman said, "Now you sleep together in one bed." And from that point on, the cook and the two girls slept together in the same bed. That was the way they lived.

4. After a month they started talking. "Perhaps because I've come, he'll let us go for a walk. Wouldn't your father allow it?" he said to the girls. "You speak to him, because you're accustomed to going for walks," they said. So he spoke to the gentleman, asking, "Would you give us permission to take a walk?" The gentleman replied, "No. You've come here and you're going to work. You stay up there [on the second floor]." That was the way it was. "We want to go for a walk because we've become women," the daughters said. "Won't God take pity on us? Let's say the rosary at three in the morning [when a quarter of the moon has vanished]. Let's ask. Let's see if God will give us something so we can make ourselves happy here," they added. They convinced the cook. They said the rosary for about two months. "How are you?" asked the cook. "Well, we are the same, just as you found us," they said. "Well, I made myself as if I were a man," replied the cook. "That's not true," the girls said. He told them to feel if he really had made himself as if he were a man. They felt that he was like a man. Someone said, "Good. Well, now let's have some fun." So he started having fun with the older girl, and then right afterwards he had fun with the younger one. And so it was day after day. He pleased himself with them and they pleased themselves with him.

5. In about eight months, the child of the oldest daughter was about to be born. Her father exclaimed, "What! Well, why has this happened?! How did my children make themselves this way?" He was furious and asked the girls how they became that way when he hadn't let them out of the house. "Our cook told us to say the rosary when the moon was a quarter vanished," they said.[7]

6. Well, that well-dressed gentleman was angry. Well now, he

liked the cook. He wanted to speak to her alone, and so he told his wife, "Take those girls of ours for a walk in the garden and let the cook stay here." The wife did as told, and the gentleman went to speak to the cook. "Well, I'll give you an answer, but only if you take a bath first," said the cook to the gentleman. "Let me bathe you so that you'll be clean when you please yourself," the cook added. "I'll bathe. Put the water on to heat," said the gentleman. "Take off your clothes and let me bathe you," said the cook. He bathed the gentleman with a lot of soap. He put soap all over him. "Now make yourself like a horse," instructed the cook, who put soap everywhere, even where he defecated. And then the cook gave it to him [had sex] and then went off.

26. THE JEALOUS MAN'S DAUGHTERS, by F. J. of Yaonáhuac

1. Once there was a little man who had three daughters. Those girls were already grown. They were virgins. Then there were three boys who decided to speak to them. But those girls were not allowed to speak to the boys. They never walked alone. When they went somewhere, they went together.

2. So those boys became impatient. "What'll we do?" they said. One of them had a plan. He told the others, "Well, there are three boys and three girls. There has to be a way to talk to them. We're going to do it this way. We're going to their house when it's dark and ask for lodging. I'm going to make my stomach look large and I'm going to put on a dress so that they'll think I'm sick with a child. You'll be like sisters. We'll all make ourselves look like girls to grab them. It's the only way." So they got themselves ready. The one who had the plan would be the oldest sister. He made himself look like a woman. He put on breasts. He had a big stomach as if he were sick with a child. The others also put on dresses.

3. They went to the little man's house and asked for lodging. "We've come a long way and we're late. We have a long way to go, and it looks like our sister is ill. We beg you for lodging," they pleaded. "Well, come inside," said the little man. They were given supper.

4. The one who dressed as a pregnant woman said, "My stomach seems to hurt me a little." He acted as if labor pains had begun. "Ask the man to light the steam bath so that I can warm myself a little. I'm very cold," he added. One of the daughters ran and told her father. "She's going to get worse," she said. Her father spoke to the pregnant one himself and asked, "How do you feel?" "I'm going to deliver. Would you give me permission to give birth here?"

asked the "woman." "Light the steam bath," commanded the father. One of the girls ran to carry out the order. "It's ready," she announced. All three boys dressed as women went into the steam bath. "Wouldn't you like to join us?" they said to the girls. "Let's warm ourselves together, and one of you can put water on [the hot stones] for us [to make steam]. We don't know where to put the water. We might burn our hands," they added. The girls told their father, "They also want us to bathe with them." "Fine," he said. They went in too and fanned the steam over the sick one to heat "her." Those girls took off all their clothes and got into the steam bath. They closed themselves in. Then each one of the boys grabbed a girl. The older girl shouted, "Papa! Papa! It's a boy!" "Blessed be God. It's a boy. She's a live one," said the father, who played a tune on his violin. When the piece ended, another daughter shouted, "Papa, it's a boy! It's a boy!" "Oh, blessed be God," he said, and he played another tune on his violin. Then he heard another daughter shout, "Papa, it's a boy!" "Blessed be God, it's another boy. Son of a whore!" he said, and he played another tune.

5. The girls came out of the steam bath and said, "Papa, you didn't come. You didn't come to help us. They weren't really girls. They were men, and each one grabbed us in the steam bath. We shouted to you from there. You never came to help. They grabbed us well." Their father listened and then asked, "Where are they now?" "They left quickly. They went off. They were fine people to have done such a thing! We all shouted to you and you didn't hear us." "F——! My violin is to blame," said the father, who smashed the instrument.

27. THE GIRL WHO KILLED HER MOTHER, by J. H. of Huitzilan

1. Once there was a girl who was very disobedient. She did not like to prepare tortillas, but she really did like men. One day her mother wanted her to eat some meat for dinner. "Eat, daughter," she said. "Well, mama, I won't eat this," replied the girl. "But what kind of meat do you want?" asked the mother. "That which I told you about. I want meat, but I want meat!" replied the girl.

2. Her mother went to bring the meat she thought her daughter wanted. She brought it home and cooked it. She put chiles on it and told her daughter to eat it. But the girl refused. "Well, I won't eat it. I don't want this meat," she said. "What meat do you want?" asked the mother. "Well, I know what meat," replied the girl. The mother bought pork and prepared another dinner and gave it to her daughter. "I don't want this meat," said the girl. "What meat do

you want?" asked the mother. She was angry now. "Chicken?" The daughter didn't say anything, so the mother killed a chicken and made another dinner. But the girl didn't want it. The mother bought mutton, but the girl didn't want that either. So her mother asked angrily, "Oh God, what meat do you want then?" The girl replied, "I want that with which a man urinates. I want it to touch here [narrator gestures to the crotch]." "Well, if you want that," said the mother, "it would have been better if you said so in the first place. If you want that with which a man urinates, then go over there in the road and look for two or three men so that you'll feel better." "Ah good, mama. I'll go," said the daughter. The girl grabbed her shawl and went off. She found two men, and they had what she wanted. It turned out fine. So she came back home and said, "I'm home, mama." She came back very pleased. "That's it, mama. It was great. I found four men," she said.

3. Then one day the mother went to wash clothes in the river. She returned home and said to her daughter, "I'm very hungry. I want you to put on the tortillas." But the girl refused and said, "But I won't." The mother replied, "But what are you going to do? Put on the tortillas and we'll eat." The girl said, "No. I'm going to look for another man, because I really want a man." So her mother got angry. Well, that girl took out a knife and gave it to [killed] her mother. After she gave it to her mother, she took out her mother's liver and ate it. She thought to herself, "Well, I'll eat this liver. But who knows where I'll go."

4. That girl liked that man who had what pleased her. She thought, "Now I'll go catch up with him so that I can keep on eating what that man has. I'll catch up to him and I'll marry him. If they want to punish me, that man will answer them so they won't." She came to the man's house. "You've come!" he said. "Yes. I've come because I've killed my mother. I've come to see if you can hide me so they won't punish me," she said. "Good. Wait for me. I'll have to ask my mother. If she agrees, then you can stay. If she doesn't agree, then you can't, because they'll punish me if you stay," said the boy. He spoke to his mother, who said to her son, "But I know that she killed her mother and ate her mother's liver. That's why she fled. She might kill you someday." But the boy said, "She won't kill me because she likes that with which I urinate." "So you asked her to try it," said the mother. The boy said yes, and the mother declared, "Then let her come."

5. So she stayed there and married the boy. Then one day she decided she wanted meat again. The girl got angry and said, "I want meat but real meat." They brought mutton. They brought beef.

They brought pork. They brought all kinds of meat, but she didn't want it. The mother thought, "She'll get angry and kill us and eat us." They brought every kind of meat, but she didn't want any of it. So the husband went to visit one of her brothers. "When she was little she really liked snake meat," said the brother. "But I can't catch snakes," protested the husband. "They'll bite me," he added. The brother explained how he could do it. "Make one of those reed flutes and go to the woods. Go to the foot of a mountain and climb a tree so the snakes don't bite you. Play the flute four times and a pile of snakes will come," he said. The husband followed the instructions. He took his carrying bag [*tenate*] and went to the place where the girl's brother told him. All kinds of snakes came. Some were small and some were large. He decided he wanted a big one. When he climbed down from the tree, only one was left. He grabbed it with a forked stick and put it into his bag. He came home and told his mother, "Here is the meat for the girl to eat." They killed the snake, skinned it, and removed the meat. It didn't have any bones. They fried it with lard. The girl ate well. It was like fried pork rinds.

6. After she had eaten well, the girl said, "We're going to make mole [a ceremonial dish] with the rest to eat this evening." They made the mole, and then the boy's father decided they would all take a steam bath. He and the mother did not eat the meat. Only the girl ate it. They prepared to go into the steam bath, and then along came a neighbor who asked to join them. "Sure," said the boy. They warned the neighbor not to touch the mole. "If you touch it, you'll soon want water," they said. But the neighbor touched the mole anyway. He picked out a piece of meat and ate it. He and his wife ate some. In about half an hour they wanted water. The girl had eaten it, but she drank a liter of *aguardiente* before she ate the meat. Then afterwards she ate two leaves of tobacco. Well, the neighbor and his wife ate tobacco and drank a bottle of *aguardiente*, but they turned over on their backs and died.

28. THE GIRL WHO KILLED HER MOTHER,
by L. V. of Yaonáhuac

1. Once there was a little girl whose mother taught her to eat meat everyday. The meat her mother bought for her was always liver. The girl always ate liver, be it cow's liver or pig's liver. That girl grew up eating liver. Each time she ate liver she liked it. She became accustomed to eating liver. But the day came when her mother couldn't find liver anywhere. "You're not going to eat liver

because there isn't any," she told the girl. "But mother, I won't be satisfied without eating it," the daughter replied. "There isn't any," said the mother. "Well, go find more wherever you'd like," demanded the girl.

2. That little woman looked for liver. She went all over, but she couldn't find it anywhere. She came home and told her daughter, "Well, there isn't any. You'll be angry, but there isn't any liver anywhere."

3. "Well, since you haven't found the liver, I'm going to eat yours," said the daughter. She pulled out a knife and killed her mother. She took out her mother's liver and cooked it. She put the rest of her mother's body into a corner, where she wrapped it in a straw mat [petate]. She made herself dinner and ate the liver.

4. Her father came. "Come eat, papa," said the girl. He came to the table. "Eat now, papa. You won't be eating with mama," said the girl. "Where did your mother go?" asked the father. "I'll wait so that we can eat together," he added. The girl replied, "She's coming later. You eat now. Don't wait." But the father insisted he would wait. He asked again, "Where is your mother? Where did she go? Did she tell you where she went?" "You'll find out where she is," said the girl. She showed her father the straw mat that covered up her mother's dead body. "Perhaps you'd like her that way," said the girl. Then she added, "If not, then you'll see what I'll have to say to you. I should kill you too." She pulled out a knife and stabbed her father. But he spoke to God and displayed the cross. The girl remained motionless. She couldn't do anything because her father spoke to God. Then they grabbed the girl and took her away as a prisoner. She was frantic and gored when they found her. In jail she began burning. She shouted filthy things. The devil spoke to her because she killed her mother.

Appendix 2. Profiles of Nahuat Storytellers

The storytelling process generally shapes narratives so they fit prevailing collective beliefs and experiences. But the degree to which this applies in each case depends on the storyteller and the length of time his stories have been incorporated into Nahuat oral tradition. This appendix contains thumbnail sketches of the fifteen narrators whose tales appear in this book, to give a perspective on these factors. One can identify a number of interesting patterns concerning the storytellers from a glance at these sketches.

All are men who are older than most members of their communities. Their average ages are 52.9 years in Huitzilan and 48.0 years in Yaonáhuac, although these figures exaggerate the differences between the ages of narrators from the two communities. I collected stories from the Huitzilan storytellers over an eight-year period between 1970 and 1978, and the average age of the narrators from this community reported above is relative to 1978. Moreover, the Yaonáhuac narrators' ages are estimated to the closest five-year interval. The fact that narrators have an average age of about 50 is significant, because the Nahuat place a great deal of importance on rank by age. Because the storytellers are older than the general population, they usually hold the position of authorities on beliefs and tradition.

Some narrators may have learned a number of their stories while temporarily living outside Huitzilan or Yaonáhuac. While all were born and lived most of their lives in these two communities, a number have histories of frequent labor migration (see table 28). Storytellers who have been labor migrants generally worked as farm laborers on Hispanic plantations in the coastal plain in the state of Veracruz. Most have migrated with others from their natal communities, but there remains the possibility that they learned stories from co-workers coming from other communities in the northern Sierra de Puebla. But on closer inspection, only two narrators (both from Huitzilan) have migrated recently out of the immediate area and beyond adjacent communities. The others migrated many years ago, and thus they have probably adapted their imported tales to local conditions.

The history of frequent labor migration appears to contribute to greater knowledge of Spanish among storytellers relative to the

Table 28. Characteristics of Storytellers, by Community

Storyteller	Age	Frequent labor migration outside the area	Knowledge of Spanish
Huitzilan			
D. A.	64	yes	much
M. A.	67	no	some
N. A. H.	33	no	much
N. C.	49	yes	little
M. F.	59	yes	some
J. H.	32	yes	some
R. M.	59	yes	some
J. P.	46	no	some
J. S.	51	yes	much
A. V.	69	yes	none
Yaonáhuac			
M. I.	55	yes	much
F. J.	35	no	much
J. M.	45	yes	much
F. V.	50	yes	much
L. V.	55	yes	much

Table 29. Bilingualism of Storytellers Relative to the Entire Population, by Community

Knowledge of Spanish	Storytellers		Entire population	
	Number	Percent	Number	Percent
Huitzilan				
None	1	10	1598	69.0
Little	1	10	219	9.4
Some	5	50	326	14.1
Much	3	30	173	7.5
Yaonáhuac				
None	0	0	152	9.6
Little	0	0	187	11.8
Some	0	0	326	20.5
Much	5	100	924	58.1

general population (see table 29). Labor migration has taken place for many decades in the northern Sierra and has probably contributed to bilingualism for a number of generations. This undoubtedly facilitated the flow of peninsular Spanish stories into Nahuat oral tradition.

Most, but by no means all, have led lives that earned them the high esteem of the members of their communities. The most prominent exceptions are two reputed thieves (one from Huitzilan and one from Yaonáhuac), and a Protestant from Huitzilan who cut himself off from his ritual kin by leaving the Catholic church. Two more have acquired bitter political enemies by their active participation in political factionalism (both come from Yaonáhuac), but most express comparatively little interest in secular politics. A few belong to or are related to those who participate in traditional dance groups which perform during religious festivals. I suspect they are among the custodians of traditional culture in their communities.

HUITZILAN STORYTELLER D. A.

1. The Tiger in the Forest, Huitzilan version 2 in chapter 9.
2. The Adulterer, chapter 9.

D. A. is 64, is married, has several grown children, and was born and has lived all his life in Huitzilan. His only land is a small ejido plot which he uses for a house site and a small coffee orchard. Consequently he has had to migrate frequently to the hot country and to the *municipios* surrounding Huitzilan to supplement his small income. He is more bilingual than most Nahuat his age, primarily because of his extensive labor migration experience outside his community. D. A. is unusual among all the storytellers whose narratives appear in this book because he is now a Protestant. When I first began fieldwork in Huitzilan in 1968, he was a Catholic with a large number of ritual kin. He had taken an active role in the religious side of the civil-religious hierarchy by assuming roles in the *mayordomía* system anchored around the ejido chapel at the northern end of this community. The participants in this system came from the families living on the 125 house sites (as of 1968) on a large ejido tract. But shortly afterwards he broke with the Catholic church and with his ritual kin and joined a Protestant sect that established a temple near the ejido chapel. A number who formerly participated in the chapel *mayordomía* system have now joined the Protestant temple along with D. A.

HUITZILAN STORYTELLER M. A.

1. The Origin of the Sun and the Moon, Huitzilan version 1 in chapter 7.
2. The Man Who Entered the Forest, Huitzilan version 3 in chapter 8.
3. Two Men, story 2 in appendix 1.

Age 67, married, and with several children, this narrator was born and has lived all his life in Huitzilan. He owns a small plot of land in fee simple which he uses as a coffee orchard, he has a small ejido plot for a house site, and he rents land for growing corn from one of the Hispanics in the community. He earns a good income by Huitzilan standards by working as a stonemason. Undoubtedly for this reason he has not had to migrate often to the coastal lowlands. He speaks Nahuat better than Spanish, although he understands both languages, but he cannot read or write. He has played a role in politics by serving as a member of the local ejido committee, but no Nahuat including M. A. has control of any branch of the local government, which is controlled by Hispanics. M. A. has played only a modest role in the religious side of the civil-religious hierarchy and rarely assumes the office of *mayordomo*. He learned most of the stories he told me from other Nahaut of his community with whom he has worked in the *milpa* and as a member of sugar-processing teams working at local sugarcane presses within the boundaries of the *municipio*.

HUITZILAN STORYTELLER N. A. H.

1. The Monster at Ištepek, chapter 6.
2. The Man Who Entered the Forest, Huitzilan versions 2 and 4 in chapter 8.
3. The Tiger in the Forest, Huitzilan version 1 in chapter 9.
4. The Lazy Husband, story 3 in appendix 1.
5. Juan Barajero, story 17 in appendix 1.
6. The Man Who Won the Hacienda, story 19 in appendix 1.

Age 33, married, with two small children, narrator N. A. H. was born and lived all his life in Huitzilan. He received a modest inheritance that consisted of a small coffee orchard. He obtained credit from local merchants and established a small store in the center of town to supplement his income. With money he saved from his share of the coffee harvest, he managed to buy a small plot for a house site in the middle of the *cabecera*. Although his income is very small by Hispanic standards, he migrated only once to the hot country and promptly returned because he did not like the food and very hot weather. N. A. H. is more bilingual in Nahuat and Spanish than any other storyteller from his community. He can read and write because he is one of the few Nahuat to have completed his primary education. He has put his bilingualism to work by serving as a prayer leader and works closely with the priest, who resides in the neighboring community of Zapotitlán, to learn Catholic doctrine and assist in the mass. He appears to be one of the most religious members of this community and has described dreams of churches in heaven. He is frail and believes he would be vulnerable to soul loss and thus avoids situations of conflict. He and his brothers have frequently assisted their cousin, who has assumed a very large number of *mayordomías* over the past two decades. N. A. H. learned most of the stories told to me from one of his brothers, who plays the flute for the Quetzal dancers who perform during the patron saint celebration in August.

HUITZILAN STORYTELLER N. C.

1. The Fisherman, story 22 in appendix 1.

N. C. is 49 years old, is married, and has unmarried children. He was born and has lived all his life in Huitzilan. Although his father owned some land, N. C. received a small inheritance that consisted of his house site, which includes a small coffee orchard. He consequently has had to migrate frequently to the hot country to supplement his income. He currently migrates to the neighboring community of Zapotitlán de Méndez to help harvest coffee on the estates of wealthy Hispanics. He speaks more Nahuat than Spanish, and he cannot read or write. Several Nahuat who know him consider him a scoundrel because he reputedly is a thief. In this respect his position in Huitzilan is like that of Yaonáhuac storyteller J. M. except that he is not an alcoholic. He does not play a role in the civil-religious hierarchy. He learned most of the stories he told me from fellow members of his community.

HUITZILAN STORYTELLER M. F.

1. The Origin of Corn, chapter 7.
2. The Origin of Corn Planting Knowledge, story 8 in appendix 1.

M. F. is 59, is divorced and was widowed, and has several children. He was born and has lived most of his life in Huitzilan. He is poor by Huitzilan standards because he owns just his small ejido that he uses for a house site and a tiny coffee orchard. M. F. has migrated more frequently and for longer periods of time to the coastal lowlands than most Nahuat of Huitzilan. He knows more Spanish than most in his community, but he speaks better Nahuat. His long and frequent absences from the community make me suspect he probably learned many of his stories outside of Huitzilan. But other Nahuat reported hearing him perform while working in sugarcane-processing groups within Huitzilan, and he asserted that he learned his tales from other Huitzilan Nahuat. M. F. has not played a major role in the civil-religious hierarchy of his community.

HUITZILAN STORYTELLER J. H.

1. The Origin of the Sun and the Moon, Huitzilan version 2 in chapter 7.
2. Adam and Eve, Huitzilan version 1 in chapter 10.
3. The Lightning-bolts Take Nawewet from Cosolin, story 5 in appendix 1.
4. The Crucifixion of Christ, story 14 in appendix 1.
5. The Girl Who Killed Her Mother, story 27 in appendix 1.

J. H. is 41, is married, and has several unmarried children. He was born and has lived all his life in Huitzilan. Like many Nahuat from his community, he is very poor, because he owns only his ejido plot that he uses for a house site and a small coffee orchard. Consequently he has migrated extensively, primarily to the large Nahuat-speaking *municipio* of Cuetzalan to the north. Most of his trips as a migrant worker took place over twenty years ago. Now J. H. primarily works to support his family within the *municipio* of Huitzilan. He speaks better Nahuat than Spanish, and he cannot read or write. Recently he took an active part in the religious side of the civil-religious hierarchy when his mother was a *mayordomo*. Of all narrators in this community, J. H. tended to stress sexual themes in his stories. He often portrayed deviant women characters as hypersexual. Thus he stands to all Huitzilan Nahuat storytellers as Yaonáhuac narrator F. J. stands to the narrators in his community because both stressed sexual themes in their stories. This is important because J. H. and F. J. each recounted versions of the Adam and Eve story compared in chapter 10.

HUITZILAN STORYTELLER R. M.

1. The Fisherman, story 21 in appendix 1.

This narrator is 59, is widowed, and has several children, two of whom are married. He was born and has lived most of his life in Huitzilan. His mother owns two plots of land which she recently passed on to her son. The plots are small, and R. M. has three sons who stand to inherit a fraction of the patrimony. Moreover, one son married several years ago and shares one of the plots which the family uses as a house site and small coffee orchard. Recently a dirt road was constructed through the middle of the house site, and the family was forced to move to borrowed land. Because R. M. is poor he has had to migrate numerous times to places outside Huitzilan, most of which lie in the hot country. The bulk of his trips took place over thirty years ago. R. M. speaks Nahuat better than Spanish, and he cannot read or write. He was reputed by many to have been a good storyteller, and a number of Nahuat mentioned that he often performed as a narrator when working in sugarcane harvesting groups at presses within the *municipio*. But he has become a heavy drinker, and his memory is failing him. R. M. has not played a major role in the civil-religious hierarchy.

HUITZILAN STORYTELLER J. P.

1. Adam and Eve, Huitzilan version 2 in chapter 10.
2. The Time the Devil Lost the Wager, story 12 in appendix 1.

This narrator is 46, is married, and has several unmarried children. He was born and has lived most of his life in Huitzilan. Although he received very little inheritance, he has more land than most Nahuat of his community. He owns a small ejido plot that he uses for a house site and a small coffee orchard. He also owns a half-hectare plot of land on which he has planted coffee trees and corn. He earned the money to buy this plot by felling trees and cutting them into lumber and selling the beams to a wealthy Hispanic merchant in Huitzilan. He supplements his income from these sources by working as a carpenter and a butcher. Consequently this narrator has not had to migrate often to the coastal lowland plantations. To be sure, he has visited the hot country several times, but he has made fewer trips out of the community than other narrators like M. F. and R. M. Although J. P. knows Spanish, he speaks more Nahuat, and he cannot read or write.

HUITZILAN STORYTELLER J. S.

1. The Jealous Man's Daughters, story 25 in appendix 1.

This narrator is 51, was widowed and has remarried, and has several children by his first wife. He is unusual among the Nahuat of both communities because he served as a conscript in the Mexican army before he married his first wife. He is moderately poor, although he owns a small plot of land in addition to his ejido plot that he uses for a house site and a coffee orchard. Several Nahuat told me that he once had more land but sold his properties to pay for his numerous ritual kinship obligations. He has acted as the ritual sponsor for more godchildren than any other Nahuat from Huitzilan who came to my attention during ten years of fieldwork in this community. He has supplemented his income by migrating to the hot country about twenty times. He made his last trip about fifteen years ago. He occasionally works in Huitzilan as a stonemason. Like all storytellers with a history of experience outside the community, J. S. speaks Spanish, but he clearly prefers to speak Nahuat. He can read and write, and he once told me a story that he read in a book. I found it particularly important to pin down the sources of the stories in his repertoire. The tale he told me that appears in this volume came from oral tradition which he picked up from other Huitzilan Nahuat.

HUITZILAN STORYTELLER A. V.

1. The Man Who Entered the Forest, Huitzilan version 1 in chapter 8.
2. The Flood, chapter 11.
3. The Man Who Said When It Would Rain, story 6 in appendix 1.

A. V. is 69, was widowed and has remarried, and has several children by both wives. He has more land than most Nahuat in his community because he owns a corn plot three-quarters of a hectare in size, in addition to his ejido that he uses for a house site and a small coffee orchard. He also frequently rents land so he can plant corn. These sources of income have enabled him to live without migrating frequently to the lowland plantations. To be sure, he has migrated as a farm worker to the coast, but when he works outside of Huitzilan, he most frequently travels to the neighboring *municipios* of Zapotitlán de Méndez and Xochitlán de Romero Rubio. Perhaps because he has less experience in the Hispanic world outside his community, A. V. is the most monolingual Nahuat speaker of all storytellers from Huitzilan. Like all monolinguals I have known, he does not read and write. A. V. is probably the most gifted storyteller of all those whose work appears in this volume. I heard him perform at a wake and watched as he held the audience in the palm of his hand. He is also a fountain of information on Huitzilan Nahuat beliefs and thus occupies a position among the storytellers in his community analogous to the position occupied by M. I. among the narrators of Yaonáhuac.

YAONÁHUAC STORYTELLER M. I.

1. The Man Who Entered the Forest, Yaonáhuac versions 1 and 3 in chapter 8.
2. The Sun and the Moon, story 1 in appendix 1.
3. The Man Who Said When It Would Rain, story 7 in appendix 1.
4. The Fisherman, story 24 in appendix 1.

M. I. is 55 years old, is married, and has a married son and unmarried children. He was born and has lived all his life in Yaonáhuac. M. I. is poorer than most in his community because he owns no land (his wife owns the house site). He consequently was forced to migrate periodically to the coastal lowlands to work as a member of the work team (*cuadrilla*) led by a local Yaonáhuac labor recruiter. Like all members of his household, he is a bilingual speaker of Nahuat and Spanish, but he cannot read or write. This narrator has an active record in local *municipio* politics because he is a member of a faction of Nahuat families which worked with the Hispanic member of the community who served as the town secretary for a number of years (see chapter 4). This faction once operated within the PRI (Partido Revolucionario Institucional), the dominant party of Mexico. But a local dispute within the Yaonáhuac branch of this party caused members of this faction to align themselves with the PPS (Partido Popular Socialista), which gained prominence by winning an election in the important commercial center of Teziutlán, twenty kilometers to the west. M. I., however, does not take a leading role in his political faction and does not know much or care about political philosophies. He has expressed a very skeptical attitude about political contests and declared on several occasions that those who seek local office want access to the local *municipio* treasury. Despite M. I.'s experience in the work team, and his political participation, he is not worldly by Yaonáhuac standards. Several consider him a fountain of information about local Nahuat beliefs, and all regard him as a master storyteller with a gift for turning a phrase. M. I. told a number of stories about lightning-bolts, and he believed that a lightning-bolt was his grandfather's animal companion spirit.

YAONÁHUAC STORYTELLER F. J.

1. The Origin of Corn, chapter 7.
2. Adam and Eve, Yaonáhuac version 1 in chapter 10.
3. The Origin of Corn Planting Knowledge, story 9 in appendix 1.
4. The Compadre and the Chile Thief, story 11 in appendix 1.
5. The Crucifixion of Christ, story 15 in appendix 1.
6. The Man Who Won the Hacienda, story 20 in appendix 1.
7. The Jealous Man's Daughters, story 26 in appendix 1.

F. J. is 35 years old, is married, and has unmarried children. He, his wife, and their children were born and have lived all their lives in Yaonáhuac. F. J. inherited enough land from his father so that he can support himself by corn farming and by selling fruit from his orchard. Consequently he has not had to migrate much to the hot country and thus is different from most of the storytellers in his community. He is a bilingual speaker of Nahuat and Spanish, but he seems much more comfortable speaking Nahuat. He can read and write, and he has expressed a strong interest in sending his children to study in secondary school in the neighboring community of Teteles de Ávila Castillo. He learned most of the stories he told me from a Yaonáhuac man, now deceased, who worked with him in local *milpa* agriculture. F. J. has taken a very modest role in local politics, and most consider him a shy man who prefers to associate with close friends, relatives, and working companions. During the recent *municipio* election (November, 1977) he expressed sympathy with the PRI faction that has taken the place of the once dominant faction, now aligned with the PPS party, that controlled the *municipio* government. Like narrator M. I. he has taken no leadership role and has preferred to stay on the sidelines of local politics.

YAONÁHUAC STORYTELLER J. M.

1. Myth of Creation, chapter 5.
2. The Time I Met the Devil, chapter 6.
3. The Origin of the Sun and the Moon, Yaonáhuac version 1 in chapter 7.
4. The Origin of Corn Planting Knowledge, story 10 in appendix 1.

J. M. is 45, is separated from his wife, and has several children. He was born and has lived most of his life in Yaonáhuac. Although he inherited some land, he is poor by Yaonáhuac standards partly because the plot he inherited is small and partly because he has not made full use of the land he owns. He has frequently joined the work teams (cuadrillas) led by the same local labor recruiter who contracted narrator M. I. and other Yaonáhuac storytellers. He is a bilingual speaker of Nahuat and Spanish, but he cannot read or write. J. M. and his brother are considered scoundrels by most of the Yaonáhuac community. J. M. is an alcoholic who frequents local cantinas (stores which sell aguardiente and other alcoholic beverages) from dawn to late evening. He reputedly engaged in ma-chete fights in his youth, and his brother is now serving a prison term for killing a man in this manner. He allegedly steals fowl and other domesticated animals. Many scoff at his claim that his ani-mal companion spirit is a lightning-bolt, but his harshest critic, narrator M. I., made the same claim for his long deceased grand-father. J. M. told more stories based on personal visions and experi-ences than any other storyteller in his community. His account of his encounter with the devil in chapter 6 is a good example of his anecdotal stories. While many Yaonáhuac Nahuat do not believe the details of his anecdotes, they express considerable agreement over the underlying concepts J. M. uses to generate his stories.

YAONÁHUAC STORYTELLER F. V.

1. The Tiger in the Forest, chapter 9.
2. The Adulterer, chapter 9.

F. V. is 50 and lives with his wife and adopted son. He was born and has lived all his life in Yaonáhuac. F. V., along with his brother L. V., is the director of traditional dance groups who perform during the festivals in honor of Catholic saints. He directs the Santiago and the flying pole dancers (kwowpatanini) who perform in Yaonáhuac and occasionally in neighboring communities in this part of the northern Sierra. He has worked periodically in the work team (*cuadrilla*) to compensate for a small inheritance. He generally joined up with the same labor recruiter who contracted the other storytellers from Yaonáhuac. F. V. is a bilingual speaker of Nahuat and Spanish, and he can read. He, along with other ceremonial specialists, can read the script (*Relación*) that is part of the Santiago dancers' performance. F. V. has traveled more widely than most Yaonáhuac Nahuat. He has been to Mexico City, and he prides himself on his worldly knowledge. He learned most of the stories told to me, however, from his father, who was also a dance master, and from his work team companions. F. V. has not taken much of a role in past or present political factions although he sides with the PRI faction that has taken the place of the once dominant faction that now aligns itself with the PPS party.

YAONÁHUAC STORYTELLER L. V.

1. The Origin of the Sun and the Moon, Yaonáhuac version 2 in chapter 7.
2. The Man Who Entered the Forest, Yaonáhuac versions 2 and 4 in chapter 8.
3. Adam and Eve, Yaonáhuac version 2 in chapter 10.
4. The Flood, chapter 11.
5. The Lazy Husband, story 4 in appendix 1.
6. The Time the Devil Lost the Wager, story 13 in appendix 1.
7. The Hunter, story 16 in appendix 1.
8. Juan Barajero, story 18 in appendix 1.
9. The Fisherman, story 23 in appendix 1.
10. The Girl Who Killed Her Mother, story 28 in appendix 1.

L. V. is 55 and lives with his wife, his widowed daughter and his married son, and their children. He was born and has lived all his life in Yaonáhuac. Like his brother F. V., he is also a dance master, and his group is the Quetzales, who perform primarily during the patron saint celebration in July. Also like his brother, he migrated periodically to the hot country with the work team (*cuadrilla*) to compensate for a modest inheritance. He was contracted by the same local labor recruiter who organized work teams with storytellers M. I., J. M., and his brother F. V. He is a bilingual speaker of Nahuat and Spanish, but he cannot read and write. He explained that his parents sent him to school, but he was very disobedient and very truant. L. V. said he learned most of the stories he told me from his father and from fellow members of the work team. He recounted how he often performed as a storyteller at the evening camp of migrant laborers in the hot country. Most of L. V.'s stories have a clear moral message, and he explained that he found this the most interesting aspect of narratives. He said he has an interest in stories because they provide examples that guide him in his own personal life. This storyteller became involved in a bitter political dispute several years ago when he opposed members of the current PPS faction when they controlled the *municipio* government. He became embroiled in a personal vendetta against the members of this faction but was calmed by a priest whom he credits with preventing him from killing his enemies and bringing grief to his family. L. V. remains active in the church and participates in church committees and aids *mayordomos* in the civil-religious hierarchy. Of all storytellers, he is the most strong-minded and outspoken.

Notes

1. INTRODUCTION

1. Various terms are applied to the non-Indian population in the northern Sierra de Puebla, and the local terms do not coincide with those that appear in the ethnographic literature on ethnic relations in Mesoamerica. The most popular local terms used in the northern Sierra are *gente de razón* (people of reason), *castellanos* (Castilians), *españoles* (Spaniards), *los ricos* (the rich ones), and *koyome* (gentlemen). Mesoamerican ethnographers frequently use the terms *Mestizo* or *Ladino* (Tax 1937, 1941; de la Fuente 1967; Colby and van den Berghe 1969), but few use them in the northern Sierra. Perhaps arbitrarily I elected to use the word *Hispanic*, which conveys the general meaning of all terms. It suggests a person whose language and culture derive from Spain. Of course, one must acknowledge that the Nahuat and the Hispanics have synthetic cultures derived from both indigenous and Spanish antecedents.

2. Carrasco (1952), Wasserstrom (1978), and Rus and Wasserstrom (1980) describe the development of the civil-religious hierarchy during the Colonial and Independence periods in different parts of Mexico. Nash (1958) and Cancian (1965) focus on the relationship between this system and internal community stratification. See Cancian (1974), Smith (1975), and Wasserstrom (1978) for discussions of changes that have taken place since World War II affecting the civil-religious hierarchies of towns in Mexico and Guatemala.

3. This study uses the method of controlled comparison to study social and cultural change. Eggan (1937, 1954) was one of the first to utilize and draw attention to this method in anthropology. Redfield (1941) applied it to the study of social and cultural change in Mexico, although he did not compare narratives to detect ideational changes for the communities in his design. Mesoamericanists have used a number of other methods to study change, including longitudinal research designs (see Hinshaw 1975; Schwartz 1977; Foster et al. 1979). See Hinshaw (1975) and Schwartz (1977) for longitudinal studies of world view in Guatemalan communities.

4. For a different but related approach to change through the study of artistic expression, see Peacock's (1968) study of proletarian drama in Java.

5. Foster (1945) recognized that Mexican Indian oral tradition is a synthetic product of peninsular Spanish and indigenous elements.

2. THE NAHUAT

1. The nineteen *municipios* of Sierra Nahuat speakers, together with their populations according to the 1970 Mexican census (México 1973), are as follows: Atempan (7,991), Chignautla (8,381), Cuautempan (5,647), Cuetzalan (24,501), Hueyapan (4,120), Huitzilan de Serdán (6,995), Jonotla (2,505), Nauzontla (3,158), Santiago Yaonáhuac (3,409), Tetela de Ocampo (19,967),

Teteles de Ávila Castillo (2,313), Teziutlán (40,742), Tlatlauquitepec (29,113), Xochiapulco (3,657), Xochitlán de Romero Rubio (8,042), Zacapoaxtla (26,134), Zaragosa (6,150), Zautla (14,464), and Zoquiapan (1,831).

2. Several ethnographers have worked among the Sierra Nahuat, and their research contributes to understanding a number of aspects of this complex region. Fabila (1949), and Nutini and Isaac (1974) give overviews of the northern Sierra de Puebla. For descriptions of economic and social organization in different communities, see Buchler (1967), Arizpe (1973), Taggart (1972, 1975a, 1975b, 1976), Slade (1975, 1976), and Murphy (1976). Torres-Trueba (1973) described political factionalism in the former district capital of Zacapoaxtla. Those who report and analyze narratives include Díaz Hernández (1945), Arizpe (1973), and Taggart (1977, 1979, 1982a, 1982b).

3. The tales gathered in this study share a number of motifs listed in Boggs's (1930) index of peninsular Spanish tales and Robe's (1973) index of Mexican tales with Spanish motifs. The Spaniards who settled in the New World came from a number of provinces depending on the period of their migration. Spaniards settled in the northern Sierra de Puebla in the late seventeenth century, and the bulk of the migration from Spain during this and the preceding century came from the southern and central provinces (Perez Bustamante 1941; Foster 1952).

3. HUITZILAN DE SERDÁN

1. This figure is based on my census of the five sections of the *cabecera*. This census was carried out in 1969 by local members of the community, who visited the homes of their fellow residents and requested their voluntary cooperation.

2. The Nahuat word *koyot* is probably derived from the Aztec word *coyotl* (coyote), which has a negative connotation. For instance, the Aztec god Huehuecoyotl (Old Coyote) was a back-biter or mischiefmaker (Vaillant 1966: 190). It makes sense that the Nahuat would apply the word *koyot*, derived from *coyotl*, to the dominant ethnic group because Hispanics brought so much disruption to the Sierra Nahuat area. They apparently added the connotation of *gentlemen* to express the wealth and status differences between themselves and Hispanics in the modern ethnically stratified society.

3. See Taggart (1975a: 42–54) for a detailed description of the civil-religious hierarchy in Huitzilan de Serdán.

4. Article 3420 of the Puebla Civil Code states that if the father dies without a testament, equal portions of his property will pass to his legally recognized children regardless of their age or sex (Puebla 1969). The Hispanics of Huitzilan who serve in the civil government are well aware of this edict and tend to apply it in cases that come to their attention.

5. Most Nahuat *ejiditarios* of Huitzilan make their preferences about inheritance of ejido plots known before their deaths, although few write their wishes in testaments. Article 162 of the Agrarian Code applies to

cases where the *ejiditario* declares his wishes. It states that the *"ejiditario* has the power to name *an* heir who will succeed to his agrarian rights from among the persons who depend economically on him, even though they are not relatives" (México 1969: 61; emphasis mine). The law is not so clear about cases where the *ejiditario* does not make his wishes known. Article 163 of the Agrarian Code applies to these cases, and it states that if no one is designated, or if the heir has died, or is permanently absent from the community, the inheritance goes to "the wife or the mistress with whom he has had children, or to the woman with whom he lived as man and wife during the six months prior to his death: and lacking a woman, the child*ren* will inherit" (México 1969: 61–62; emphasis mine).

6. Patrilineal land inheritance and virilocality do not always mean women have a weak position in the social structure. Leis (1974) describes an African case where women who live in virilocal polygynous extended families and who work land from their husbands' patrimony have a strong position in their society. Women's political power in this society derives from their solidarity as co-wives, and their independence from their husbands in economic matters.

4. SANTIAGO YAONÁHUAC

1. The figure of 2,487 is reported in the 1970 Mexican census for the six sections of the *municipio* located in the highlands. I conducted my own census of the community to obtain data on social structure comparable with that collected in Huitzilan. The census covered 1,663 individuals who live in the northern half of section 1, and most of sections 2 through 5. Census takers in Yaonáhuac were members of the local community who visited their neighbors and obtained information on a voluntary basis in 1978.

5. SPACE AND TIME

1. See appendix 1, story 1, episode 1.
2. Ambiguities and gaps in the ancient Aztec data leave room for different interpretations of the relationship among the cardinal directions (particularly north and south), the times of the year, and the times of the day. Graulich (1981: 49, 58) connects north with midnight and south with noon, but his interpretation rests on two assumptions not accepted by a number of other Mesoamerican scholars. First, he assumes that by 1519, the Aztec ritual calendar had become out of step with the solar year by 209 days. Second, he correlates the cardinal directions, the seasons, and the times of the day in a clockwise, rather than counterclockwise, direction.
3. See Yaonáhuac versions 3 and 4, items 2 and 3 in chapter 8.
4. See appendix 1, story 1.
5. See appendix 1, story 2.
6. See appendix 1, stories 3 and 4.
7. See appendix 1, story 5.

8. See appendix 1, stories 6 and 7, episode 3.
9. See appendix 1, stories 8, 9, and 10.
10. See appendix 1, story 11.
11. See appendix 1, story 12.
12. See Taggart (1977: 282–284).
13. See appendix 1, stories 14 and 15, episodes 8 and 10.
14. See appendix 1, stories 12 and 13, episode 3.
15. See appendix 1, story 12, episode 6. The narrator indicates that the devil returns at night from the periphery in two ways. First, he mentions that the devil returns when God's dogs are sleeping. Second, he says the devil returns when God is holding a celebration, and most Huitzilan Nahuat commence their celebrations around midnight.

7. NARRATIVE ACCULTURATION

1. Krickerberg (1971: 211) suggests this is the bone of a sacrificial victim and represents a composite of all the dead who lived in the underworld.
2. See appendix 1, story 1, episode 6.
3. See the Yaonáhuac version of The Flood, in chapter 11.
4. See the Yaonáhuac version of The Flood, in chapter 11.
5. See appendix 1, stories 6 and 7, episode 3.
6. Krickerberg (1971: 39) found this belief in *Historia de los Mexicanos por sus pinturas*.
7. See appendix 1, story 16, episode 5.
8. Krickerberg (1971: 30) notes that this belief appears in *Historia de los Mexicanos por sus pinturas*.
9. See appendix 1, story 16, episodes 5 and 6.
10. Krickerberg (1971: 39) found this belief expressed in *Historia de los Mexicanos por sus pinturas*.
11. See appendix 1, story 7, episode 3.
12. Krickerberg (1971: 37).
13. Compare episode 3 in stories 17 and 18, in appendix 1.

8. MEN WHO ENTER THE FOREST

1. The idea of an Orpheus-like myth in which Piltzintecuhtli pursues Xochiquetzal into the land of corruption originated with Seler (Krickerberg 1971: 212).
2. Ten judges, who were professional colleagues at Franklin and Marshall College, read the items in this table and rated the lightning-bolt relative to the man. If they believed the lightning-bolt took the initiative, assisted, commanded, caused fear, threatened, or instructed the man, they scored the item with a positive number on an open-ended scale. If they believed the lightning-bolt was neutral, then they scored the item with a zero. If they judged the man took the initiative, assisted, commanded, caused fear, threatened, or instructed the lightning-bolt, then they scored

the item with a negative number on an open-ended scale. Judges followed exactly the same procedure when rating the behavior of the mouse relative to the hawk in table 23. The positive and negative numbers were added for each item, and the sums for the parallel items in the versions from Huitzi- lan and Yaonáhuac were compared to determine if the judges generally rated the lightning-bolt or the mouse stronger in the stories from one of the two communities.

3. The low number of events for the means compared in this table does not permit their standard deviations to be equal. Consequently I used a formula from Blalock (1960: 175–176) which does not assume equal stan- dard deviations for computing the test statistics in tables 21 and 23.

9. LIGHTNING-BOLTS WHO PUNISH SIN

1. See appendix 1, stories 6 and 7.

10. ADAM AND EVE

1. See appendix 1, story 23, episode 6.

11. MEN : WOMEN : : CULTURE : NATURE

1. See MacCormack (1980) for a critique of this argument.

2. Drummond (1977) interpreted a South American version of this metaphor in terms of inter-ethnic rather than sexual relations.

3. The Laymi Indians, an Aymara-speaking group in central Bolivia, have a number of parallels with the Yaonáhuac Nahuat. They express the moral weakness of women with a metaphor in which men : women : : sun : moon, but they do not take the additional step of placing women closer to nature, in part because of comparatively egalitarian sexual rela- tions (Harris 1980). It would be interesting to know if variations in sexual ideology exist among different Aymara-speaking groups concordant with their social structure.

12. CONCLUSIONS

1. This debate primarily concerned societies with dual organizations that regulate marriage. See Maybury-Lewis (1979) for a re-examination of societies in Central Brazil with dual organizations, including the Bororo, who figured prominantly in the debate. The Bororo and a number of other Central Brazilian societies have a dual social structure, in part because they have exogamous moieties. Other types of dual organizations regulat- ing marriage do exist in contemporary Mesoamerica, although they are not strictly parallel to the Bororo. The largest settlement in the Mayan *muni- cipio* of Amatenango del Valle has two endogamous sections which func- tion for allocating civil and religious offices and pasturage on communal lands, and which act as a factor in the etiquette of social interaction (Nash

1970: 2–10). Neither type of dual organization regulating marriage exists among the Nahuat of Huitzilan and Yaonáhuac, who define incest as sex or marriage with anyone recognized as a blood or spiritual relative and who have no positive marriage rules. The reader can find a description of Huitzilan marriage rules in Taggart (1975 a: 91–95) that applies equally well to Yaonáhuac.

Despite the obvious difference between dual organizations regulating marriage and the social structure of Huitzilan and Yaonáhuac, the debate between Lévi-Strauss and Maybury-Lewis raised a number of general issues. Aside from the relationship between social relations and dyadic and triadic symbolic structures, it raised questions about the fit between the symbolic and the social domains of experience. Questions about this fit particularly arise in the Nahuat case, because Huitzilan and Yaonáhuac have experienced considerable change during the last 100 years. Redfield and Villa Rojas (1962: 87) observed a lack of isomorphism between ideal (symbolic) and real social behavior in another Mesoamerican community undergoing rapid change. However, the Nahuat data illustrate a tight fit between ideational constructs and social relations under changing conditions.

2. See Dumond (1970) for an interesting discussion of how different patterns of ethnic relations in the Yucatan could account for some of the differences reported for the communities in Redfield's (1941) comparative design.

3. Semiotics and other theories of communication point out that dialogue takes place with a myriad of signs and symbols (see Singer 1980), only a fraction of which probably make their way into narratives. It is well known that different speech genres can express different although complementary facets of a world view (Gossen 1972, 1974). Moreover, Nahuat narratives are told by men and thus express a masculine view of experience. In short, little of a Nahuat's private personality, and only a portion of his public personality, may appear in this specialized vehicle of communication. But I contend that narratives contain many of the invariant ideas that underlie the process of communication in Nahuat society.

APPENDIX 1. STORY SUMMARIES

1. Nawewet in Huitzilan stories is the counterpart of Nanawatzin in Yaonáhuac oral tradition.

2. The Cosolin, also known as Cosoltepet, is a mountain to the south of Huitzilan. The narrator noted it has a lot of water, and even has a spring on its summit.

3. Tuxtla is a Totonac community to the north of Huitzilan.

4. Nawewet's former home at Cosolin was above Huitzilan, and the lightning-bolts took him north to a point in the Zempoala River below the community where he cannot destroy the Nahuat with a flood.

5. The Yaonáhuac Nahuat assert that Nanawatzin, their character par-

allel to Nawewet, lives in the sea to the north of their community, and they, like the Huitzilan Nahuat, refer to him as San Juan.

6. The *cayime* accompany the Santiago dancers, and they wear long, dark dress coats, black masks, and swords.

7. The narrator changed the character. Earlier in this episode, he told how the daughters convinced the cook to join them in saying the rosary when the moon was a quarter vanished.

Bibliography

ADAMS, KATHLEEN
1980   Personal communication based on unpublished field notes.
AGUIRRE BELTRÁN, GONZALO
1973   *Regiones de refugio: El desarrollo de la comunidad y el proceso dominical en Mestizoamérica*. México: Instituto Nacional Indigenista.
ARDENER, EDWIN
1977*a* "Belief and the Problem of Women." In *Perceiving Women*, ed. Shirley Ardener, pp. 1–17. New York: John Wiley and Sons.
1977*b* "The 'Problem' Revisited." In *Perceiving Women*, ed. Shirley Ardener, pp. 19–27. New York: John Wiley and Sons.
ARIZPE, LOURDES
1973   *Parentesco y economía en una sociedad nahua: Nican pehwa Zacatipan*. México: Instituto Nacional Indigenista.
BARNES, J. A.
1973   "Genetrix : Genitor : : Nature : Culture?" In *The Character of Kinship*, ed. Jack Goody, pp. 61–73. Cambridge: Cambridge University Press.
BLAFFER, SARAH D.
1972   *The Blackman of Zinacantan*. Austin: University of Texas Press.
BLALOCK, HERBERT M.
1960   *Social Statistics*. New York: McGraw-Hill.
BOGGS, RALPH S.
1930   *Index of Spanish Folktales*. Helsinki: Academia Scientarium Fennica.
BRANDES, STANLEY
1980   *Metaphors of Masculinity: Sex and Status in Adalusian Folklore*. Philadelphia: University of Pennsylvania Press.
BRICKER, VICTORIA REIFLER
1977   "Historical Dramas in Chiapas, Mexico." *Journal of Latin American Lore* 3: 227–248.
BRUNDAGE, BURR CARTWRIGHT
1979   *The Fifth Sun: Aztec Gods, Aztec World*. Austin: University of Texas Press.
BUCHLER, IRA R.
1967   "La organización ceremonial de una aldea mexicana." *América Indígena* 27: 237–264.
CANCIAN, FRANK
1965   *Economics and Prestige in a Maya Community: The Religious Cargo System in Zinacantan*. Stanford: Stanford University Press.
1974   "New Patterns of Stratification in the Zinacantan Cargo System." *Journal of Anthropological Research* 30: 164–173.
CARO BAROJA, JULIO
1973   *The World of Witches*. Chicago: University of Chicago Press.

CARRASCO, PEDRO

1952   *Tarascan Folk Religion: An Analysis of Economic, Social and Religious Interaction.* Publication No. 17, pp. 1–64. New Orleans: Tulane University Middle American Research Institute.

1961   "The Civil-Religious Hierarchy in Mesoamerican Communities: Pre-Spanish Background and Colonial Development." *American Anthropologist* 63: 483–497.

1964   "Family Structure in Sixteenth Century Tepoztlán." In *Process and Pattern in Culture: Essays in Honor of Julian H. Steward,* ed. Robert A. Manners, pp. 185–210. Chicago: Aldine.

1975   "La transformación de la cultura indígena durante la colonia." *Historia Mexicana* 25: 175–203.

1976a "Las bases sociales del politeísmo mexicano: Los dioses tutelares." *Actes du XLIIᵉ Congrès International des Amèricanistes* 6: 11–17.

1976b "The Joint Family in Ancient Mexico: The Case of Molotla." In *Essays on Mexican Kinship,* ed. Hugo G. Nutini, Pedro Carrasco, and James M. Taggart, pp. 45–64. Pittsburgh: University of Pittsburgh Press.

1979   "Las fiestas de los meses mexicanos." In *Mesoamerica: Homenaje al Doctor Kirchoff,* ed. Barbara Dahlgren, pp. 52–56. México: Instituto Nacional de Antropología e Historia.

CASO, ALFONSO

1967   *The Aztecs: People of the Sun.* Norman: University of Oklahoma Press.

CHANG, KENNE H-K

1970   "The Inkyo System in Southwestern Japan: Its Functional Utility in the Household Setting." *Ethnology* 9: 342–357.

COLBY, BENJAMIN

1966   *Ethnic Relations in the Chiapas Highlands of Mexico.* Santa Fe: Museum of New Mexico Press.

COLBY, BENJAMIN N. and PIERRE L. VAN DEN BERGHE

1969   *Ixil Country: A Plural Society in Highland Guatemala.* Berkeley: University of California Press.

COLLIER, GEORGE ALLEN

1975   *Fields of the Tzotzil: The Ecological Basis of Tradition in Highland Chiapas.* Austin: University of Texas Press.

COLLIER, JANE FISHBURNE

1974   "Women in Politics." In *Women, Culture and Society,* ed. Michelle Zimbalist Rosaldo and Louise Lamphere, pp. 89–96. Stanford: Stanford University Press.

DAVIES, CLAUDE NIGEL BYAM

1968   *Los señorios independientes del imperio azteca.* México: Instituto Nacional de Antropología e Historia.

DÍAZ HERNÁNDEZ, VICENTE

1945   "Nanawatzin, Hueyapan Puebla." *Tlalocan* 2: 64.

DRUMMOND, LEE

1977   "Structure and Process in the Interpretation of South American

Myth: The Arawak Dog Spirit People." *American Anthropologist* 79: 842–868.

DUMOND, D. E.
1970   "Competition, Cooperation and the Folk Society." *Southwestern Journal of Anthropology* 26: 261–286.

DWYER, DAISY HILSE
1978a   "Ideologies of Sexual Inequality and Strategies for Change in Male-Female Relations." *American Ethnologist* 5: 227–240.
1978b   *Images and Self-Images: Male and Female in Morocco.* New York: Columbia University Press.

EDMONSON, MUNRO S.
1971   *Lore: An Introduction to the Science of Folklore and Literature.* New York: Holt, Rinehart and Winston.

EGGAN, FRED
1937   "Historical Changes in the Choctaw Kinship System." *American Anthropologist* 39: 34–52.
1954   "Social Anthropology and the Method of Controlled Comparison." *American Anthropologist* 56: 743–763.

FABILA, ALFONSO
1949   *Sierra Norte de Puebla.* México: Imprenta de la Nación.

FELICIANO VELÁZQUEZ, PRIMO (ed. and trans.)
1975   *Codice Chimalpopoca: Anales de Cuauhtitlan y Leyenda de los Soles.* Traducción directa del náhuatl. México: Universidad Nacional Autonoma de México.

FERNANDEZ, JAMES
1974   "The Mission of Metaphor in Expressive Culture." *Current Anthropology* 15: 119–145.

FISCHER, J. L.
1956   "The Position of Men and Women in Truk and Ponape: A Comparative Analysis of Kinship Terminology and Folktales." *Journal of American Folklore* 69: 55–62.
1958   "Folktales, Social Structure and Environment in Two Polynesian Outliers." *Journal of the Polynesian Society* 67: 11–36.

FOSTER, GEORGE M.
1945   "Some Characteristics of Mexican Indian Folklore." *Journal of American Folklore* 58: 225–235.
1948   *Empire's Children: The People of Tzintzuntzan.* Publication No. 6. Washington, D.C.: Smithsonian Institution Institute of Social Anthropology.
1952   "The Significance to Anthropological Studies of the Places of Origin of Spanish Emigrants to the New World." In *Selected Papers of the XXIXth International Congress of Americanists,* ed. Sol Tax, pp. 292–298. Chicago: University of Chicago Press.

FOSTER, GEORGE M., THAYER SCUDDER, ELIZABETH COLSON, and ROBERT V. KEMPER (eds.)
1979   *Long-Term Field Research in Social Anthropology.* New York: Academic Press.

FRISCH, ROSE E.
1978 "Population, Food Intake, and Fertility." *Science* 199: 22–30.

FUENTE, JULIO DE LA
1967 "Ethnic Relations." In *Handbook of Middle American Indians*, vol. 6, ed. Manning Nash, pp. 432–448. Austin: University of Texas Press.

GARIBAY, ANGEL M.
1970 *La literatura de los aztecas.* México: Editorial Joaquín Mortiz.

GEORGES, ROBERT A.
1969 "Toward an Understanding of Storytelling Events." *Journal of American Folklore* 82: 313–328.

GISSI BUSTOS, JORGE
1976 "Mythology about Women with Special Reference to Chile." In *Sex and Class in Latin America*, ed. June Nash and Helen Icken Safa, pp. 30–45. New York: Praeger.

GOSSEN, GARY H.
1972 "Chamula Genres of Verbal Behavior." In *Toward New Perspectives in Folklore*, ed. Américo Paredes and Richard Bauman, pp. 145–167. Austin: University of Texas Press.
1974 *Chamulas in the World of the Sun: Time and Space in a Maya Oral Tradition.* Cambridge, MA: Harvard University Press.

GRAULICH, MICHAEL
1981 "The Metaphor of the Day in Ancient Aztec Myth and Ritual." *Current Anthropology* 22: 45–60.

HARRIS, OLIVIA
1980 "The Power of Signs: Gender, Culture and the Wild in the Bolivian Andes." In *Nature, Culture and Gender*, ed. Carol P. MacCormack and Marilyn Strathern, pp. 70–94. Cambridge: Cambridge University Press.

HELMS, MARY W.
1975 *Middle America: A Cultural History of Heartland and Frontiers.* Englewood Cliffs, NJ: Prentice-Hall.

HINSHAW, ROBERT E.
1975 *Panajachel: A Guatemalan Town in a Thirty-Year Perspective.* Pittsburgh: University of Pittsburgh Press.

HUNT, EVA
1977 *Transformation of the Hummingbird: Cultural Roots of a Zinacantan Mythical Poem.* Ithaca and London: Cornell University Press.

KRICKERBERG, WALTER
1971 *Mitos y leyendas de los aztecas, incas, mayas y músicas.* México: Fondo de Cultura Economica.

LEHMANN, WALTER (ed. and trans.)
1906 "Traditions des anciens Mexicains: Texte inédit et original en langue náhuatl avec traduction en latin." *Journal de la Société des Américanistes de Paris* n.s. 3: 239–297.

LEIS, NANCY B.
1974 "Women in Groups: Ijaw Women's Associations." In *Women, Cul-*

ture and Society, ed. Michelle Zimbalist Rosaldo and Louise Lamphere, pp. 223–242. Stanford: Stanford University Press.

LEÓN-PORTILLA, MIGUEL
1974   *La filosofía náhuatl.* México: Universidad Nacional Autónoma de México.

LÉVI-STRAUSS, CLAUDE
1960   "On Manipulated Sociological Models." *Bijdragen tot de Taal-, Land-, en Volkenkunde* 116: 45–54.
1963   *Structural Anthropology.* New York: Basic Books.
1967   "The Story of Asdiwal." In *The Structural Study of Myth and Totemism*, ed. Edmund Leach, pp. 1–47. London: Tavistock.
1969   *The Raw and the Cooked: Introduction to a Science of Mythology*, vol. 1. New York: Harper and Row.

LEWIS, OSCAR
1949   "Husbands and Wives in a Mexican Village: A Study of Role Conflict." *American Anthropologist* 51: 602–611.
1951   *Life in a Mexican Village: Tepoztlán Restudied.* Urbana: University of Illinois Press.

LONGACRE, ROBERT
1967   "Systematic Comparison and Reconstruction." In *Handbook of Middle American Indians*, vol. 5, ed. Norman A. McQuown, pp. 117–159. Austin: University of Texas Press.

MACCORMACK, CAROL P.
1980   "Nature, Culture and Gender: A Critique." In *Nature, Culture and Gender*, ed. Carol P. MacCormack and Marilyn Strathern, pp. 1–21. Cambridge: Cambridge University Press.

MAYBURY-LEWIS, DAVID
1960   "The Analysis of Dual Organizations: A Methodological Critique." *Bijdragen tot de Taal-, Land-, en Volkenkunde* 116: 2–43.

MAYBURY-LEWIS, DAVID (ed.)
1979   *Dialectical Societies: The Ge and Bororo of Central Brazil.* Cambridge, MA: Harvard University Press.

MÉXICO
1969   *Código Agrario y leyes complementarias.* México: Editorial Porrua, S.A.

MÉXICO, SECRETARÍA DE INDUSTRIA Y COMERCIO
1973   *IX Censo General de Población: 1970, 28 de enero de 1970.* México: Dirección General de Estadistica.

MICHAELSON, EVALYN JACOBSON and WALTER GOLDSCHMIDT
1971   "Female Roles and Male Dominance among Peasants." *Southwestern Journal of Anthropology* 27: 330–352.

MINTZ, SIDNEY W. and ERIC R. WOLF
1950   "An Analysis of Ritual Co-Parenthood (Compadrazgo)." *Southwestern Journal of Anthropology* 6: 341–368.

MOLINA, FRAY ALONSO DE
1966   *Vocabulario náhuatl-castellano, castellano-náhuatl.* México: Ediciones Colofón, S.A.

MURPHY, TIMOTHY D.
1976   "Marriage and Family in a Nahuat Speaking Community." In *Essays on Mexican Kinship*, ed. Hugo G. Nutini, Pedro Carrasco, and James M. Taggart, pp. 187–205. Pittsburgh: University of Pittsburgh Press.

NASH, JUNE
1970   *In the Eyes of the Ancestors: Belief and Behavior in a Maya Community*. New Haven: Yale University Press.

NASH, MANNING
1958   "Political Relations in Guatemala." *Social and Economic Studies* 7: 65–75.

NICHOLSON, HENRY B.
1971   "Religion in Pre-Hispanic Central Mexico." In *Handbook of Middle American Indians*, vol. 10, ed. Gordon F. Ekholm and Ignacio Bernal, pp. 395–446. Austin: University of Texas Press.

NUTINI, HUGO G.
1968   *San Bernardino Contla: Marriage and Family Structure in a Tlaxcalan Municipio*. Pittsburgh: University of Pittsburgh Press.

1976a   "The Demographic Functions of *Compadrazgo* in Santa María Belén Azitzimititlán and Rural Tlaxcala." In *Essays on Mexican Kinship*, ed. Hugo G. Nutini, Pedro Carrasco, and James M. Taggart, pp. 219–236. Pittsburgh: University of Pittsburgh Press.

1976b   "Syncretism and Acculturation: The Historical Development of the Cult of the Patron Saint in Tlaxcala, Mexico (1519–1670)." *Ethnology* 15: 301–321.

NUTINI, HUGO G. and BARRY L. ISAAC
1974   *Los pueblos de habla nahuatl de la región de Tlaxcala y Puebla*. México: Instituto Nacional Indigenista.

ORTNER, S. B.
1974   "Is Female to Male as Nature Is to Culture?" In *Women, Culture and Society*, ed. Michelle Zimbalist Rosaldo and Louise Lamphere, pp. 67–88. Stanford: Stanford University Press.

PASO Y TRONCOSO, FRANCISCO DEL (ed. and trans.)
1903   *Leyenda de los Soles*. Florencia: Tipografía de Salvador Landi.

PEACOCK, JAMES L.
1968   *Rites of Modernization: Symbolic and Social Aspects of Indonesian Proletarian Drama*. Chicago: University of Chicago Press.

PEREZ BUSTAMANTE, C.
1941   "Las regiones españoles de la población de América (1509–1534)." *Revista de Indias* 2: 81–210.

PROPP, V.
1979   *Morphology of the Folktale*. Austin: University of Texas Press.

PUEBLA
1969   *Código Civil del Estado L. y S. de Puebla*. Puebla: Editorial José M. Cahica, Jr., S.A.

QUINN, NAOMI
1977   "Anthropological Studies on Women's Status." In *Annual Review*

of *Anthropology*, vol. 6, ed. Bernard J. Siegel, Alan R. Beals, and Stephen A. Tyler, pp. 181–225. Palo Alto: Annual Reviews.

REDFIELD, ROBERT

1941   *The Folk Culture of Yucatan.* Chicago: University of Chicago Press.

REDFIELD, ROBERT and ALFONSO VILLA ROJAS

1962   *Chan Kom: A Maya Village.* Chicago: University of Chicago Press.

ROBE, STANLEY L.

1973   *Index of Mexican Folktales, Including Narrative Texts from Mexico, Central America, and the Hispanic United States.* Folklore Studies No. 26. Berkeley: University of California Press.

ROBINSON, DOW F.

1966   *Sierra Nahuat Word Structure.* Santa Ana, CA: Dow F. Robinson.

ROGERS, SUSAN CAROL

1975   "Female Forms of Power and the Myth of Male Dominance: A Model of Female/Male Interaction in a Peasant Society." *American Ethnologist* 2: 727–756.

RUS, JAN and ROBERT WASSERSTROM

1980   "Civil-Religious Hierarchies in Central Chiapas: A Critical Perspective." *American Ethnologist* 7: 466–478.

SAHAGÚN, FRAY BERNARDINO DE

1950   *Florentine Codex: General History of the Things of New Spain, Book 1—The Gods,* translated from the Aztec original into English by Arthur J. O. Anderson and Charles E. Dibble. Santa Fe, NM: School of American Research and University of Utah.

1951   *Florentine Codex: General History of the Things of New Spain, Book 2—The Ceremonies,* translated from the Aztec original into English by Arthur J. O. Anderson and Charles E. Dibble. Santa Fe, NM: School of American Research and University of Utah.

1953   *Florentine Codex: General History of the Things of New Spain, Book 7—The Sun, Moon, and Stars, and the Binding of the Years,* translated from the Aztec original into English by Arthur J. O. Anderson and Charles E. Dibble. Santa Fe, NM: School of American Research and University of Utah.

1961   *Florentine Codex: General History of the Things of New Spain, Book 10—The People,* translated from the Aztec original into English by Charles E. Dibble and Arthur J. O. Anderson. Santa Fe, NM: School of American Research and University of Utah.

1969   *Florentine Codex: General History of the Things of New Spain, Book 6—Rhetoric and Moral Philosophy,* translated from the Aztec original into English by Arthur J. O. Anderson and Charles E. Dibble. Santa Fe, NM: School of American Research and University of Utah.

1978   *Florentine Codex: General History of the Things of New Spain, Book 3—The Origin of the Gods,* translated from the Aztec original into English by Arthur J. O. Anderson and Charles E. Dibble. Santa Fe, NM: School of American Research and University of Utah.

1979   *Florentine Codex: General History of the Things of New Spain,*
       Book 4—The Soothsayers, Book 5—The Omens, Book 8—Kings
       and Lords, translated from the Aztec original into English by
       Arthur J. O. Anderson and Charles E. Dibble. Santa Fe, NM: School
       of American Research and University of Utah.

SAPIR, J. DAVID
1977a "The Anatomy of a Metaphor." In *The Social Use of Metaphor,* ed.
       J. David Sapir and J. Christopher Crocker, pp. 3–32. Philadelphia:
       University of Pennsylvania Press.
1977b "The Fabricated Child." In *The Social Use of Metaphor,* ed. J. David
       Sapir and J. Christopher Crocker, pp. 193–223. Philadelphia: Uni-
       versity of Pennsylvania Press.

SCHWARTZ, NORMAN B.
1977   "A Pragmatic Past: Folk History, Environmental Change, and
       Society in a Peten Guatemala Town." *American Ethnologist* 4:
       339–358.

SILVA ANRACA, HECTOR
1960   *Tetela de Ocampo: O la lucha de un pueblo por la libertad y la*
       propiedad de la tierra. Puebla: Silva Anraca.

SINGER, MILTON
1980   "Signs of the Self: An Exploration in Semiotic Anthropology."
       American Anthropologist 82: 485–507.

SLADE, DOREN
1975   "Marital Status and Sexual Identity: The Position of Women in a
       Mexican Peasant Society." In *Women Cross-Culturally: Change*
       and Challenge, ed. Ruby Rohrlich-Leavitt, pp. 129–148. The
       Hague: Mouton.
1976   "Kinship in the Social Organization of a Nahuat-Speaking Commu-
       nity in the Central Highlands." In *Essays on Mexican Kinship,* ed.
       Hugo G. Nutini, Pedro Carrasco, and James M. Taggart, pp. 155–
       186. Pittsburgh: University of Pittsburgh Press.

SMITH, WALDEMAR R.
1975   "Beyond the Plural Society: Economics and Ethnicity in Middle
       American Towns." *Ethnology* 14: 225–244.

SOUSTELLE, JACQUES
1970   *La vida cotidiana de los aztecas.* México: Fondo de Cultura
       Económica.

TAGGART, JAMES M.
1972   "The Fissiparous Process in Domestic Groups of a Nahuat-Speaking
       Community." *Ethnology* 11: 132–149.
1975a *Estructura de los grupos domésticos de una comunidad de habla*
       nahuat de Puebla. México: Instituto Nacional Indigenista.
1975b "'Ideal' and 'Real' Behavior in the Mesoamerican Nonresidential
       Extended Family." *American Ethnologist* 2: 347–358.
1976   "Action Group Recruitment: A Nahuat Case." In *Essays on Mex-*
       ican Kinship, ed. Hugo G. Nutini, Pedro Carrasco, and James M.
       Taggart, pp. 137–153. Pittsburgh: University of Pittsburgh Press.

1977   "Metaphors and Symbols of Deviance in Nahuat Narratives." *Journal of Latin American Lore* 3: 279–308.
1979   "Men's Changing Image of Women in Nahuat Oral Tradition." *American Ethnologist* 6: 723–741.
1982*a* "Animal Metaphors in Spanish and Mexican Oral Tradition." *Journal of American Folklore* 95: 280–303.
1982*b* "Class and Sex in Spanish and Mexican Oral Tradition." *Ethnology* 21: 39–53.

TAX, SOL
1937   "The Municipios of Midwestern Highlands of Guatemala." *American Anthropologist* 39: 423–444.
1941   "World View and Social Relations in Guatemala." *American Anthropologist* 43: 27–42.

THOMPSON, STITH
1955–58   *Motif-Index of Folk-Literature*, vols. 1–6. Bloomington: Indiana University Press.

TORRES-TRUEBA, HENRY
1973   "Nahuat Factionalism." *Ethnology* 12: 463–474.

TURNER, PAUL R.
1974   "Highland Chontal Women: Myth and Social Structure." Unpublished paper presented at the 73rd Annual Meeting of the American Anthropological Association in Mexico City.

VAILLANT, GEORGE C.
1966   *Aztecs of Mexico: Origin, Rise, and Fall of the Aztec Nation.* Harmondsworth: Penguin Books.

VELASCO TORO, JOSÉ
1979   "Indigenismo y rebelión totonaca de Papantla, 1885–1896." *América Indígena* 39: 81–105.

VILLA ROJAS, ALFONSO
1947   "Kinship and Nagualism in a Tzeltal Community, Southern Mexico." *American Anthropologist* 49: 578–587.

VOGT, EVON Z.
1969   *Zinacantan: A Mayan Community in the Highlands of Chiapas.* Cambridge, MA: Harvard University Press.

WARREN, KAY B.
1978   *The Symbolism of Subordination: Indian Identity in a Guatemalan Town.* Austin: University of Texas Press.

WASSERSTROM, ROBERT
1978   "The Exchange of Saints in Zinacantan: The Socioeconomic Bases of Religious Change in Southern Mexico." *Ethnology* 17: 197–210.

WOLF, ERIC R.
1958   "The Virgin of Guadalupe: A Mexican National Symbol." *Journal of American Folklore* 71: 34–38.
1959   *Sons of the Shaking Earth.* Chicago: University of Chicago Press.

Index

1AAL1528   11/24/97   hi